Kinship and Marriage in Early Arabia

A History of Arabian Tribes and Culture from the time of Mohammed

By William Robertson Smith

**PANTIANOS
CLASSICS**

Published by Pantianos Classics

ISBN-13: 978-1-78987-464-8

First published in 1885

This reprint is based upon the expanded edition of 1903

Contents

Editor's Preface

The present edition of *Kinship and Marriage in Early Arabia* is no mere reprint of the work, which from its freshness and originality attracted the attention of Semitic scholars and anthropologists in 1885 and laid the foundation of all subsequent research in this department of studies. During the nine years which elapsed between its publication and his lamented death, Robertson Smith had collected additional notes and references in his own interleaved copy, and there were indications that he contemplated the preparation of a second edition, and had even marked out for himself certain features and lines of argument which he proposed to develop.

When, in course of time, the call for a second edition began to make itself heard, it was felt that his new material — however incomplete — ought not to be withheld, and Professor Ignaz Goldziher of Budapest, a valued personal friend of the author, and the writer of a careful and discriminating review of the book in the *Literatur-blatt für Orientalische Philologie,* was invited to see the proposed work through the press. This task he unfortunately found himself unable to complete, and, when it passed into the hands of the present writer in May 1901, he very generously placed at the disposal of the latter such notes as he had already collected.

In the discharge of this somewhat delicate task, the present editor's aim has been to give effect, in the first instance, to all the author's corrections, alterations, and additions, all other matter whether contributed by himself or others being placed within square brackets. *Kinship and Marriage* itself arose out of that epoch-making paper in the *Journal of Philology* referred to below, and simply marks a stage in the author's investigation of Semitic organisations, which was brilliantly followed up by the lectures on the fundamental institutions of the Semites. If in the *Religion of the Semites* primitive ritual rather than primitive society forms the chief theme, yet the two works are in a large degree complementary, and several points which are only lightly touched upon in *Kinship and Marriage* receive fuller treatment in the later work. Accordingly, it has seemed desirable to introduce into the present edition all necessary references to *Religion of the Semites*, more particularly in those cases — though few in number — where the author had modified his views.

Throughout his life Professor Robertson Smith's position was in the vanguard of critics. He was quick to assimilate fresh material and to test his theories in the light of new evidence. The criticisms that were passed upon his suggested derivation of the name Terah were sufficient to cause him to erase three lines upon p. 220 of the first edition — after consultation with well-known scholars — it can hardly be doubted that effect has only been given to what would have ultimately been his own wish. Some notice has also been taken of other criticisms, notably of Professor Nöldeke in the *Zeitschrift der Deutschen Morgenländischen Gesellschaft*, vol. 40, pp. 148 *sqq.*, and of Professor Wellhausen in his "Die Ehe bei den Arabern," in the *Nachrichten v. d. kgl. Gesellsch. d. Wissenschaffen* (Göttingen, 1893, no. xi. p. 432). In one or two instances the author's notes have been developed or a suggestion has been worked out, [1] but these cases are exceptional. Into the whole question of blood-feud Robertson Smith fully intended to go more thoroughly, but he has left no notes to indicate the lines he intended to pursue, and we can only regret that here again his purpose remained unaccomplished. [2]

No doubt parallels, criticisms, and bibliographical notes might have been easily multiplied. [3] The book, as we know, resolves itself into the theory that the primitive organisation of the Arabs — and indeed of all the Semites — finds its explanation in the assumption that they had passed through the totem stage. The whole theory of totemism no longer stands where it did in McLennan's day. Fresh discoveries are constantly being made, and the new facts call for at least a reconsideration of the opinions which were held ten or fifteen years ago. It is impossible to say to what extent Robertson Smith might not have been led to recast his views and what of the following pages might not have been rewritten — but his was the only hand which could modify his own statements, and it will be recognised that his additions and corrections even in minor points have their importance. After all, the totem theory is not the most prominent feature of the present work, and the value of the facts which he has brought together from his unsurpassed stores of knowledge are in no degree dependent upon a particular attitude towards this theory.

The preparation of the new edition has been felt to be a privilege, but also a responsibility. Every effort has been made to maintain that degree of accuracy, which marked all Robertson Smith's published writings, and the time involved in the verification of references in the new material — apart from heavy pressure of other work — has delayed the publication until now. It remains for the present writer to express his thanks to Dr. J. S. Black, Dr. J. G. Frazer, and Professor Nöldeke, for advice and suggestions, to Professor A. A. Bevan for the notes signed with his initials on pp. 9, 32, 2,s, 48, and above all to acknowledge his profound gratitude to Professor Ignaz Goldziher for his numerous notes (all of which are distinguished with the initials I. G.), and for his goodness in reading the proofsheets. [4]

S. A. COOK.

London, *October* 10, 1903.

[1] *E.g. Additional Note* D.
[2] How important the subject is for the history of primitive Semitic organisation is abundantly evident from Procksh's essay, *Uber die Blutrache bet den vorislamischen Arabern* (Leipzig, 1899); reference may also be made to W. M. Patton, "Blood-revenge in Arabia and Israel" in *the American Journal of Theology*, October 1901, pp. 703-731.
[3] This is particularly true of evidence from the Babylonian field, a department to which only slight attention is paid in *Kinship and Marriage*. Some idea of its importance may perhaps be obtained from the present writer's *The Laws of Moses and The Code of Hammurabi* (chaps. iv.-vi.), where the earliest Babylonian family and marriage-laws appear to be highly instructive for the study of primitive Semitic society.
[4] The present writer may perhaps be allowed to refer to his article "Israel and Totemism" in *The Jewish Quarterly Review* April 1902, pp. 413-448, where the endeavour was made to estimate Robertson Smith's theory of Semitic totemism in the light of the present position of totemism generally.

Author's Preface

The object of the present volume is to collect and discuss the available evidence as to the genesis of the system of male kinship, with the corresponding laws of marriage and tribal organisation, which prevailed in Arabia at the time of Mohammed; the general result is that male kinship had been preceded by kinship through women only, and that all that can still be gathered as to the steps of the social evolution in which the change of kinship law is the central feature corresponds in the most striking manner with the general theory propounded, mainly on the basis of a study of modern rude societies, in the late J. F. McLennan's book on *Primitive Marriage*. The correspondence of the Arabian facts with this general theory is indeed so close that all the evidence might easily have been disposed under heads borrowed from his exposition; and for those who are engaged in the comparative study of early institutions this would probably have been the most convenient arrangement. But the views of my lamented friend are not so widely known as they deserve to be, and several of the Essays in which they are expressed are not very accessible. Moreover I wished to speak not only to general students of early society but to all who are interested in old Arabia; for if my results are sound they have a very important bearing on the most fundamental problems of Arabian history and on the genesis of Islam itself. I have therefore thought it best to attempt to build a self-contained argument on the Arabian facts alone, following a retrogressive order from the known to the unknown past, and not calling in the aid of hypotheses derived from the comparative method until, in working backwards on the Arabian evidence, I came to a point where the facts could not be interpreted without the aid of analogies drawn from other rude societies. This mode of exposition has its disadvantages, the most serious of these being that the changes in the tribal system which went hand in hand with the change in the rule of kinship do not come into view at all till near the close of the argument. In the earlier chapters therefore I am forced to argue on the supposition that a local group was also a stock-group, as it was in the time of the prophet; while in the two last chapters it appears that this cannot have always been the case. But I trust that the reader, if he looks back upon the earlier chapters after reaching the end of the book, will see that this result has been tacitly kept in view throughout, and that the substance of the argument involves nothing inconsistent with it.

The first chapters of the book do not, I think, borrow any principle from the comparative method which cannot be completely verified by Arabian evidence. These chapters are rewritten and expanded from a course of public University lectures delivered in the Easter Term of the current year, and my original idea was to confine the present volume to the ground which they cover. I found, however, that to break off the argument at this point would be very unsatisfactory both to the author and to the reader, and that, to round off my results even in a provisional way, it was absolutely necessary to say something as to the ultimate origin of the tribal system. And here it is not possible to erect a complete argument on the Arabian evidence alone. But it is, I think, possible to show that the Arabs once had the system which McLennan has expounded under the name of totemism (chap, 7.), and if, as among other early nations, totemism and female kinship were combined with a law of exogamy, it is also possible to construct, on the lines laid down in Primitive Marriage, a hypothetical picture of the development of the social system, consistent with all the Arabian facts, and involving only *verae causae, i.e.,* only the action of such forces as can be shown to have operated in other rude societies in the very way which the hypothesis requires (chap. viii.). I have thought it right to limit myself, in this part of the subject, to the briefest possible outline. The general principles of the hypothesis, as laid down by J. F. McLennan, are not, I believe, likely to be shaken, but it is premature to attempt more than the most provisional sketch of the way in which they operated under the special historical conditions existing in the Arabian peninsula.

The collection of the evidence on which my arguments rest has occupied me at intervals since the autumn of 1879, when I put together a certain number of facts about female kinship and totemism in a paper on "Animal worship and animal tribes among the Arabs and in the Old Testament," which was published in the *Journal of Philology,* vol. ix. At that time I had access to no good library of Arabic texts, so that I could only pick up what lay on the surface of the unsearched field; but the results of this provisional exploration appeared so promising that it seemed desirable to publish them and to invite the cooperation of scholars better versed in the early literature of Arabia. Several orientalists of mark responded to this invitation; in particular Prof. Th. Nöldeke sent me some valuable observations, which have since been incorporated in his review of Prof. G. A. Wilken's book, *Het Matriarchaat bij de oude Arabieren* (Oester. *Monatschrift f. d. Orient,* 1884), and Prof. Ignaz Goldziher contributed a list of important references to the hadith and other sources in a letter to the *Academy,* July 10, 1880, The *hadīth* (traditions of the prophet) was not used at all in my paper, but I had begun to search through it in the winter of 1879-80, when a visit to Cairo enabled me also to procure extracts from Tabarī's Coran commentary, of which some specimens are given in the notes to the present volume. The next contribution to the subject was Prof. Wilken's book, already cited, which appeared at Amsterdam in 1884. Most of the facts on which Prof. Wilken builds are simply copied from my paper and Dr. Goldziher's letter, but he adds a very useful collection of the traditional evidence about *mot'a* marriage, for which he had the assistance of Dr. Snouck Hurgronje. On this topic I had briefly touched in a note to my *Prophets of Israel* (1882), p. 408; but Prof. Wilken was the first to bring it into connection with the rule of female kinship. Another new point to which Prof. Wilken devotes considerable attention is the importance attached in ancient and modern Arabia to the relationship of maternal uncle and nephew; and what he has said on this head plays a chief part in the controversy between him and Dr. Redhouse, which has produced the two latest publications on the subject of female kinship in Arabia (J. W. Redhouse, *Notes on Prof. E. B. Tylor's "Arabian Matriarchate"* [1885]; G. A. Wilken, *Eenige Opmerkingen naar anleiding eener critiek van mijn "Matriarchaat bij de oude Arabieren,"* The Hague 1885). Some points in both these papers are touched on in the following pages, but I have not found occasion to go into the controversy in detail, as my interpretation of the whole evidence differs fundamentally from that of the Dutch scholar. It will be seen from this survey that by much the larger part of the evidence which I have used had to be collected without assistance from any predecessor, and I have not been able to extend my search over more than a moderate part of the vast field of early Arabic literature. On the other hand, while I have tried to give specimens of all the types of evidence that have come under my observation, I could easily have multiplied examples of many of these types.

The notes appended to the volume contain a variety of illustrative matter, and in some cases take the shape of excursuses on topics of interest which could not have been brought into the text without breaking the flow of the argument. [1]

In conclusion I desire to express my thanks to my friend and colleague Prof. W. Wright for valuable help in all parts of the book, and to my friend Mr. D. McLennan for many important criticisms and suggestions on the first six chapters.

W. ROBERTSON SMITH.
Christ's College, Cambridge,
Oct. 26, 1885.

[1] [For the greater convenience of the reader the majority of these notes now appear in their proper place as footnotes.]

Chapter One - The Theory of the Genealogists as to the Origin of Arabic Tribal Groups

At the time when Mohammed announced his prophetic mission, and so gave the first impulse to that great movement which in a few years changed the whole face of Arabian society, the Arabs throughout the peninsula formed a multitude of local groups, held together within themselves not by any elaborate political organisation but by a traditional sentiment of unity, which they believed or feigned to be a unity of blood, and by the recognition and exercise of certain mutual obligations and social duties and rights, which united all the members of the same group to one another as against all other groups and their members.

The way of life of these groups was various; some were pastoral and nomadic, others were engaged in agriculture and settled in villages or towns, and in some towns again, as in Mecca and Taif, a chief occupation of the citizens was trade. This of course implies that some communities were much more advanced in civilisation than others: the difference between a wild Bedouin and a rich merchant of Mecca was perhaps nearly as great then as it is now. And with this there went also considerable variety of law and social custom; thus the Traditions of the Prophet and the commentators on the Coran often refer to diversities of 'āda, that is of traditional usage having the force of law, as giving rise to discussion between the Meccans who followed Mohammed to Medina and the old inhabitants of that town. But all through the peninsula the" type of society was the same, the social and political unit was the group already spoken of.

This is not to be taken as meaning that there was no such thing as a combination of several groups into a larger whole; but such larger combinations were comparatively unstable and easily resolved again into their elements. In the greater towns, for example, several groups might live together in a sort of close alliance, but each group or clan had its own quarter, its little fortalices, its own leaders, and its particular interests. The group-bond was stronger than the bond of citizenship, and feuds between group and group often divided a town against itself So too among the nomadic Arabs we find that a certain number of groups might form a confederation presenting the semblance of something like a nation; but the tendency of each group to stand by its own members in every quarrel was fatal to the permanence of such unions. This was the case not only where the confederation rested on a treaty (casāma) and was limited in scope by the nature of the contract, but also where neighbouring and allied groups regarded themselves as brothers, united by a bond of blood. In such cases, indeed, quarrels were not willingly pushed to an open rupture; the cooler and wiser heads on both sides were willing to strain a point to keep the peace; but if the principals in the quarrel proved intractable the outbreak of open hostilities between their respective groups was usually a mere question of time. And then all other considerations disappeared before the paramount obligation that lay on every family to stand by its own people, that is, by its own ultimate group.

It is the constitution of these ultimate groups, out of which all larger unions were built up, and into which these constantly tended to resolve themselves again, which must form the starting-point of the present enquiry.

According to the theory of the Arab genealogists the groups were all patriarchal tribes, formed, by subdivision of an original stock, on the system of kinship through male descents. A tribe was but a larger family; the tribal name was the name or nickname of the common ancestor. In process of time it broke up into two or more tribes, each embracing the descendants of one of the great ancestor's sons and taking its name from him. These tribes were again divided and subdivided on the same principle, and so at length that extreme state of division was reached which we find in the peninsula at the time of the prophet. Between a nation, a tribe, a sept or sub-tribe, and a family there is no difference, on this theory, except in size and distance from the common ancestor. As time rolls on the sons of a household become heads of separate families, the families grow into septs, and finally the septs become great tribes or even nations embracing several tribes.

It is proper to observe here that in the earliest times of which we have cognisance the ultimate kindred group, which in the last resort acted together against all other groups, was never a single family or homestead (*dār*), and that the group-bond was, for its own purposes, stronger than the family or household bond. Thus, if a man was guilty of homicide within his own group, the act was murder and his nearest relatives did not attempt to protect him from the consequences, but the whole group usually stood by a manslayer who had killed an outsider, even though the slain was of a brother group. In such a case they might recognise that some atonement was necessary, but they interested themselves to make for their kinsman the best terms they could. This observation, it will readily be seen, does not square well with the theory that the kindred group is only the family grown large; at all events if we accept the theory it appears necessary to supplement it by an> explanation of the reason why the blood-bond creates absolute obligations between all the families which form a single group, and only very modified obligations towards children of the common ancestor beyond this limit. On the theory one would expect to find that the family was the real social unit, beyond which the feeling of kinship obligation was never quite absolute, but grew continuously weaker as the degree of kinship was more remote; whereas we actually find a certain group of families within which kinship obligations are absolute and independent of degrees of cousinship, while beyond this group kinship obligations suddenly become vague. But this is a point on which the genealogists have nothing to say; they content themselves with offering a scheme of the subdivision of patriarchal tribes by which all Arabs who possess a *nisba* or gentile name can trace back their genealogy to one of two ultimate stocks, the Yemenite or S. Arab stock, whose great ancestor is Cahtan, and the Ishmaelite or N. Arab stock, whose ancestor is 'Adnan, a descendant of Abraham through Ishmael. The latter stock bears also indifferently the names of Ma'add or Nizar, the former being represented as the son and the latter as the grandson of 'Adnān. [1] Ma'add, indeed, has according to the genealogists a brother 'Akk; but the 'Akk are regarded as having married into Yemen and become Yemenite (B. Hish. p. 6), or even the Yemenites and the 'Akk in Khorāsān gave themselves a different descent, deriving their father 'Adnan or 'Odthan from the Asd (*ib.* 1. 18). Ma add, again, has four sons (B. Hish. p. 6 ult.), of these the first is Nizar, the second Codā'a (really the firstborn, but on him see *Additional Note* A), the third Conos, who is regarded as extinct (p. 7, 1. 9), and the fourth Iyād, who, however, is reckoned also as son of Nizār (so Wüstenfeld's tables). Thus the three, 'Adnān, Ma'add, and Nizār are practically identical.

The elaboration of this genealogical scheme falls mainly within the first century of the Flight — though it was hardly completed so early — and is probably connected (as Sprenger has pointed out in his Life of Mohammed) with the system of registers introduced by the Caliph 'Omar I. for the control of the pensions and pay distributed among believers from the spoil of the infidel. The pension system, as Sprenger [2] has explained at length, afforded a direct stimulus to genealogical research, and also, it must be added, to genealogical fiction; while the vast registers connected with it afforded the genealogists an opportunity, which certainly never existed before, to embrace in one scheme the relations of a great circle of Arab kindreds. At the same time, in consequence of the victories of Islam many tribes, or at least large sections of them, migrated to distant lands, where they received estates or were settled in military colonies and frontier stations. The military organisation closely followed the old tribal grouping; the feuds of the desert were transplanted to Syria and Iraq, to Spain and Khorāsān, and in all the numerous factions and civil wars that rent the old Arab empire tribal alliances and kinship played a conspicuous part. Every ambitious chief therefore was anxious to include as wide a kinship as possible among his dependents and allies, while a weak group found it advantageous to discover some bond of connection with a stronger neighbour. As the old groups were, in the various provinces, shuffled through each other in very various combinations, it plainly became an object of interest to reduce to system the relationships of all the Arab tribes. From time immemorial the population of Arabia had been divided into two great races — the same which the genealogists refer to Cahtan and 'Adnan respectively. In all parts of the empire these two races maintained their ancestral traditions of bitter and persistent feud, and this race-antagonism was a dominating feature in the whole stormy politics of the Omayyad dynasty. In such circumstances the task of the genealogists, who undertook to trace out and reduce to system all the links of kindred connecting the tribes of 'Adnan and Cahtan respectively, had a very practical interest; the questions involved were not mere matters of archaeological curiosity, but had a direct bearing on the political combinations of the time. Scientific impartiality therefore was not to be looked for; even if the genealogist himself was an incorruptible judge — and hardly any Oriental is so — he was certain to have much spurious evidence laid before him.

An example will make this clear, and at the same time show how uncertain is even the main structure of the genealogical tree. In the form of the genealogies which ultimately prevailed, 'Adnan, Nizar, Ma' add, Ishmaelite Arabs are identical terms and embrace one great nation. All other Arabs are Yemenites or sons of Cahtan, and these again, if we neglect the remote tribes of Hadramaut, may be taken as forming two main groups: (a) the tribes of Kahlan, and (b) the tribes known under the common name of Coda'a, which are traced to Cahtan through Himyar, the eponym of the race whom the Greeks and Latins call Homerites. At first sight all this seems to be quite correct and to correspond with the historical fact that under the Omayyads there was a great and enduring hatred between the Caisites, a branch of Nizār or Ma'add, and the Kalbites, a branch of Codā'a; the feud of Caisites and Kalbites seems to be simply a local form of the feud of Yemen and Ma'add. But when we turn to the *Aghānī, 777 sq.* we find that "the genealogists are at variance as to Coda a, some maintaining him to be a son of Ma' add and brother of Nizar, while others make him to be Himyarite." The evidence on each side consists of verses in which Coda a is referred to Ma add or to Himyar respectively. The later singers of Codā'a maintained the Himyarite genealogy and made a number of verses to support it; [3] but this, says Moarrij (a noted scholar who died A.H. 195), dates only from the last days of the Omayyads, and all older poets before and after Islam refer Codā'a to Ma add. [4] And accordingly the *Aghānī* shows that the famous Codaite poet Jamil, of the tribe of Sa'd Hodhaim (died A.H. 82), repeatedly speaks of his race as Maaddite.

It appears then that in this case the genealogy that ultimately prevailed was based on a deliberate falsification of old tradition. The motive is explained by the noted genealogist Abū Ja'far Mohammed ibn Habīb (died A.H. 245), quoted in the *Tāj*, 5461: "Codā'a was always known as Maaddite till the feud between Kalb and Cais-'Ailan arose in Syria in the days of Merwān ibn Al-Hakam; then the Kalbites inclined to the Yemenites and claimed kin with Himyar to get their help the more readily against Cais." In point of fact, at the battle of Marj Rāhit (A.H. 64) Merwān's party included besides the Kalbites the Kahlanite tribes of Ghassān, Sakun, and Sakasik. [5]

What was done on a large scale in the case of Codā'a was doubtless done on a smaller scale in other cases. Indeed Hamdānī tells us that he found it to be the regular practice of obscure desert groups to claim kinship with more famous tribes of the same name (*Jezīrat,* p. 90). But for our purpose the point to be noticed is that it still was possible in the later days of the Omayyads to make a radical change in the pedigree of great tribes like the Kalb and other Codā'a. For this shows that the whole system of pedigrees was still in a state of flux, at least as regarded its remoter members and the connections between distant tribes. The Northern Arabs called themselves Maaddites even before the time of the prophet; but if this term had then conveyed the definite genealogical conceptions that went with it in later times, it would not have been possible to transfer a series of great tribes from Ma'add to Himyar. Undoubtedly the genealogists found in oral tradition and official registers a large mass of sound information as to the old affinities and subdivisions of tribes, but this material was not sufficient for their task; it was fragmentary in character and its range was limited by the notorious shortness of the historical memory of the Arabs. To make a complete system out of such materials it was necessary to have constant recourse to conjecture, to force a genealogical interpretation on data of the most various kinds, and above all to treat modern political combinations as the expression of ancient bonds of kinship. The backbone of the system was the pedigree of the prophet — itself one of the most obviously untrustworthy parts of the whole scheme — and round this all the other Northern Arabs were grouped on the principle that every connection, real or imaginary, between two tribes was to be explained by deriving them from a common ancestor, who in turn was brought into the prophet's *stemma* as brother or cousin of some ascendant of Mohammed. To link all known tribal and gentile names together in this way, and at the same time make the lines connecting historical contemporaries with the common father tolerably equal in length, it was necessary to insert a number of "dummy" ancestors. These were got by doubling known names or using personal names of no tribal significance. The places in which the imaginary names should come in were of course largely arbitrary; it was known what were the actual sub-tribes and septs included in any greater tribe, and all these had to appear by their names as descendants of the father of the tribe, but it was comparatively indifferent whether they should be sons or grandsons, though in a general way it was desirable that the eponyms of the more populous groups should stand nearer the common ancestor. Accordingly when one compares different authorities one finds continual variations in matters of this sort; A is indifferently represented as the brother, the cousin or the uncle of B; and then perhaps a later genealogist comes in and solves the difficulty by saying that there are three A's, who are brother, cousin and uncle of B respectively.

No one who has worked through any part of the material in detail, comparing Wüstenfeld's tables with the notices in the *Aghānī,* the *'Ied,* the Hamāsa, the Hodhalite poems and similar sources, can fail to conclude that the system of the genealogists and the methods by which traditional data are worked into the system are totally unworthy of credit. The actual genealogical materials which the authors of the lists had before them embraced pedigrees of individual men, seldom going back more than two or three generations before the prophet, and notices of the subdivisions and second or third sub-divisions of tribes, or, what amounted to the same thing, of the various *nisbas* (gentile surnames) and war-cries that one man might use. All the rest was more or less arbitrary conjecture.

It may, however, be maintained that although the system breaks down as a whole, owing to the imperfection of historical tradition, the principles which underlie it are so far sound that they really do explain the origin of individual groups, and to some extent at least the relations subsisting between nearly-connected groups. It may be maintained (1) that the groups which formed social and political units at the time of Mohammed were really, as the system supposes, groups of kinsmen descended in the male line from a common an-cestor, and (2) that groups which, though living and acting separately, and at times perhaps even at war with one another, yet acknowledged that they were brethren — such groups let us say as the Bakr and the Taghlib, or the Aus and the Khazraj — were really the descendants of brother eponymi, that Bakr and Taghlib for example were sons of an historical personage called Wāil, as the genealogists have it.

It will be observed that if the tribal groups were strictly kindred groups and if kindred was always reckoned in the male line, these two positions stand or fall together. If all Bakrītes were descendants of Bakr and all Ta-ghlibites descendants of Taghlib, and if at the same time brotherhood always meant kinship on the father's side, then the brotherhood of the two tribes can mean nothing else than that Bakr and Taghlib were themselves brothers. But, this being so, two cases are possible. Either the genealogists knew by historical tradition that two brothers Bakr and Taghlib, sons of Wail, had ac-tually lived, or on the other hand the logic of their theory led them to infer the existence of two such brothers from the fact that in historical times the two tribes spoke of each other as "our brethren (*Hārith, Moall.* 1. 16). The latter beyond all question is the real case. Arabic tradition has nothing to tell about the personalities of Bakr and Taghlib that is not obviously mere fable. A story told in the *Aghānī* about Bakr and Zaid Manāt ibn Tamīm I condense in a note as a fair sample of what the Arabs used to relate of their mythical ancestors. [6] About Taghlib on the other hand I find only a notice in Wüsten-feld, the authority for which I have not traced, that his true name was Dithar, and that once in his boyhood, having repelled an attack on his father's house, he was greeted with the cry *Taghlib,* "thou art victorious." But according to all Semitic analogy the name derived from such an incident should have been in the third person masculine, Yaghlib "the victorious," like Yadhkor, Yashkor and the like in Arabic, or Jacob "the supplanter," Isaac "the laugher," and so forth in the Bible. And beyond doubt Taghlib must be taken not as the second person masculine but as the third person feminine imperfect of *ghalaba* — feminine (by an ordinary rule of grammar) because it is the name of a tribe and not of a man. The gender shows that the tribal name existed before the mythical ancestor was invented, and indeed, as Nöldeke has pointed out, the older poets down to the time of Al-Farazdac personify Taghlib as the daughter not as the son of Wail. [7]

It appears therefore that the acknowledgment that two tribes are brothers does not necessarily imply any historical tradition of a common ancestor. No one indeed who was not tied by a theory would suppose that it did. Brotherhood in the Semitic tongues is a very loose word; even covenant relations may make men brothers. Thus, in ancient times, Amos (19) speaks of Tyre and Israel as connected by a "covenant of brotherhood," and to this day the blackmail paid by Syrian peasants to their Bedouin neighbours is called *khūwa,* "brotherhood-money." In ancient Arabia it was not otherwise; a man whom one is bound to protect is *akhū mohāfaza,* a brother in virtue of this bond ('Alcama, ed. Socin, 8 1).' Brotherhood between tribes might therefore arise by integration as well as by differentiation, by covenant between alien stocks as well as by the division of a single stock into two, as Sprenger (*Alte Geogr. Ar.* p. 203) has shown by examples from Hamdānī. On the other hand) the conditions of nomad life must often have compelled one group to divide into two, as in the bible story Lot parts from Abraham. But here again the fact that the two sections are called brothers is no proof that before its division they formed two patriarchal clans or sub-tribes tracing descent from two brothers germane; for in the language of the Arabs all the members of a tribe are brethren, and you can say indifferently "one of the sons of Hodhail," or "brother of the sons of Hodhail," or "brother of Hodhail." [8]

It appears therefore that the zeal of the genealogists has pressed the word brother far beyond what it can bear. But does it stand better with the terms father and son?

Here again the genealogical system appears at first sight to be securely based on the *usus loquendi,* for we find the same tribe indifferently spoken of as Bakr or Sons of Bakr, Taghlib or Sons of Taghlib. But according to the laws of Semitic speech this usage is by no means conclusive in favour of the theory of patronymic tribes. For on the one hand the head or founder of any society or group is called its father, as in the Bible Jonadab son of Rechab is the father of the religious order of the Rechabites. And so even in Arabic clans of quite recent origin, which are certainly named after an historical person, it would be an entire mistake to suppose that all the Sons (let us say) of Hosein are really sprung from the loins of Hosein. And on the other hand all the members for the time being of a permanent guild or other social unity are sons of that unity. Thus in the Bible we have "sons of the prophets" meaning simply members of the prophetic order, "sons of the Exile" meaning simply members or descendants of the body of exiles. So when we find an Arab tribe which is called Khozā'a, that is "separated ones," we shall not easily agree with the genealogists who, in deference to the logic of their system, insist on giving an individual ancestor named Khoza a to the "sons of the separated ones," especially as they themselves are aware of the tradition that the Khoza a were so called because they broke off from the Asd (Azd) in the great

Yemenite dispersion. A still clearer case is that of the Kholoj (Kholj, Khalj). [9] It was quite well known that these had their name, which means "transferred," because the Caliph Omar I. transferred them from 'Adwān to Al-Hārith (Ibn Cotaiba, p. 33) I nevertheless Kholoj is to the genealogists a nickname of Cais son of Al-Hārith (*Tāj*, 2 35). Cais is one of those "dummy" names which are always turning up to fill blanks in a genealogy, and Al-Hārith is made to be the son or grandson of Fihr the father of the Coraish, who stands in the pedigree of the prophet eleven generations before the time of Omar.

As most of the considerable Arabian tribes date from pre-historic times one cannot hope to be often able to lay one's finger on the genealogical fiction as clearly as in these two cases. But many tribal names are so plainly collectives that we can have no hesitation in classing them with Khozā'a and the Kholoj. [10] Among such we may reasonably include not only plural or collective forms of adjectives, but also, as we have just seen, feminine verbal forms with adjective force, like Taghlib and Tazīd. To these, moreover, must be added plural animal names like Panthers, Dogs, Lizards, Spotted Snakes (Anmār, Kilāb, Dibāb, Arācim), which are exactly similar to the Totem names found in so many parts of the world. The genealogists derive the Banū Kilāb from an ancestor whose name was Kilāb, that is "dogs," but really the phrase means nothing more than sons, *i.e.* members, of the dog tribe. [11]

In like manner place-names are transformed by the genealogists into the names of ancestors or ancestresses (Hadramaut, Hauab, etc.) — more often the latter, because it is common Semitic idiom to call a land or town the mother of its inhabitants. Again very many Arab tribes are named after gods or goddesses and the euhemerism which explains this by making the deity a mere deified ancestor has no more claim to attention in the Arab field than in other parts of the Semitic world. No one accepts the euhemeristic explanations of Phoenician deities in Philo Byblius, and the case is not a whit better in Arabia, where we find Children of the Sun [12] and Children of the Moon side by side with such groups as Servant of Cais, Sons of Cais, Gift of Manāt, Slave of Al-Lāt. Some of these god-names it is true ultimately became personal names, but there can hardly be a question that in such a case the group-name Cais is older than Cais as the name of an individual man. In truth such personal names as Cais afford perhaps the oldest evidence of Arabic euhemerism and the earliest traces of the way of explaining tribal names which becomes universal in the genealogical system. The Arabs were fond of naming their children after ancestors, and yet hardly any old tribal name, unless it were also a divine name, appears in historical times as the personal name of a member of the tribe. This is tolerably conclusive proof that tribal names not taken from gods were not originally understood to be derived from ancestors; and with this it agrees that though the Arabs paid the greatest respect to the graves of their forefathers, as has been illustrated at length by Goldziher in his *Culte des Ancétres chez les Arabes* (Paris, 1885), there is hardly one well-authenticated case of a tribe which possessed a really ancient tradition as to the place where the tribal ancestor was interred. [13]

In S. Arabia later ages pointed out the tomb of Cahtan, who however is not the eponym of an ancient tribe, but stands on the same line with the prophet Hud, the sage Locman, and others whose tombs are also commemorated in the *Iklīl*. Abulfeda tells us that the tomb of Codā'a was shown in Jebel Shihr in Hadramaut, but this appears to be a still more modern invention, corresponding with the late and spurious genealogy of the tribe, and inconsistent with the fact that the name Codā'a means simply "far removed from their kin," and cannot originally have been derived from an eponym hero. There is better *prima facie* evidence for the tomb of Tamīm in Marrān, two marches from Mecca on the way to Al-Basra, which is mentioned by Ibn Cotaiba (p. 37) by Bakrī and Yācūt in their articles on Mārran. But here also closer examination of the witnesses shows that they are not speaking from knowledge, but merely drawing an inference from two passages of the poet Jarīr in which he speaks of Marrān as containing a sacred tomb which the warriors of his house regarded as an inviolable asylum, so that by taking refuge at it he could secure the aid of a brave and powerful clan against the Caliph himself (Bakrī, p. 522, *Yāc.* 4 478, compared with the historical explanation in *Agh.* 8 179). This is quite in accordance with the general Arab doctrine of asylum at a tomb; but the other instances of such asylum drawn from the same period lead us to think not of a remote ancestor, but of a chieftain of comparatively recent date — of a member of Jarīr's more immediate kindred, rather than the mythical head of that vast and scattered nation of Tamīm, of which Jarīr's was not the main branch. In fact the poet seems to have had personal associations with Mārran (see a verse in Bakrī, p. 243), and that his family buried their dead there is rendered probable by the fact that 'Āmr ibn 'Obeid, who was interred at Mārran in A.H. 144, was a client of theirs (Ibn Khallikān, ed. Wüst. no. 514). Al-Farazdac (*Kāmil*, p. 272 *sq.*, comp. p. 280) speaks of his father's tomb much as Jarīr speaks of that at Mārran. [14]

In the case of Tamīm it is very doubtful whether the personification of the tribe as an eponym hero had become fixed in mythological or quasi-historical form as early as the time of Jarīr and Al-Farazdac. At this date, as we have seen in the case of Bakr and Taghlib, it was often not settled whether a tribe should have a male or a female eponym, though the tide was running towards the former. Thus Al-Farazdac who says "Taghlib daughter of Wail" can say also "Bakr son of Wāil" (*Agh.* xix. 43 16). These two forms of speech do not really mean anything different; the poet does not connect a mythological or historical idea with either, and the personification is for him a merely verbal one. In like manner while Al-Farazdac certainly says "Tamīm son of Morr" (*Kāmil*, 765 5), he might equally well say "Tamīm daughter of Morr," and so one is tempted to read in *Agh.* viii. 1897. At any rate the *Tāj* bears witness that that expression is known to the poets. [15] One need not argue from this that a myth once existed in which Tamīm was a woman or goddess: the personification may be merely poetic, but at any rate it is one which could not have arisen side by side with a definite tradition or myth about a hero Tamīm. Such words as those of *Kāmil*, 248;, "Tamim has been destroyed, alike her Sa'd and her Ribāb," could never have been written if there had been a real belief that Tamīm was Sad's grandfather as the genealogists teach. It is clear, therefore, not only that the genealogical theory of the origin of all tribes and tribal names is not based throughout on definite historical tradition, but that it is not the expression in quasi-historical form of an old mythology. That in many cases the tribe had an eponym god who was thought of as an ancestor is likely enough, or rather certain, as we shall see by and by. But in others the personification of the tribal unity was either merely verbal, without mythological content, so that at first it could be taken indifferently as male or female, or if there was a real personification, that is, a real belief in a mythological person or deity of the tribal name, the personification was feminine. Very often we find that the sex of an eponym is matter of discussion among the genealogists themselves. Thus in *Agh.* 16 47 it appears that Madhhij is variously taken as another name for Malik son of Odad, or as mother of Mālik, or as "neither father nor mother" but the name of a mound or cairn at which the tribe assembled. [16]

We find then many reasons for refusing to accept the theory of the origin of tribal groups offered by the genealogists; but we must not rest content with this merely negative result. It is plain that in adopting the system of patronymic groups as the key to the whole tribal system, the genealogists must have had something to go on; there must have been, about the time of the prophet, a tendency to accept this as the natural explanation of the origin of tribal groups, I believe that the reason why this was so can be made out clearly enough. The patronymic theory was no mere arbitrary hypothesis, no mere idea borrowed from the Jews; it was not even an arbitrary extension to all tribes of an explanation really applicable to some of them; it followed inevitably from the assumption that the tribal bond and the law of tribal succession had always been what they were at the time of the prophet.

At that time the tribal bond all over Arabia, so far as our evidence goes, was conceived as a bond of kinship. All the members of a group regarded themselves as of one blood. This appears most clearly in the law of bloodfeud, which in Arabia as among other early peoples affords the means of measuring the limits of effective kinship. A kindred group is a group within which there is no blood feud. If a man kills one of his own kin he finds no one to take his part. Either he is put to death by his own people or he becomes an outlaw and must take refuge in an alien group. On the other hand if the slayer and slain are of different kindred groups a blood-feud at once arises, and the slain man may be avenged by any member of his own group on any member of the group of the slayer. This is the general rule of blood-revenge all over the world, and with certain minor modifications it holds good in Arabia at the present day, in spite of Islam, as it held good in the oldest times

19

of which we have record. And as the greater part of the traditions of the Arabs turns on blood-revenge and war, the rule now laid down affords a sure practical test of what kindred meant and how it was counted.

Under such a system the ultimate kindred group is that which always acts together in every case of blood-revenge. And in Arabia this group was not the family or household, not the relatives of the slayer and the slain within certain degrees of kinship, as we reckon kinship, but a definite unity marked off from all other groups by the possession of a common group-name. Such a group the Arabs commonly call a *hayy,* and the fellow-members of a man's *hayy* are called his *ahl* or his *caum.* To determine whether a man is or is not involved in a blood-feud it is not necessary to ask more than whether he bears the same group-name with the slayer or the slain. The common formula applied to manslaughter is that the blood of such a *hayy* has been shed and must be avenged. The tribesmen do not say that the blood of *M* or *N* has been spilt, naming the man; they say "our blood has been spilt." The call to vengeance is no doubt felt most strongly by the father, the son or the brother of the slain, and they may be more reluctant than distant cousins to accept a composition by bloodwit. But this has nothing to do with the principle of the blood-feud. No man who is within the group can escape responsibility merely because he is not a close relation of the slayer or the slain. If there is blood between Libyan and 'Adi there is war between every man of Lihyān and every man of 'Adī till the blood is atoned for. And conversely if a man of Kinda sheds the blood of another man of Kinda it makes no difference whether he can actually count kin with his victim on our way of reckoning descents: "he has shed the blood of his people" and must die or be cut off from the name and place of his tribe. Kinship then among the Arabs means a share in the common blood which is taken to flow in the veins of every member of a tribe — in one word, it is the tribal bond which knits men of the same group together and gives them common duties and responsibilities from which no member of the group can withdraw.

But, again, at the time of the prophet the usual rule throughout Arabia, or at least in the parts of the country which were most advanced and have had most influence on the development of the race, was that, even when a man took a wife from outside his own tribe, the son followed the tribe of his real or putative father. Strictly speaking this rule only applied when the foreign wife left her own tribe and came to reside with her husband among his kin, but this too was the customary practice in the leading centres of Arab life, and thus as a rule the son was of his father's tribe. Take now these two things together — that the tribe is all of one blood, and that the son is of the blood and therefore of the tribe of his father; assume further that these two principles had held good through the whole past history of the Arabs, and the conclusion of the genealogists is inevitable that the tribes were in their origin patronymic tribes formed by male descents from a common ancestor.

I think it will be admitted that this argument sufficiently explains how it came about that genealogists, and indeed tribesmen themselves, came to extend the patronymic theory to all tribes, even where there was no primitive tradition of descent from a common father who gave his descendants their tribal name. But it does more than this: it affords a presumption little short of certainty that the rule which reckoned a son to his father's kin cannot have prevailed at all times and in all parts of Arabia. To bring this out it is necessary to develop the argument further.

The doctrine that all the tribe is of one blood and the rule that the son is of his father's blood taken together are the sufficient conditions for the rise of the theory that the whole tribe is sprung from a common male ancestor. And generally speaking any variation in these conditions would have led to a different theory. If, for example, the doctrine of one tribal blood remaining as before, the rule had been, as it is in some parts of the world, that the children belong to their mother's tribe and therefore are of their mother's blood, theory would have led not to a common father but to a common mother being taken as the eponym of the tribe. Or if, and this too is a case which has occurred in actual usage, it was matter of arrangement whether the father's or the mother's tribe should claim the children, the motive for a theory of eponymous ancestors would be considerably weakened, and we might expect to find that where such ancestors were believed in, some would be men and some women. Conversely, if a kinship tribe derives its origin from a great father, we may argue with confidence that it had the rule that children were of their father's tribe and kin; while on the other hand if we find, in a nation organised on the principle of unity of tribal blood, tribes which trace their origin to a great mother instead of a great father, we can feel sure that at some time the tribe followed the rule that the children belong to the mother and are of her kin. Now among the Arabs the doctrine of the unity of tribal blood is universal, as appears from the universal prevalence of the blood-feud. And yet among the Arab tribes we find no small number that refer their origin to a female eponym. Hence it follows that in many parts of Arabia kinship was once reckoned not in the male but in the female line. [17]

An attempt is sometimes made to meet the force of this argument by observing that in a polygamous state of society the children of one father may be distinguished into groups by the use of their mother's name. The point before us, however, is not the use of the mother's name by individuals, for purposes of distinction, but the existence of kindred groups whose members conceive that the tie of blood which unites them into a tribe is derived from and limited by descent from a common V ancestress. That the existence of such a group proves kinship through women to have been once the rule is as certain as that the existence of patronymic groups is evidence of male kinship. In most cases of the kind the female eponym is mythical no doubt, and the belief in her existence is a mere inference from the rule of female kinship within the tribe, just as mythical male ancestors are inferred from a rule of

21

male kinship. But even if we suppose the ancestress to be historical, the argument is much the same; for where the bond of maternity is so strong that it binds together the children of the same mother as a distinct kindred group against the other children of their father, there also we may be sure that the children of one mother by different fathers will hold together and not follow their father. And this is the principle of female kinship. [18]

Nöldeke, in the *Oestr. Zeitsch. f. Orient*, 1884, p. 302, [19] has proposed to explain the existence of female eponyms among the Arabic tribes in another way. Collective terms in Arabic are constantly feminine and Arabic grammar treats all tribal unities as such. Names like Tamīm, Taghlib, etc., whether feminine in form or not, take feminine verbs and are referred to by feminine pronouns singular. According to Nöldeke this grammatical rule is the sufficient explanation of feminine eponyma, the grammatical personification of a tribe as feminine being enough to lead people ultimately to think of an ancestress eponyma. The explanation is at first sight plausible, and if there were nothing more to be explained than the purely verbal personifications of later poets like Al-Farazdac with his "Taghlib daughter of Wāil" there would be nothing to say against it. But the personification of the tribal unity as mother of the stock is not an arbitrary fiction of later poets; [21] it is one of the old standing figures of Semitic speech. In Hebrew *ēm* is "mother" but also "stock, race, community" (2 Sam. 20 19, Hosea 45); in Arabic *omm* is mother, and the derived senses are expressed by *omma*. [22] So again the bonds of kinship are expressed alike in Arabic and in Hebrew by the words *rehem, rakim,* the womb; in Amos 1 11, שחת רחמיו does not mean "he cast off all pity" but "he burst the bonds of kinship," Ar. *'acca 'l-rahim, cata'a 'l-rahim,* just as שחת ברית means "he broke through a covenant." [22] It appears then that mother-kinship is the type of kinship, common motherhood the type of kindred unity, which dominate all Semitic speech. We cannot separate these linguistic facts from the other fact that the oldest way of speaking of a tribe as a whole was in the feminine gender, and that this way was so deeply rooted in language that it survived as a law of grammar in spite of the universal adoption of the patronymic theory. It will not serve to say that tribes are feminine because all collectives are so; there can hardly be a question that tribal names are quite the earliest of collective names and that all collectives were thought of as a kind of tribes. [23] If at the time when the use of genders was taking shape the effective bond of blood had been reckoned through the father, it is simply incredible that the tribal unity could have been personified as mother of the stock; the very fact that tribal names were and continued to be treated as feminine collectives is a strong argument for an early and universal prevalence of mother-kinship.

It is true, and so much must be conceded to Professor Nöldeke's argument, that after this old mother-kinship died out and was replaced by a system of kinship through males the merely grammatical and meaningless personification of tribes as women might still go on; we cannot argue that there was female kinship in Taghlib at the time of Al-Farazdac because he says "Taghlib daughter of Bakr." But then also in this case the genealogists did not assume a female but a male eponym. And in general the system of male eponyms everywhere triumphed over the grammatical rule that tribes are feminine collectives. When therefore we find that in spite of all the pressure of the patronymic theory the genealogists were forced to admit a certain number of female eponyms, and to say that the sons of Khindif, the sons of Jadīla, and so forth, bore their mother's name and not that of their father, we may feel sure that in these cases they found themselves face to face with some stronger fact than a mere rule of grammar, *i.e.*, either with an actual tradition of female kinship, or with such a well-established myth of an eponym heroine as could only arise under a rule of female kinship. With this it agrees that such female eponyms are frequently referred to a very remote antiquity, just as in Hebrew Leah is more ancient than Levi and Sarah than Israel. [24]

In not a few instances we can show that the original affinities of a group are expressed in the genealogy of its mother while the paternal tree exhibits its relations to other tribes in more modern times. Examples of this have been given in a note to what was said above about Codā'a. [25] Let us now consider what this means in a case where the tribes actually call themselves by a metronymic name. The 'Āmila were originally a branch of Codā'a but, with the other Ribāb, were reckoned to Tamīm in later times. How could they have been persuaded to believe that 'Āmila their mother was daughter of Codā'a unless they had had the memory of a time when tribal affinities naturally went through the mother? If mother-kinship was the old rule and was gradually superseded by paternal kinship, the fact that 'Āmila was once of Codā'a and afterwards of Tamīm was well enough expressed by saying "Your mother is of Codā'a but your paternal kin is Tamīm"; but if father-kinship was the old rule such a phrase would have been at open variance with the actual history of the tribe. So again we find a section of the 'Adī incorporated in the Hanzala branch of Tamīm and calling themselves sons of the Adawite mother (Banu 'l-'Adawīya, Ibn Cot. p. 37) [26] and in Maidānī, 1 292 (Freyt., *Ar. Pr.* 1 608), we find a legend about this Adawite woman, Nawār wife of Malik, showing that she was not a mere grammatical personification. But this group which held itself to be Adawite only through the mother had the same tribal worship as 'Adī in general; 'Adī is of 'Abd-Manāt and Hanzala is of Zaid-Manāt. This is exactly parallel to the case in which the sons of Morr, who through their mother are referred to Kalb, have at the same time for their paternal grandfather Odd, that is Wodd the god of the Kalb. In both cases the religion of the group is that of its mother, and it need hardly be said that when a man is of his mother's religion he is also of his mother's kin. These are not things that can be mere inventions of genealogists helped by an accident of grammar.

Strong as these arguments appear to be, they are too abstract to afford conviction in so complicated a matter without experimental verification. Of

23

this we shall have enough by and by, but meantime it will be not unprofitable to press the abstract argument a little further.

Assuming provisionally that tribal eponyms like Khindif, Mozaina, Caila must probably be explained as pointing to groups of female kinship, let us observe that all over Arabia the rule of female kinship must gradually have given way to a rule of male kinship; for we find that the groups named after an eponym heroine are not only incorporated by the genealogists in their general system of male descents, but lend themselves to genealogical subdivision in the male line. There is no tribe with a female eponym in which the main groups have not male eponyms, and though this may be partly due to the inventive genius of the genealogists, it must also be taken to mean that in later times the rule of kinship had changed, and that so the tribe itself was able to accept without opposition a genealogical scheme foreign to its original constitution. This is quite in accordance with what is observed among other races which have once had a rule of female kinship. Everywhere as society advances a stage is reached when the child ceases to belong to the mother's kin and follows the father. Accordingly we may be tolerably sure that the law of female kinship in Arabia was once much more widely spread than appears from the recorded instances of tribes with female eponyms. That female eponyms might often be changed to male ones appears from such cases as those of Madhhij and Khasafa; and in this way the true nature of ancient communities of mother's blood was readily disguised. But we are riot dependent on the argument from eponyms alone; we have the general argument already adduced from the words *omma* and *rahim,* and another not less significant from the fact that in all parts of Arabia one of the technical terms for a clan or sub-tribe is *batn,* literally the belly, and particularly the mother's belly. The exact difference in usage between the various Arabic words for tribe and sub-tribe has never been clearly made out, and the theories of the genealogists on this head, which may be read in the lexicons or in an extract from 'Obaidallī given in Wüstenfeld's *Register,* p. 9 *sq.,* are highly imaginative. But it is safe to say that *batn* can originally have meant nothing else than a tribe constituted or propagated by mother-kinship — indeed this sense of the word still lives, according to Wetzstein (in Delitzsch, *Iob,* p. 520, 1st ed., 1864), in the spoken Arabic of Damascus. Hence, as Nöldeke has observed, *batn* may be taken as the counterpart of the word *fakkidh,* "thigh," which is used to mean a clan in the Palmyrene inscriptions and also (though less commonly than *batn*) in Arabic literature. The sense of *fakhidh* is unambiguously indicated by the Hebrew phrase which speaks of children as "proceeding from the thigh" of their father (Gen. 46 26 etc.), and by the Syriac phrase *shācā d' malkē,* the seed royal, literally "the kings' thigh" (Hoffmann, *Syrische Acten Pers. Märt.,* note 833.) Thus the "thigh" or clan of male descent stands over against the "belly" or clan of mother's blood. But *batn* in literary Arabic is applied to tribes of male kinship, just as *rahim* is no longer confined to mother-kinship — a clear indication that there has been a change in the

24

rule of descent and that mother-kinship is the older type. The technical sense of the word *batn* appears to be very old and to be known in Hebrew as well as in Arabic. At all events it supplies the most natural explanation of בְּנֵי בִטְנִי, "sons of my womb," *i.e.* my clan, in Job 19 17. And here it may be added that just as Laban says of his sister's son Jacob, "thou art my bone and my flesh," [27] so according to Hamdānī 165 10 *lohūm*, pl. of *lahm* "flesh" is a synonym of *botūn*, pi, of *batn*.

[1] A convenient view of the whole system, printed in the shape of a series of genealogical tables, is to be found in F. Wüstenfeld, *Genealogische Tabellen der Arabischen Stämme tend Familien* (Göttingen, 1852). The tables are accompanied by an index volume, *Register zu den Tabellen,* which contains a very useful accumulation of traditional material, put together without criticism of the sources, so that a good deal of sifting is necessary.
[2] [*Das Leben u. Lehre d. Mohammad,* iii. pp. cxx *sqq.* (Berlin, 1865).]
[3] So B. Hish. p. 7, I. 7.
[4] [Cp. Jarīr's Dīwān (Cairo), i. 10710. — A. A. B.]
[5] See *Additional Note A.*
[6] Zaid Manāt and Bakr b. Wail went together as suitors to a certain king. Zaid Manāt, who was of a greedy envious nature, was determined to be first with the king, and persuaded Bakr to put on his best clothes before presenting himself at court, thus gaining time to occupy the king's ear with unfavourable accounts of his friend. But Bakr has his revenge, for when both appear before the king together and Zaid Manāt has craved as his boon that whatever is given to his comrade he shall have double, Bakr, whose right eye was blind, though it looked sound, begs that it may be put out. He therefore leaves the king seeing as well as when he came, while Zaid retires with the loss of both eyes. Socin, *Gedichte des Alcama,* p. 19 *sq.* — There is some fault in 20 9; Brünnow's edition of *Agh.* bk. 21 (p. 172, 1. 21) has شِيمة, which is clearly right.
[7] Bakr and Taghlib together are the sons of Hind as Nöldeke, *Delectus,* p. 45, 1. 10, rightly reads with *Agh.* against Hamāsa, p. 9. She is bint Morr b. Odd and sister of Tamīm. Nöldeke in *Oesterreichische Monatschrift für den Orient,* 1884, p. 302, cites 'Āmr b. Kolthūm (Agh. 9 184), Al-Akhnas b. Shihāb (*Ham.* 346), and Al-Farazdac (*ib.* 420). (Cp. Ibn al-Athīr, 1 373. To these add a verse of Al-No'mān b. Bashir, *Agh.* xiii. 154 10.) The last passage is given in Tāj, 1 134, with the variant ورد for دخل in the last hemistich, together with a verse of Walid b. 'Ocba, who was taxmaster among the Taghlib under 'Omar I.

According to Goldziher [*Literatur-blatt für Orientalische Philologie,* 3 (1885-87) 23*], the use of "brother" here is like that in Prov. 74, or *akhu l'hadr, Agh.* ii. 36 20 (cp. *ib.* 52 11), akhu thicat, or *ikhwān assafa* "the pure ones." See further Goidziher's remark, *Muh. Stud.* 1 9.
[8] Tebrīzī, *Hamāsa,* p. 284, says, "their brother, *i.e.* one of them, as one says 'O brother of Bakr or Tamīm.'" Cp. *Kāmil,* 288 20, 289 1. So in *Diw. Hodh.* 331, Hobshī is called "the Sobhite brother of the sons of Zolaifa," but in 25 introd. "one of the sons of Zolaifa b. Sobh." The phrase is common in this collection, and seems sometimes to be expressly chosen to denote a tribesman by affiliation — so no.

130 introd. In no. 106 Hodhaifa is brother both of the Banū 'Āmr. b. al-Hārith and the Banū 'Abd b. 'Adī. The latter are his mother's tribe (no. 103 introd.). [It is even said of a married couple: *baina akhawai* Banī 'Ajlān, *i.e.* a man and woman of the tribe 'A. (Bokhārī, *Kitāb al-Talāc*, no. 31). — I. G.]

[9] [On the Kholoj, see fully *Agh.* 4 102. — I. G.]

[10] The existence of metronymic tribes is admitted by Ibn Doraid, 130 13, 251 9 (Goldz. *Lit.blatt f. Orient. Phil.* 3 26*.) [Goldziher, however, would qualify the term metronymic. As he points out, what Ibn Doraid admits is the existence of tribal names with Banū which have an apparent genealogical form, but in reality have no relationship with any male or female ancestor.]

[11] It is natural to explain such a term as Kilāb on the analogy of forms like al-Nomairūna, on which compare *Kāmil*, p. 622 *sq.* The members of the tribe of No-mair are "the Nomairs" or "little panthers," each one having a right to the name of the tribal "father," Nomair. Such at least is Mobarrad's explanation, assuming the patronymic theory: but the thing is equally consistent with the theory of to-tem tribes, and much more natural under it. Accordingly, the Kilāb are not really different in name from the Kalb, and Kalb (sing.), not Kilāb (plural), ought to be the eponym of the former as well as of the latter. In later times we occasionally find plural personal names derived from animals. Thus in Ibn Hishām, 563 17, we have Sibā' (wild beasts), son of a freedwoman called "Mother of Panthers." The *konya* Abū Sibā' is found in *Diw. Hodh.* 165 2. Among the Bedouins of the Hijāz at the present day, Dhiāb "wolves" is a man's name. But it is almost certain that such names are a mere efflux of the patronymic theory. In *Diw. Hodh.* 83 the collector supposes Anmār to be the name of the poet, but what the poem itself says is, "I am the son of Anmār, that is my war-cry," and we know that the usual Arab war-cry was the clan name. But see Nöld. *ZDMG* 40 163, n. 4, who denies that *zabrī* signifies a war-cry and makes it to mean "name"; Dozy, however, ac-cepts the scholiast to 40, who renders by ح ‏ .

[12] The Σαμψηνοί are connected by Staph. Byz. with a town σάμψα. He explains σάμψα as "sun."

[13] [But see *RS,* p. 156, n. 2], Yācūt, ii. 343 13 sqq. The himā of Dariya, where also the cattle grazed, was the hima of Kolaib b. Wail, and his grave was in a cor-ner of it. See Wellh. Heid. (1) 163, (2) 184. The supposed grave of Modar ibn Nizār was at ‏الروبا‏ (Bakri, *s.v.,* p. 425, end of article). [The grave of the ancestor of the B. Dabba is said to have been in the district of the B. Tamīm (Yacūt, iv. 91 12), the grave of Kolaib Wāil in Dhanāib (near Zabid in S. Arabia, *Agh.* iv. 142 12, Yāc. ii. 723 12). — I. G.]

[14] Similarly Nābigha (16 Ahlw.; 36 Derenb.) speaks of the tomb at Jillic, which, according to Hassān b. Thābit (C. de Percival, 2 241), is that of the son of Māriya, *i.e.* Al-Hārith b. Jabala, 569 (Nöldeke, Ghassān. *Fürsten,* 22 *sq.*) On the second grave spoken of in the same verse, cp. Wetzstein, *Reisebericht über den Hauran,* 117 (Berlin, 1860), cited by Nöld. *op. cit.* 50.

[15] According to the *Taj,* 1 134, the poets say "Tamim daughter of Morr," and from this statement it seems legitimate to correct the line of Al-Farazdac, *Agh.* viii. 189 7, by reading ‏مر‏ for ‏بنت مر‏ a feminine being more appropriate to the grammatical context [but see Nöld. *ZDMG* 40 170.] A very different form of the verses is given in *Agh.* xix. 10 *sq.* In the *Kāmil*, 278 4, Abū Moshamraj, the Yashkorite, says, "Would that the mother of Tamīm had never known Morr but had been as one whom time sweeps away" — another form of feminine personification.

[16] For Madhhij compare further Yācūt, *s.v.*, and 4 1023, *Kāmil*, 266. Another example of eponyms of uncertain sex is Khasafa (*infra*, 31, n. 1). In *Agh.* 8 179, the branch of the Ribāb called the 'Āmila are made descendants of Al-Hārith, and the author says in the same breath that Al-Hārith is 'Āmila and that 'Āmila is Al-Hārith's wife. So, again, Ibn Cotaiba (p. 36) says, Mozaina son of Odd; but Al-Nawawī, 568, makes Mozaina the daughter of Kalb and wife of 'Āmr b. Odd.

[17] A few examples will suffice: (1) The two great branches of Modar are Cais and Khindif, and the latter is said to be wife of Al-Yās and great-granddaughter of Codā'a. Al-Yās is not a tribal name, but Khindif is so, and Yāla Khindif is a battle-cry, or cry for help (*Ham.* 194). (2) The joint-name of the Aus and Khazraj is Banū Caila (Ibn Hishām, 140). She also is made a descendant of Codā'a. Caila seems to be the feminine of the well-known Hiniyarite battle Call. The Banāt Caila (Ibn Sa'd, 102) are different. They appear to be an independent family, and Wellhausen formerly conjectured that they had matriarchy (*Skizsen*, 4 16, n. 4, 1889). (3) The sons of Jadīla are one of the two great branches of the Tayyi (Ibn Doraid, 228), and they are named after their mother. (4) At the battle of Bu'ath the Banū 'Abd al-ashhal shout: We are the sons of Sakhra — but Mon-a bint Zafar is their ancestress (*Agh.* xv. 165 10). (5) The Fezārites are named Manūla after the wife of Fezāra (al-Hādira, ed. Engelmann, p. 4, line 10; cp. Nābigha, 21 7). Many other examples may be found in Ibn Doraid, *Kitāb al-Ishticāc*, Ibn Cotaiba, *Kitāb al-Ma'ādrif,* or in Wüstenfeld's *Register* ('Adawīya, To*hayy*a, Bajīla, Bāhila, 'Adasa, etc.).

[18] The explanation of metronymic tribal names from polygamy was pressed by Dr. Redhouse, in his defence of the theory of the Arab genealogists against Professor Wilken [cp. *JRAS* 17 282]. But the old Arab explanation of the phenomenon, as given in the *Aghānī*, 4 128 *sq.*, is different. "Al-Kalbī, following his father, says that Khasafa was not, as is usually said, son of Cais b. 'Ailān and father of 'Ikrima, but that 'Ikrima, was son of Cais and Khasafa was his mother or foster-mother; and that Cais dying when 'Ikrima was a little child, he was reared by Khasafa, and his people used to say, This is 'Ikrima son of Khasafa, and the name stuck to him; and then ignorant people said 'Ikrima son of Khasafa son of Cais, just as the Khindif are named from Khindif wife of Al-Yās." This explanation is of course purely imaginary. According to old Arab custom Khasafa on her husband's death would either have returned to her own kin or been married again to one of her husband's kinsmen. In the former case the child would have belonged to her tribe, in the latter to her husband's tribe.

[19] [Cp. also *ZDMG* 40 169 *sq.*]

[20] [See the verse of Ghallac ibn Marvvan, referring to the feud between the tribes of 'Abs and Dhobyān in pre -Islamic times (Hamdsa, 224) — "Oh would that they (*i.e.* the hostile clan) were the children of some other woman, and that thou, O Fatima, hadst given birth to none of them!" — A. A. B.]

[21] Omina is "community" according to Fleischer, the community that has a common Imam. The sense "religion" or rather "religious community" appears in Nābigha (ed. Derenb.) 2 21 ذُو أُمَّة. For religion pure and simple Nābigha says دِين, 6 6, 3 24.

[22] [To be noted also is the expression: *unshiduka allāha walrahima, Agh.* xiv. 16 15; cp. also *shacca,* Ibn Hish. 539 13; *Agh.* 1 10 ult., *Ham* 437 5 *'arhāmun tushaccacu* — with the variant *tumazzacu* (Ibn abī Osaibi'a, i. 116 4). — I. G.]

[23] [There is an illuminating example of this in Cor. *Sur.* 6 38. — A. A. B.]

[24] For Levi as the patronymic corresponding to Leah, see Wellhausen, *Prolegomena,* (4) 141 (E.T. 145). I do not remember to have seen it pointed out that Sarah corresponds just as closely with Israel. The masculine name corresponding to Sarah is Seraiah (inniy), which stands to Israel as Hezekiah does to Ezekiel. Now it is well known that Judah was not originally included in the name of Israel, but was only a brother tribe; see the books of Samuel *passim,* and especially 2 Sam. 5 1. It is also known that Abraham was originally a Judean hero; thus we understand how Sarah as the eponyma of Israel was Abraham's sister before she came to be called his wife and the mother of Israel and Judah alike.

[25] See *Additional Note* A.

[26] So the B. Sāma are called on the mother's side B. Nājiya (*Agh.* 9 104 *sq.,* Masūdī, 7 250; cp. Goldz. *Lit.blatt f. Or. Phil.* 26*).

[27] So in later Arabic "he is thy flesh and thy blood," 'Antara, 467 1. 2, cp. *ib.* 62 1. 7 [cp. the other parallels cited by Goldz. (*Lit. blatt* p. 26*)].

Chapter Two - The Kindred Group and Its Dependents or Allies

The two principles underlying the genealogical system of the Arabs are, as we have seen, that every tribe is a homogeneous group, *i.e.* a collection of people of the same blood, and that the son is of the blood of the father.

If these two principles can be held to have always been in force as they were in the time of Mohammed, only real patronymic tribes are possible; and so every indication that some tribes were not patronymic goes to show that at some time or other there was either a different law of kinship, or a possibility of forming a tribe on another principle than that of unity of blood. We have already seen that if the principle of the homogeneous tribe is really ancient the existence of tribes with female eponyms affords a strong argument that male descent was not always the law of kinship; but it is obvious that before pursuing this line of argument further we must first make sure that we have a clear insight into the constitution of an Arab tribe, and that homogeneity or oneness of tribal blood is really as fundamental a factor in its constitution as the law of blood-revenge has hitherto inclined us to suppose. The present chapter will be devoted to this topic.

The Arab kindred group or *hayy,* as we know it, was a political and social unity, so far as there was any unity in that very loosely organised state of society. The nomadic Arabs, whose way of life supplied the type on which all Arabian society was mainly moulded, are not to be thought of as roaming quite at large through the length and breadth of the peninsula. Each group or confederation of groups had its own pastures, and still more its own waters, beyond which it could not move without immediate risk of a hostile encounter (*e.g. Agh.* xvi. 49 9). Within these limits families wandered at large with their cattle and tents wherever they could find water and forage. But generally these movements — say from summer to winter pasture — were made by the whole *hayy* together, and no small body felt itself to be safe at a great distance from its brethren. In ordinary circumstances, it is true, the free Bedouin does what he pleases and goes where he pleases, but the law of self-preservation has dictated that in war all must act together. "The cause of the annihilation of tribes," says a poet cited in the *Kāmil,* 170 7, "is the violation of the duties of blood." It is only by mutual help, by avoiding intestine quarrels and subordinating individual interests to those of the kin, that, in the hard conditions of desert life, and in a state of constant war with outsiders, a tribe can hope to hold its own (comp. *Agh.* 2 170 1, i). To get the full benefit of this mutual support, the group or *hayy* must not only fight together, but as far as possible move together. In time of peace indeed this was dictated not by binding custom, but only by convenience and mutual advantage. A man, a family, or even a small group might find it convenient for a time to part from the main stock and sojourn with some other kin. But if war broke out between the stranger's hosts and his own stock his part was at once to regain his tribe. If his own sense of duty did not force him to do this he was likely to receive a peremptory summons from his people (*Diw. Hodh.* nos. 63, 210), or might get from his hosts three days' notice to quit ('*Icd,* 3 68, *Agh.* 16 28). We must, therefore, think of the kindred group as a central mass of kinsmen ordinarily living near one another, but with some members temporarily absent in other groups subject to recall, and a certain fringe of wandering parties (*tawāif,* — *Diw. Hodh.* ed. Kosegarten, pp. 49, 223) which felt themselves strong enough to move about alone at a distance from their brethren. When the group became very large it necessarily broke up into two or more masses, for a large horde cannot find subsistence together in the desert. When this took place the different hordes gradually acquired independent interests, and at length each became a separate *hayy,* even exercising blood-feud against their old brethren. For the unity of the *hayy* was maintained only by the principle that all must act together in war (*i.e.* blood-feud), and that no one must protect his kinsman for the murder of a man of his own blood. But a sub-group or horde which habitually lived apart from its brethren was very likely to form covenants with aliens, and this often led to a conflict of obligations in case of war and loosened the old tribal bond (*Diw. Hodh.* 47, 128, etc.). And again, in a case of murder, where the slayer was of the same kin, but of a different horde from the slain, his horde was very likely to stand by him. The cooler heads were ready no doubt to pay blood-money and keep the peace, but they would not give up their brother altogether. Hence arose such fratricidal wars as those of the Aus and the Khazraj, Bakr and Taghlib, 'Abs and Dhobyān. But there were some conventional limitations on quarrels between near kinsfolk. The Aus and the Khazraj, for example, came at length to fight *à outrance,* but for long their rule was not to pursue fugitives beyond the nearest homestead — the *dār* was not invaded. [1] In the long run then the strict bond of kinship could not maintain itself except within the limits of a local group habitually moving together, and though the word *hayy* is sometimes used in a very comprehensive sense, *e.g.* of the Azd (*Kāmil,* 35 12) or Tamīm and Kalb (Al-Farazdac in *Agh.* 19 25), it usually means such a kindred group as was guided in war and on the march by one chief (*Agh.* 4 141 1. 25, 16 50 1. 6, 53 1. 23), migrating together (*ib.* 2 163, last line, 16 24 1. 18 *sq.*), and forming generally a single settlement (*Agh.* 16 29 1. 10, 52 1. 4, 4 151 1. 12; *Diw. Hodh.* ed. Kos. 110 12), which might, however, consist of several *dārs,* or groups of tents, at some distance from one another (*Diw. Hodh.* 103 introd., 143 introd.). As the *hayy* had its own chief, so also it had its own war-cry — usually the tribal name, or that of its god — and its own flag (Harith, *Moall.* 1. 59). [2]

The local unity of the *hay* [3] is so marked an element in the conception of a kindred group that the word ultimately comes to mean no more than a dwelling-place, and Wilken in his latest paper on Arabic kinship believes that this is the original sense and that the sense of kindred is secondary, as in our "house" or the Hebrew בֵּית אָב. But this seems a hasty conclusion. Unambiguous instances of *hayy* in the sense of dwelling-place belong to later Arabic; even De Goeje's reading has supplied Wilken with none earlier than the time of Al-Farazdac (*Agh.* 19 25). In the case of so very common a word, it is obviously inadmissible to suppose that the primitive sense is one which is familiar to late writers, but for which no early authority can be found, especially as it is easy to show early passages (*e.g.* 'Antara, 18 1, Imrau 'lCais, *Moall.* 1. 4) which indicate the mode of transition from the sense of a kindred group to that of a dwelling-place. And, to make the point quite clear, it appears that the same word meant kindred in Hebrew, for in 1 Sam. 18 18, חַיָּי (so we must point with Wellhausen, *Text der BB. Sam,* p. 111) [4] is explained to mean "my father's clan." The literal sense of *hayy* is simply "life" or "living," and the application of such a name to a group which is of one blood is at once explained by the old Semitic principle that "the life of flesh lies in the blood" (Lev. 17 11). The whole kindred conceives itself as having a single life, [5] just as in the formula "our blood has been spilt" it speaks of itself as having but one blood in its veins. [6]

That the word *hayy* occurs in the same sense in Hebrew and Arabic affords a strong presumption that the group founded on unity of blood is a most ancient feature in Semitic society. Certainly no Semitic race had any remembrance of an earlier time when society was not yet constituted of kindred groups united by blood-bond and common blood-feud. And down to the time of Mohammed, the Arabs formed no enduring communities based on a higher principle. In some cases, as at Mecca, there was a sort of approximation to political incorporation of several kins. But even here the several branches of the Coraish never became incapable of having blood-feuds with one another, though in practice the occurrence of blood-feud was much restricted by regard to common interests. Similar aggregations among desert tribes were still more loosely knit together and always ready to break up again into their component kindred groups. By and by we shall find reason to think that at one stage, in prehistoric times, local groups ordinarily consisted of such unstable aggregates of fractions of different stock-groups. But in pursuing our enquiry from the known to the unknown we must first see how far back we can go on the assumption, which is true for historical times, that men of one kindred either lived together or could be called together to assert their common interests. The results so reached will not, I believe, require much modification to adapt them to remoter possibilities.

At the same time an Arabic group might and generally did contain in addition to pure-blooded tribesmen (*sorahā*, sing, *sarīh*, Heb. *ezrāh*) a certain number of slaves and clients. The clients again, *mawālī*, were of two kinds, freedmen and free Arabs of other kins living under the protection of the tribe or of its chief or some other influential man. In modern Arabia a protected stranger is called a *dakhīl*, from the phrase *dakhaltu 'alaika*, "I have come in unto thee," that is, have sought the protection of thy tent. For it is a principle alike in old and new Arabia that the guest is inviolable. This applies especially to one who has eaten or drunk with him whose protection he claims — in *Agh.* 16 51 even the thief who has surreptitiously shared the evening draught of an unwitting host is safe. [7] Nay, it is enough to touch the tent-ropes, [8] imploring protection — "tent-rope touching tent-rope" (sc. insures protection) is still a fundamental maxim of desert law (*al-tunub bi 'l-tunub*, comp. *Agh.* 19 79 last line). [9] In old Arabic the act of seeking such protection is *istijāra*, and the protected stranger is a *jār*, pi. *jīrān* (Heb. גֵּר). Now men were constantly being cut off from their own tribe, generally for murder within the kin, sometimes for other offences against society (*Agh.* 19 75), or even for dissipated habits (Tarafa, *Moall.* 1. 54, and the exclusion might be publicly proclaimed at 'Okath as in the case in *Agh.* 13 2 1. 7). Such outlaws (*khola'ā, Diw. Hodh.* 33) usually sought the protection of another tribe, which was seldom refused. There were, however, many other circumstances that might lead free Arabs, either individually or in a body, to seek the protection of another tribe and become its *jīrān*. Thus the several Jewish clans of Medina were compelled by their weakness to become *jīrān* of the Aus and Khazraj (*Agh.* 19 97). Or a group might attach itself to its cousins, *Banū 'l-'amm* (*Diw. Hodh.* 47 introd.), *i.e.* to a tribe with which it reckoned kindred; or very often a man settled in his wife's tribe, or with his mother's people (*akhwāl*). In these last cases the stranger had a special claim (comp. Ibn Hishām, 244 15, 275), but even absolute strangers were freely admitted to protection, and in the insecure life of the desert a strong tribe or a strong chief could not fail to gather a great number of dependents. [10]

The relation between protector and protected must in the nature of things have varied according to circumstances. Sometimes it was quite temporary, at other times it was permanent and even hereditary. At one time the protector only promised to aid his jar against some particular enemy; at another time he undertook to protect him against all enemies, or even against death itself, which meant that if the stranger died under his protection the host undertook to pay blood-money to his family. [11] Sometimes the protectors seem to have claimed the right to dismiss their *jīrān* at will (*Agh.* 19 75, Barrād), even though the relation was strengthened by some measure of kinship, short of that absolute blood-bond which did not extend beyond the *hayy* (*Diw. Hodh.* 192 *sqq.*); at other times — as in certain Meccan examples — protection is constituted by a public advertisement and oath at the sanctuary, and holds good till it is renounced at the sanctuary (Quatremère, p. 326 *sqq.*; Ibn Hishām, p. 243 *sq.*). The strongest case of all is where a man grants his *jār* blood-revenge against his own full-brother. [12]

We can hardly hope to reconstruct from scattered notices a complete account of the law of protection or *jiwār,* especially as many of the examples known to us, *e.g.* at Mecca, date from a time when the old tribal system and the old social order generally were falling into decay along with the old religion. For our present purpose, however, we may neglect the mere temporary relations formed by a man who had not renounced his old kin, and was liable at any moment to be recalled by or sent back to them. The permanent and hereditary dependents of a tribe other than slaves may then be roughly classified as (*a*) freedmen, (*b*) refugees outlawed from their own tribe, (*c*) groups like the Jews at Medina who were not strong enough to stand by themselves.

The principle that each Arab kindred held by itself and did not allow aliens to make a permanent settlement in its midst was not seriously compromised by the presence of freedmen and refugees, for these had no other tribal connection which could come into competition with 'their relation', to their protectors. As regards freedmen, indeed, the only point that concerns us here is that they were often adopted by their patrons. The commonest case was no doubt that of which the poet 'Antara furnishes an illustration. 'Antara was the son of a black slave girl, and therefore by old law was born a slave. But when he gave proof of prowess his father recognised him as his son and then he became a full tribesman. The right of adoption, however, was not limited to the legitimation of the offspring of a free tribesman by a slave girl. Mohammed, for example, adopted his freedman Zaid, a lad of pure Arab blood who had become a slave through the fortune of war. Here, then, a man is incorporated by adoption into a group of alien blood; but we learn that to preserve the doctrine of tribal homogeneity it was feigned that the adopted son was veritably and for all effects of the blood of his new father. For when Mohammed married Zainab, who had been Zaid's wife, it was objected that by the prophet's own law, laid down in the Coran, it was incest for a father to marry a woman who had been his son's wife, and a special revelation was required to explain that in Islam the *da'ī* or adopted son was no longer, as he had been in old Arabia, to be regarded as a son proper. As there was no difference between an adopted and real son before Islam, emancipated slaves appear in the genealogical lists without any note of explanation, just as if they had been pure Arabs: Dhakwān for example, who is entered as son of Omayya, and whom the Omayyads themselves always called the son of Omayya, in spite of Mohammed's new law, was really, as the genealogist Daghfal once reminded the Caliph Mo'awiya, the slave who used to lead Omayya by the hand in his blind old age (*Agh.* 1 8). [13]

In like manner refugees were frequently admitted to the tribe of their protector by adoption. The relation of protector and protected was constituted by a solemn engagement and oath, so that the *jār* is also called *halif* or *hilf* (pl. *holafā, ahlāf*), from the verb *halafa,* to swear. The exact nature of this engagement might vary, [14] but very often the covenant made the outlaw the son of his protector and gave him all the rights and duties of a tribesman, Micdād ibn Al-Aswad for example, a contemporary of the prophet, of whom there is a notice in Nawawi's biographical dictionary (p. 575), was by birth of the tribe of Bahrā. But having shed blood in Bahrā he fled to Kinda and exchanged the *nisba* or tribal name of Bahranite for that of Kindite. Once more he shed blood in his new kin and fled to Mecca, where he was adopted by Al-Aswad the Zohrite, and was thenceforth known as Micdād ibn Al-Aswad the Zohrite. The story is told somewhat differently in the *'Icd*, 2 72, where he is said to have been a captive among the Kinda before Al-Aswad adopted him. Both versions correspond with known usage and it is not necessary for our purpose to ask which is correct. The adoption of individual protégés to full tribesmanship must in later times have been very common, for hilf and dcti, sworn ally and adopted son, are often taken as synonymous terms (Nawawī, *l.c.*; 'Icd, 3 301 1. 17 *sq.*) [15]

When a whole group was taken into dependent alliance the terms of alliance would naturally be governed by circumstances, and complete fusion would not be so easy, especially if there were religious differences, such as separated the worshippers of Al-Lāt and Manāt in Medina, the Aus Manāt and the Taim al-Lāt, from their Jewish *holafā*. Nevertheless the obligations that united protector and protected were not much less stringent, at least as regarded the duty of help against outsiders, than those which united full tribesmen. The Jews of Medina are said to be "between the backs" of the protecting clans (*baina azhorihim, Agh.* 19 97 — the same phrase which in *'Icd,* 3 272 is applied to a daughter of the tribe), that is, could not be reached by a foe except over the bodies of their supporters. Protector and protected shared the risks and benefits of the blood-feud; the protector was bound to avenge his *halīf's* blood, and he himself or any of his people was liable to be slain in the *halīf's* quarrel, as the latter was in the quarrel of his protector (*Agh.* 19 75 *sqq.*, Ibn Hishām, p. 543). [16] The only difference was that the blood-money for the death of a dependent was not so high as for a *sarīh* (Agh. 2 170; C. de Perceval 2 657, 1. 662). Further, in Medina at least, the sworn ally had a claim on the inheritance of his protector. According to the commentators on Sura, 4 37, a man's *holafā* took one -sixth of his estate. For another rule Goldziher (*loc. cit.*) cites Tabarī, 1 12 1. 3.

Now duties of blood-feud and rights of inheritance, such as we see here extended to covenant allies, are in Arabia regarded as properly flowing from unity of blood. And accordingly we find evidence that a covenant in which two groups promised to stand by each other to the death (*ta'ācadū 'ala l'maut*), that is took upon them the duties of common blood-feud (Ibn Hishām, 1 125), was originally accompanied by a sacramental ceremony, the meaning of which was that the parties had commingled their blood. [17] It must be remembered that all our evidence from Arabic writers is of comparatively late date and comes from a time when the old religion was in decay. The point for which I am making can therefore be reached only by a combination of fragments of evidence, but by one which seems to be raised above the possibility of reasonable question.

We have already seen that a covenant of alliance and protection was based upon an oath. Such an oath was necessarily a religious act; it is called *casāma* (*Diw. Hodh.* 87, 128), a word which almost certainly implies that there was a reference to the god at the sanctuary before the alliance was sealed, and that he was made a party to the act. So we have already seen that at Mecca protection was publicly constituted and renounced at the Ka'ba. Now at Mecca within historical times such a life and death covenant was formed between the group of clans subsequently known as "blood-lickers" (*la'acat al-dam*). [18] The form of the oath was that each party dipped their hands in a pan of blood and v tasted the contents. But the use of blood in sealing a compact was not confined to Mecca. In *Agh.* 4 151, at the conclusion of peace between Bakr and Taghlib, we find the phrase "when the blood was brought nigh and they proceeded to close the compact." Again Lane, p. 1321, quotes a verse of Al-A'shā—

"Two that have sucked milk from the breasts of the same foster-mother have sworn
   By the dark flowing blood, We will never part."

Blood, therefore, was employed in making a life and death compact generally. The custom was so well established that there is a technical word, asham [19] for blood so used, and that "he dipped his hand in oath with such a one's people" (*ghamasa halifan fī āli folān*) is as much as "he entered into covenant with them." What was the meaning then of the blood? To understand this we must first compare certain other forms of covenant. In *Agh.* 16 66 we find that the covenant known as the *hilf al-fodūl* was made by taking Zemzem water and washing the corners of the Ka'ba with it, after which it was drunk by the parties. Again, the allies called the Motayyabūn, "perfumed," swore to one another by dipping their hands in a pan of perfume or unguent, and then wiping them on the Ka'ba, whereby the god himself became a party to the compact. [20] All these covenants are Meccan and were made about the same period, so that it is hardly credible that there was any fundamental! difference in the praxis. We must rather hold that they are all types of one and the same rite, imperfectly related and probably softened by the narrator. The form in which blood is used is plainly the more primitive or the more exactly related, but the account of it must be filled up from the others by the addition of the feature that the blood was also applied to the sacred stones or fetishes at the corners of the Ka'ba. And now we can connect the rite with that described in Herodotus 3 8, where the contracting parties draw each other's blood and smear it on seven stones set up in the midst. Comparing this with the later rite we see that they are really one, and that Herodotus has got the thing in its earliest form, but has omitted one trait necessary to the understanding of the symbolism, and preserved in the Meccan tradition. The later Arabs had substituted the blood of a victim for human blood, but they retained a feature which Herodotus had missed, they licked the blood as well as smeared it on the sacred stones. Originally therefore the ceremony was that known in so many parts of the world, in which the contracting parties become one by actually drinking or tasting one another's blood. The seven stones in Herodotus are of course sacred stones, the Arabic *ansāb,* Hebrew *massēbōth,* which like the sacred stones at the Ka'ba were originally Baetylia, Bethels or god-boxes. So we find in *Tāj,* 3 560 a verse of Rashīd ibn Ramīd of the tribe of 'Anaza, "I swear by the flowing blood round 'Aud, and by the sacred stones which we left beside So'air." [21] So'air is the god of the 'Anaza (Yācūt, 3 94) and 'Aud of their allies and near kinsmen Bakr-Wail (Bakrī, p. 55). [22]

We see then that two groups might make themselves of one blood by a process of which the essence was that they commingled their blood, at the same time applying the blood to the god or fetish so as to make him a party to the covenant also. Quite similar is the ritual in Exod. 24, where blood is applied to the people of Israel and to the altar. In certain cases in Arabia a man still seeks protection by drawing his own blood and wiping his gory hands on the doorpost of the man whose favour he intreats, but here the act is at the same time one of deprecation and atonement. For the significance which the Arabs down to the time of Mohammed attached to the tasting of another man's living blood there is an instructive evidence in Ibn Hishām, p. 572. Of Mālik, who sucked the prophet's wound at Ohod and swallowed the blood, Mohammed said, "He whose blood has touched mine cannot be reached by hell-fire."

The commingling of blood by which two men became brothers or two kins allies, and the fiction of adoption by which a new tribesman was feigned to be the veritable son of a member of the tribe, are both evidences of the highest value that the Arabs were incapable of conceiving any absolute social obligation or social unity which was not based on kinship; for a legal fiction is always adopted to reconcile an act with a principle too firmly established to be simply ignored. But of the two forms of the fiction that of blood brotherhood would seem to be the older, having much earlier attestation and a manifestly primitive character. And in this there seems to lie an indication that in the oldest times the social bond was not necessarily dependent on fatherhood. In the case of adoption a man becomes a tribesman by becoming a tribesman's son, in the other case the allies directly enter into the fellowship of the blood of the tribe as a whole.

This difference corresponds to a very clearly marked distinction between the antique view of kinship and that which is found gradually to supplant it, in all parts of the world, as the family begins to become more important than the tribe. To us, who live under quite modern circumstances and have lost the tribal idea altogether, kinship is always a variable and measurable quantity. We have a strong sense of kindred duty towards parents or children, not quite so strong a one towards brothers, and a sense much less strong towards first cousins; while in the remoter degrees kinship has hardly any practical significance for us. Something of this sort, though not nearly so developed, is occasionally found in Arabia before Mohammed, when beyond question family feeling was getting the upper hand of tribal feeling. But in Arabia the kind of kindred feeling which is weaker or stronger according to the distance of the kindred persons from their common ancestor always shows itself as a disturbing feature in the social system; the obstinate father who refuses to be guided by his tribesmen and take blood-money for his son's death, the fellow-tribesman who will not come to the help of a distant relative, all people in short who think of counting degrees instead of considering the whole *hayy* as a single unity of blood, are the men who break up the old society and bring in that growing chaos which made the prophet's new law a welcome reformation. The law of blood-revenge operated so strongly for the disintegration of society in the fraternal wars that rent Arabia in the century before the Flight, because people had begun to think of it as the affair of the immediate kindred and not of the whole kindred group. Nothing can be clearer than that the original doctrine of kinship recognised no difference of degree. Every tribesman risked his life equally in the blood-feud, and every tribesman might be called upon to contribute to the atonement by paying which blood-feud could be healed. This is still the rule of the desert, [23] and so we often read of the "collection" of the blood-wit and find that it is afforded not by the manslayer himself but by his people (*Diw. Hodh.* 31 introd., 35 7). There is a very instructive case for this in Bokhārī (Būlāc vocalised edit., 4 219 *sq.*), in a feud between two Meccan clans, where the manslayer has the

36

alternative of paying a hundred camels, or bringing fifty of his kin to take the oath of purgation, or abiding the blood-feud. He chooses the oath and his kinsmen cannot refuse, but one of them escapes the perjury by paying two camels as his share of the atonement. [24]

Conversely it is Mohammedan law and was doubtless ancient practice — for there is no express revelation on the point — that the blood-wit is distributed to the kin of the slain within the limits of inheritance. Under Mohammedan law the details of inheritance depend on degrees of kinship, near relations receiving certain fixed shares (*farāid*); and very probably certain provisions of this sort, though in less fixed shape, existed before Islam, as regarded both inheritance and the division of bloodwit. But it is the limits of heirship that indicate the original basis of the system of inheritance, and these, even in Mohammedan law, are defined in a way which shows that the right of inheritance originally lay with the *hayy* as a whole, or rather with the active members of it. For Mohammed enjoins that after the fixed shares are paid a gratuity shall be given to every kinsman who is present at the distribution of a dead man's estate. And when there are no near heirs, or something remains over after they have got their due, the reversion falls to the *'asaba,* a word which primarily means those who go to battle together, *i.e.* have a common blood-feud. Similarly in the old law of Medina, women were excluded from inheritance on the principle that "none can be heirs who do not take part in battle, drive booty and protect property" (Beidh. on Sur. 4 8 126, *Kāmil,* 678 15, 679). [25] Accordingly in Medina, as we have seen, even the *halīf* took a share in his protector's inheritance, because he shared the risks of battle and the responsibility of blood-feud. [26] But further we see from the law of Medina that there are three things that run parallel, and in which the whole *hayy*, or its active members, have a common interest — the rights and duties of blood-feud, the distribution of inheritance and the distribution of booty. The last point brings the communal origin of the whole institution into still clearer relief, for the warriors did not take booty each man for his own hand, but the spoil was divided after the campaign, the chief of the *hayy* taking a fourth part (*Ham.* p. 458, *Agh.* 16 50), and so *sohma* means at once relationship and a share of booty (comp. *Diw. Hodh.* 197). That the law of inheritance should follow the law of booty is easily intelligible, for among the nomads waters and pastures were and still are common tribal property, and moveable estate was being constantly captured and recaptured. Plainly the original theory was that it also, since no man was strong enough to keep his own without help, was really tribal property of which the individual had only a usufruct, and which fell to be divided after his death like the spoils of war. Thus the whole law of the old Arabs really resolves itself into a law of war — blood-feud, blood-wit, and booty are the points on which everything turns.

And as it was with tribal law so it was also with tribal organisation; up to the present day, among the Bedouins, it is only in war, or on the march, which is conducted with all the precautions of war, that the sheikh of a tribe exercises any active authority. In other words the tribe is not organised except for offence and defence; except in war and in matters ultimately connected with war the licence of individual freewill is absolutely uncontrolled. There cannot be a greater mistake than to suppose that Arab society is based on the patriarchal authority of the father over his sons; on the contrary there is no part of the world where parental authority is weaker than in the desert, [27] and the principle of uncontrolled individualism is only kept in check by the imperious necessity for mutual help against enemies which binds together, not individual families but the whole *hayy*, not kinsmen within certain degrees but the whole circle of common blood. The only permanent social unit is such a *hayy* as is strong and brave enough to protect itself without having recourse to outsiders, and this is what the Arabs call an *'imāra* or *hayy 'imāra,* a tribe that is able to subsist by itself. [28]

The key to all divisions and aggregations of Arab groups lies in the action and reaction of two principles: that the only effective bond is a bond of blood, and that the purpose of society is to unite men for offence and defence. These two principles meet in the law of blood-feud, the theory of which is that the blood-bond, embracing all men who bear a common *nisba* or group-name, constitutes a standing obligation to take up the quarrel of every tribal brother; and the practical limit to the working of this principle is simply that a group which is too weak to stand alone must seek to create a fictitious bond of blood with another group, while on the other hand, a group that is too large habitually to move and act together, too large for common offence and defence, must subdivide, and that then the subdivisions lose that sense of absolute unity which is kept alive not by counting degrees of kinship but by the daily exercise of the duties of common blood.

The type of society in which the stock or kinship-tribe and not the family is the basis of reciprocal duties no longer appears in its purity in our documents, which belong to a date when the old tribal system had begun to break down along with the old tribal religion which formed an integral part of it. The Arabs before Mohammed had not been able to rise to any conception of the state superseding the tribal system, but that system, as we shall by and by see more fully, was being broken up from within by the growth of the idea of family as opposed to stock ties, and of private as distinct from stock rights.

If our sources had begun only a little later it might have been impossible to reconstruct the older type of Arab society at all; but fortunately our information begins at a time when its main outlines were not obliterated but only blurred, and when careful comparative study makes it still possible to distinguish the old from the new. That this is so has I hope appeared to a certain extent in the course of the present chapter, in closing which I shall add only one more argument, derived from language, in illustration of one of the most important points that have come before us. I have tried to show that in old Arabia relationship cannot originally have been reckoned by counting degrees from a common ancestor, but was something common to a whole group. And with this it agrees that the language does not possess the terms necessary to reckon degrees of kin in our sense. The word *khāl,* which is usually translated "maternal uncle," really means any member of the mother's group. [29] This is not a mere term of address which a man uses out of politeness in speaking to his mother's kin; in every kind of context a man's *akhwāl* are simply his mother's people. Here, therefore, we see quite clearly that relationship is a relation between a man and a group, not between a man and an individual. The words *'amm,* "paternal uncle," and *ibn 'amm,* "son of a paternal uncle," are used in an equally wide way; thus in *Diw. Hodh.* 47 introd., the words "a kin cannot give up the sons of its *'amm*" are used by the Sahm, a branch of the Hodhail, when they refuse to desert the Lihyān, another branch of the same stock. In fact the word *'amm,* identical with the Hebrew עַם, "a people, a kin," seems to mean etymologically nothing else than an aggregate or community; the *ibn 'amm,* therefore, is literally a man of the same stock-group, and *'amm* in the sense of paternal uncle, which is a use of the word peculiar to Arabic, seems to be a comparatively late development.

[1] *Agh.* 15 162 1. 24; cp. Wellh. *Skizzen u. Vorarbeiten,* 4 18 (1889).
[2] For the war-cry see *Diw. Hodh.* 83, *ib.* 155 1. 3, "Kāhil," "'Āmr"; Ibn Hishām, 127, "Yāla Dārim." The same chief might use several war-cries. At the second battle of Kolāb (*Agh.* 15 74), Cais b. 'Āsim first cries "Yāla Sa'd"; but this cry his adversary returns; so Cais now cries "Yāla Ka'b" and finally "Yāla Mocā'is." The story is told somewhat differently by Ibn Doraid (*Ishticāc,* 150), where it is the sons of Al-Hārith who, finding that their adversaries also cry "Yala Hārith," adopt "Yala Mocā'is" (Moca'is = one who dwells apart from his comrades). Sad, Ka'b, and Mocā'is are successive divisions of the Tamīm, but Sa'd is also a well-known god, and the point seems to be that it was useless for both sides to invoke the same god. A panic seizes the hostile standard-bearer when he finds that Cais raises a cry he cannot return. So at Ohod the Meccan war-cry is "Yala 'Ozzā," "Yāla Hobal" (*Maghāzī,* ed. Kremer, 237). This, however, is a religious war. In *Agh.* 16 57, Zaid al-Khail, fighting for his guest-friend the Tamīmite chief Cais — the same who himself calls "Yāla Sa'd," etc. — shouts "Yāla Tamīm," and uses the *konya* of Cais (يا التميم ويتكنى بكنية قيس يجعل يدعو) every time that he smites an enemy. The use of the *konya* of Cais by his *jār* supplies an exact parallel to Is. 44 5. [But see Nöld. *ZDMG* 40 186, head of page.] The use of the name of the *hayy* as a war-cry explains *Diw. Hodh.* 142 7, "the shouting of the *hayy* and the screaming of the women." *Hayy* does not mean men as opposed to women, but the cry that brings the *hayy* together for resistance is contrasted with the screams of the noncombatants. The battle-cry is in form identical with the summons by which a man calls his kindred to him for any sudden emergency (*Agh.,* 16 109 1. 24).

Whether جَشِع used as a summons to gather people, comes from this, or is a mere interjection, seems doubtful. Goldziher cites Hātim (ed. Hassoun, p. 28, 1. 4) for oath by the *ši'ār.* This is important. He also cites Antara, 25 2, where the poet speaks of rushing to aid when called without even recognising whether he is in-

39

voked by his name or his *konya*. What was the difference? Goldziher distinguishes the *ši'ār* from. the case (as in Antara, *l.c.*) where a single hero is called on. The latter is *du'a* (Antara, *Moall.* 66 [ed. Arnold], 73, [ed. Ahlw.], Append., Ant. 19 14 *sq.* Nab. 2 15-16, ed. Ahlw.). See, further, Goldz. *Lit. bl.* 27*, *Muh. Stud.* 161 *sq.* [For specimens of modern war-cries among the N. Arabian tribes see Huber, *Journal d'un voyage en Arabic*, 176; for S. Arabia, Landberg, *Arabica*, 417-22 (*sarkha, 'azwa*), and vol. 5, index *s.v. sarakha.* For a parallel to the use of the tribal name as a war-cry, see Plutarch, *Marius,* chap. 19. — I. G.]

[3] For *hayy* with more of a local sense see Mofadd. 2 2; *Agh.* 18 210 1. 5, 19 3 1. 9.

[4] Cp. also Num. 32 41 [see *Ency. Bib.* col. 1901, and add also Ps. 68 11 with Cheyne, Baethgen, Driver, and others].

[5] [Cp. the interesting passage, *Agh.* iv. 152 5: *cātilatun mactūlatun.* — I. G.]

[6] [On the view that *hayy* probably meant "life," and rested on the idea that one life runs through the veins on the whole group, see *Religion of the Semites,* (1) p. 256, n. 2.]

[7] [See Tabarī, 2445, where the wife of Mas'ūd ibn 'Āmr secures protection for 'Obaidallah ibn Ziyād by surreptitiously supplying him with food and dressing him in her husband's clothes. — A. A. B. Cp. taharramtu bi-ta'āmika, Baihacī, ed. Schwally, 190 8; *hurmat al-mu'ākala,* Jāhiz, ed. van Vloten, 155 5 (Leyden, 1900). — I. G.]

[8] Cp. *Agh.* 2 161 1. 8 (Cais and Khidāsh his father's friend).

[9] For the touching of the tent-rope Goldziher (*Lit. bl.* 26*) cites 'Orwa b. al-Ward (ed. Nöld. 23 1) and *habl,* see *Zeit. f. Völkerpsychologie,* 13 251 ff.; and, for the joining of garments, *Agh.* 15 117, with Imrau'l-Cais, *Moall.* 21. See Lane, p. 2169, last col. It may be interesting to give here the explanation of the modern Arabic law of protection as it was set forth to me by Sheikh 'Alī Cāsim, who for many years was tax-gatherer for the Sherīf of Mecca among the inland pastoral tribes. The explanations of terms as well as the statement of law are his. The nomads have three great principles which they call the three white rules (ثلاث البيض) — "white," in the sense in which you say of a good man that his face is white, (1) بالطنب الطنب, pronounced *attimb bettimb.* The man whose tent-rope touches yours is your *jār,* and under your protection. *Timb* is here equivalent to جيران. If you can quietly approach an Arab and pitch by him thus you are under his protection. (2) رفيق الجنب, *i.e.,* he who journeys with you by day and sleeps beside you at night is also sacred. (3) اضيف السارح — where خرج في أموره سبلا = سرح — *I.e.,* the guest who has eaten with you is under your protection till he has eaten with another. If you are in blood-feud with a body of Arabs and yet have to pass their place, you may approach cautiously and call a little boy, giving him a small present to accompany you. He must take hold of your chin and you carry him through the tribe on your camel. They have no right to molest you. [The man who receives protection by touching the tent-rope becomes *tānib* or *tānīb*; cp. Hot. 1 20, and the extremely important passage *Agh.* 2

184 1. 19. In Darimi, 39, Sunan (ed. Cawnpore, 1293), the phrase runs *al-olfa wa-atnāb al-fasātit.* — I. G.]

[10] There is a valuable collection of material as to the ancient Arab law of protection by Quatremère, "Les Asyles chez les Arabes," *Mém. Acad, Inscr. et Belles Let.* xv. 2 (1845), p. 307 *sqq.* I have not thought it necessary to cite proof texts for points fully illustrated in this memoir. [Reference may be made also to *RS*, pp. 75 *sqq.* On *jār* and *jiwār* see Goldz. *Muh. Stud.* 1 13 n. 4, 69 n. 3; Proksch, *Ueber d. Blutrache bei d. vorislam. Arabern*, 33 *sqq.* (Leipzig, 1899). It is to be noted that not only the protected one but also the protector might be called *jār*, Ibn Hish. 344 4, *inna Allāha jārun liman barra*, "Allah is the protector of the righteous." — I. G.]

[11] So it is explained in *Agh.* 8 83 1. 16 (in the case of Ash'a).

[12] 'Omair did so after the *jār* had made an appeal to the grave of his patron's father (*Kamil*, p. 203).]

[13] For Dhakwān's story see the introduction to the *Dīwān* of al-Hotai'a, no. 10 (*ZDMG* 46 475, 1892). Certain traces of houses originally servile but afterwards incorporated in pure Arab tribes perhaps survive in the genealogical lists. There is a well-known class of Semitic tribal or personal names, like 'Abd Cais, 'Abd al-Lāt, Obed-Edom, etc., in which the group or man is called the servant of some deity. But names of this form also occur in which the second member is not a god-name. Examples of this are found even in the Nabataean inscriptions, where Prof. Clermont-Ganneau conjectures that the names are borne by freedmen of kings who had been deified after death (*Recueil d'Arch. Orient.* 1 39 *sqq.*, 1885). But names like 'Abd al-Mondhir (Ibn Hish. 493) are not to be thus explained: see, however, Euting, *Nabat. Inschr.* p. 33 (1885). Even the name 'Abd al-Mottalib, grandfather of the prophet, who was reared with his mother at Medina, is traditionally explained by the statement that when his uncle, Al-Mottalib, first brought the boy to Mecca, the people took the lad for his slave and named him accordingly.

[14] In B. Hish. 288 14 the Cawācil (Ghanm b. Auf) are said to have given the man who sought protection an *arrow* as symbol of admission to the rights of a protected stranger. [On the *hilf* see also *Muh. Stud.* I 63-69. — I. G.]

[15] *Da ī*, according to Goldziher (*Lit. blatt*, p. 26*, see also *Muh. Stud.* 1 134-137), is the same as *zanīm*, one who smuggles himself into a tribe (Bokhārī, *Manākib*, 6; *Farā'id*, 28). It is often a term of reproach (*Agh.* 13 19 19 2 1. 4). See also *Lisān, s.v.* دَعِيّ, vol. ix. p. 297, 1 2 from foot.

[16] There is a striking case of blood-revenge in *Agh.* 13 69 (head); Khowailid, a Khozāite, kills a brother of 'Abbas b. Mirdās, who is *jār* of 'Āmir the Khozāite. On an appeal from 'Abbās 'Āmir swears vengeance. When Khowailid is slain by certain of the B. Nasr, they propose to set his blood against that of a certain kinsman of theirs whom Khozā'a had slain. But 'Āmir will not allow his death to be reckoned except as revenge for his *jār.* Thus, of course Khozā'a lies open to further blood-feud.

[17] For the form of covenant cp. Ibn Hish. 297 2, *Lisān, s.v.*, مَحْلُوم . The addition in Lisān, 12 89 1. 5 seems to mean, "your blood (feud) is mine, and the blood you leave unavenged, I leave unavenged."

[18] [According to *Agh.* 7 26 1. 21, in the days of the *Jāhiliya* the B. 'Āmir b. 'Abdmanāt of the Kināna were called "blood-lickers," they were the bravest of all the clans of the Kināna. — I. G.]

[19] [But the use of *asham* as a technical term is criticised by Nöldeke, p. 184. On the use of blood in covenants see *RS* 314 *sq.* Goldziher writes that the same is found among the Monbuttu (Schweinfurth, *Im Herzen v. Afrika*, 1 571, ch. xii., Leipzig, 1874), and the peoples of the East African mainland (Decken, *Reisen in Ostafrika*, ed. O. Kersten, 1 252, Leipzig, 1869).]

[20] Goldziher (*Lit. blatt*, p. 24* *sq.*) cites Zoh. *Moall.* 19 i, and observes that the perfume is not fluid. The note in Arnold is not satisfactory, Freytag, Ar. Prov. 1 155 692. For covenant by fire sprinkled with salt Goldziher refers to Jauharī (under the head of *nār al-hūla*). The *hūla* is said to be the sacred fire of the tribe before which tribesmen were made to swear to make up quarrels, the priests throwing salt on the fire. Verses are quoted, but it does not appear from Jauharī whether it was, as the authorities say, confined to tribesmen. Whether the term *mihās* (cited by Goldziher, *loc. cit.*) from Nabighā (Ahlw. 241, see Derenb. 17 1 and scholion) has anything to do with fire is not certain; it seems rather to refer to *branding* (cp. *wasm*). [See, further *RS* 479 *sq.*]

[21] On the oath by blood cp. Lane, *s.v. dumya*, p. 917*b*. For the blood covenant Goldziher adds Zohair, 1 50, Mofadd. 21 3. One or two additional references may be here given for the forms of covenant illustrated in the text. The emasculated form by dipping the hands in a bowl of water appears in Wācidī (Wellh. *Moh. in Med.*, p. 334)Sometimes, apparently, fruit-juice (*robb*) was taken to imitate blood; such, at least, is one of the explanations offered of the alliance called the Ribāb (see Lane, p. 1005, Ibn Doraid, p. 111). We may compare the use of bean juice to smear the face (Lydus, *de Mens.* 4 29); this seems to go with Faba as a totem, Fabii; compare the Attic hero, Κυαμίτης [cp. *RS* 480]. In *Hamāsa*, 190 15 there is an obscure oath, which Freytag and Osiander (*ZDMG* 7 489) confess that they do not understand, بالعزيين وشجرة تتصبب بأيدى مجزرة. Here *mathjara* is not a proper name, but must be the same as thajir, the dregs of fruit used to make wine or *nabīdh* (*sicera*). The dictionaries say that this is a foreign word; it is in fact the Talmudic שיגרא (comp. Löw, *Aram. Pflanzennamen*, p. 124). *Majzara* is *abattoir*. A tradition given in the Sīhāh says that 'Omar warned his Moslems to beware of the *majāzir*, because one becomes as unable to avoid them as to abstain from wine when the habit is formed (cp. Maid. 2 22, no. 4: wine and flesh are the two things that seduce men). This has puzzled the commentators, but Al-Asma'ī not wrongly remarks that some sort of gathering is meant, since it is only where men assemble that beasts are slaughtered. I have no doubt that 'Omar had in view some sort of heathenish sacrificial rite, and in our passage "the flanks of the *majzara*" differ little from "the base of the altar," where in the Old Testament we read of the sacrificial blood being poured. The oath then is "by the two 'Ozzā" (*i.e.*, the goddess Al-'Ozzā and her companion, possibly Al-Lāt — not necessarily two forms of the same goddess, perhaps, rather like 'Anathoth, two images of 'Ozzā, twin-pillars, like those of Hercules), "and by the wine-dregs that are poured out by the sides of the altar," or *nosb*. The dark dregs take the place of gore, as the *robb* did. Similar is the verse cited by the lexicographers, *s.v.* عزّى

(compare Osiander, *ut sup.*), "by streams of gore that look like dragon's-blood on the cippus of Al-'Ozzā and on the (idol) Nasr" (cp. Tab. 1 7 1. 91, there is a better reading in *Līsān, s.v.* اَبِيل). The wine-dregs point to a sacrificial feast, and doubtless this accompanied every covenant (Gen. 31 54, Exod. 24 11). From *Diw. Hodh.* 87 it appears that it required a casama to enable two tribes to eat and drink together.

[22] For 'Aud, compare also Ibn al-Kalbī, cited by Jauharī and in *Tāj*, 5 58. The latter seems to misunderstand; Ibn al-Kalbī does not ascribe the verse of Rashid to Al-A'shā, but uses it to explain the use of *'audo* as an asseverative particle in the words of Al-A'shā, *'ando la natafarraco*, "we will never part" (the verse of Al-A'shā in its context, *Agh.* 8 80; C. de Percival, 2 400). [See Ibn Rashic, ed. Tunis, 25. — I. G.] And this seems to be correct, *i.e.*, the particle صَوْتُ is simply a shortened form of the oath by the deity, 'Aud, which must therefore have been widely spread. 'Aud, I imagine, was a great god and not different from the Hebrew עוּץ (Uz). In Gen. 10 23, 22 21 Uz is an Aramaean eponym, while in Gen. 36 28, he appears among the pre-Edomite inhabitants of Seir, in a chapter which contains numerous god and totem names. In Lam. 4 21 Edom dwells in the land of Uz. In Jer. 25 20, again, "all the kings of the land of Uz," which is absent from the LXX., is a gloss on אֵת כָּל הָעֶרֶב, and seems to make Uz a group of Arab tribes. These various data, as Nöldeke has recognised (*Bibel-Lex., s.v.* Aram), cannot be all referred to one region, and therefore we have to think of scattered tribes — or rather of various tribes worshipping the same god. Now the LXX. form from Uz the adjective Αὐσῖτις, which points to a pronunciation 'Aus = 'Aud — the Hebrews knowing no distinction between S and D). [For Robertson Smith's remarks on Nöldeke's objections (*ZDMG* 40 184 [1886]), see *RS*, p. 42 *sq.* n. 4.]

[23] Sheikh 'Alī says, "The blood-money between tribe and tribe is now eight hundred dollars, which is contributed by all the tribesmen of the slayer, and, in virtue of the entire solidarity of the *cabīla*, who have but a single hand (*yad wāhid*), it is equally divided among all the males of the tribe. The blood-revenge may fall on any tribesman, even on a distant member in a remote town who knew nothing of the occurrence."

[24] On the *casāma*, or judicial oath, see further Bokh. 8 40 *sqq.* Its proper application was when a man was found slain; then the people of the place had to swear that they were not the murderers. This is exactly as in Deut. 21 1 *sqq.* The following case is curious. An outlaw of the Hodhail was slain by a Yemenite in the act of attempting a nocturnal theft. This was in the Jāhilīya. Subsequently the Hodhalites got possession of the Yemenite and brought him before 'Omar. The defence was that the slain was an outlaw. This the Hodhail denied, and they were called on to bring fifty men to swear to their statement. One of the fifty redeemed his oath with a thousand dirhams, and his place was taken by a substitute, who gave the money to the brother of the slain and, joining hands with him, became his *carin* or partner. This last act seems to have transferred the guilt of the perjury to the brother, for the divine judgment which is related to have followed, by the falling in of a cave in which the party had taken shelter from rain, spared the

substitute. The judicial oath is very common in early law, but the permission to an individual to buy himself off is peculiar.

[25] That the paternal uncle is the heir as against the daughter is affirmed in Moslem times in the verses *Kāmil*, 284 14 *sq.*

[26] That only warriors could inherit is regarded by Al-ʿAbbās as a custom of the heathen Arabs parallel with female infanticide. On this point see *Additional Note C*. Sheikh ʿAlī states that blood-money goes to all the males of the tribe (see note 21), which is against Moslem law. Here, therefore, we have in central Arabia a relic of the same law of inheritance as at Medina — a survival of pre-Islamic law, rendered easier by Sūra, 4 94, only saying that the blood-money of a believer goes to "his people." The commentators explain, "in the same shares as the rest of the inheritance."

The exclusion of women from inheritance was not therefore confined to Medina, and we shall see by and by that it was probably nearly if not quite coextensive with marriage by contract or purchase. The same law seems to have existed in other Semitic countries along with marriage of the same type. The Mosaic law gives daughters a share only in default of sons, and even this law is one of the latest in the Pentateuch. That a similar principle must have held good in Syria and passed from native law into the famous Syro-Roman law-book, which so long regulated the legal affairs of the Christians under the Arab empire, has been shown at length by Bruns, to whom I refer for the details of the Syrian system, and for a clear indication of the fundamental difference between the theory of Semitic and Roman law. The Roman civil law does not put women *in manu* in a worse position than sons *in manu*; the Semitic law knows nothing of *patria potestas*, and puts women as such behind men. The Roman married daughter falls out of inheritance because she is transferred to another kin and *patria potestas*; the Semitic wife retains her own kin, and her incapacity to inherit is therefore independent of her marriage. Of course these regulations appear in their purity only before the use of testamentary dispositions, which existed to a certain extent at the time of the prophet. After testaments came into force, it is only the law of inheritance in case of intestacy that can be used as a key to the original theory about property and inheritance.

[27] Even in *Agh.* 19 102 *sqq.* parental authority is so weak that a chief who wishes his only son to divorce a barren wife has first to vow that he will never speak to him, and then to call in all the elders and warriors of the *hayy* to persuade him. [Cp. *Rel. Sem.* 60, n. 1.]

[28] The sense of the word *ʿimāra* in actual usage is fixed by *Kamil*, 35 12, "a *hayy imāra*, having no need of any outside of themselves"; compare *Hamāsa*, p. 346, 3rd verse: "every group of men belonging to Maʿadd who form an *ʿimāra* have their own place of refuge from enemies"; and similarly Yācūt, 4 387 1. 7, *Agh.* 19 34 1. 15, "Tamim is my *ʿimāra*." Wilken (*Opmerkingen*, p. 8) suggests that the word originally meant a settlement or clearing. [Cp. Nöldeke, *ZDMG* 40 176.] In point of fact *ʿimāra* is often used for cultivated ground (examples are given by De Goeje in the glossary to Belādhorī). But it is scarcely credible that the Arabs should derive a name for a tribe from an agricultural term; the language of Arab agriculture is largely taken from the Aramaic, and the forms and phrases, in which the root *ʿamāra* refers not to life in general but to agricultural life, must

have had their origin with an agricultural people. Grammatically *'imāra* is a *nomen verbi* of *'amara* in two quite distinct senses; in the sense of settlement it belongs to عَمَرتِ الأرَضُ, "the country was stocked or inhabited," but it is also the infinitive of عَمَرَ رَبَّهُ, "he worshipped his god." The latter sense is very old, for the word *'Omra* (religious visit to the Ka'ba), which was already obscure in the time of the prophet, seems to mean simply "cultus" (Snouck Hurgronje, *Het Mekkaansche Feest,* p. 116). And so the adjuration عَمَرَكَ, or more fully عَمَرَكَ اللهَ (*Kāmil,* 760 12 *sq.*), means "by thy religion," or in the full phrase, "by thy worship of Allah," where Allah is of course a modern substitute for the name of some particular god. [But that *'Āmr* in such expression does not mean the cultus follows from such a formula as *la 'Āmru-bnat al-Murri,* Mofadd. 27 15: "by the life of" cp. also Nöldeke's criticisms in *ZDMG* 40 184. — I. G.] I imagine that the proper names 'Āmir and 'Omar simply mean "worshipper" — the object of worship being left out as in the names Aus and 'Abd — and that 'Āmr has a similar sense; 'Abd 'Āmr will be servant of the worship of some god, like 'Abd al-Dār. So in Hebrew עָמְרִי, Omri, is simply "worshipper of Jehovah," cp. 'Āmr al-Lāt, Azra'cī, 123 I, Wellh. Heid (1) 3, (2) 7. The corresponding feminine name is הָעַמֹר on an inscription at Bostra which De Vogüe (*Syr. Centr.,* p. 102 [*CIS* 2 173]) renders "worshipper." *'Imāra* is a formally correct collective from *'Āmir,* and so naturally means the circle that practises a common tribal religion.

[29] [See the criticisms of Nöldeke, *op. cit.* 172 *sq.*, on the *khāl* and *'amm.*]

Chapter Three - The Homogeneity of the Kindred Group in Relation to the Law of Marriage and Descent

We have seen that an Arab tribe regarded itself as a group of kindred united by the tie of blood for purposes of offence and defence. In a society thus constructed no one, it is obvious, can belong to two groups; the commentator on the *Hamāsa,* p. 124, says expressly that the same man cannot belong to more than one *hayy.* Before a man can enter a new *hayy* by adoption, he must "strip off" his old tribal connection (*khala'a*) or be expelled from it. A rule, therefore, is needed to determine whether for social duties — but not necessarily to the exclusion of all sense of kinship in the other line — a child belongs to the father's or the mother's stock; unless; the law of marriage forbids unions between people not of the same stock.

Among tribes like those of Arabia, that is tribes composed of people who call themselves of one kin, three kinds of marriage custom are possible:

(*a*) the tribe is endogamous, *i.e.* a man is not allowed to marry outside of his own stock;

(*b*) the tribe is exogamous, *i.e.* a man is not allowed to marry a woman of his own stock;

(*c*) marriage is allowed with kinsfolk and aliens indifferently.

45

There is ample evidence that there was no law of endogamy among the Arabs at and before the time of Mohammed; they could contract valid marriages and get legitimate children by women of other stocks, *i.e.* of other tribes. There is also some evidence that parents were often unwilling to give their daughters to be possible mothers of enemies to their tribe. This reluctance, however, would not greatly diminish the frequency of marriages with aliens, since women were continually captured in war and marriages with captives were of constant occurrence. Moreover, a man might often find a wife by agreement in a friendly tribe, where there could be no political reason for the woman's kin objecting to the match. So far as the husband was concerned marriage with a woman not of the kin was often preferred, because it was thought that the children of such a match were stronger and better, and because marriage within the *hayy* led to ugly family quarrels (see the passages cited by Goldziher in *Academy*, 1880, no. 427, and *Tāj*, 5 510). [1] And to the woman's kin, as we shall see later, the price paid by a husband was often important. It does not seem likely that strict endogamy was practised by any Arab tribe in historical times. For the capture of women was always going on in the incessant wars that raged between different groups, and there was also an extensive practice of female infanticide. These two causes taken together would render a law of endogamy almost impossible when every tribe was anxious to have many sons to rear up as warriors. [2]

The question then which we have now to consider is, what system of marriage and what law of kinship, working together, we may expect to find in a kinship tribe living together without a rule of endogamy.

A marriage between persons of different tribes may take various forms and have various degrees of permanency. We may suppose (*a*) that the woman leaves her tribe and finds a permanent home in a strange kin. Where marriage takes this shape we may be sure that the tribe which receives the woman into its midst will desire to keep her children, and ultimately will contrive to do so unless there is a special contract to restore the offspring of the marriage to the mother's people. They will therefore come to have a rule by which the children of an alien woman, who has come among them by marriage, are of their kin and not of the mother's. This rule may affect the children only, leaving the mother to retain her own kinship. Or for greater security the rule of Roman law may be followed, by which the woman on marriage renounces her own kin and *sacra* and is adopted into the kin of the husband. This latter course, it may be at once observed, was not followed by the Arabs. A married woman did not change her kin. [3]

But it is also possible (d) that by tribal rule a woman is not allowed to leave her own kin but may entertain a stranger as her husband. In this case we may expect that the children will remain with their mother's tribe, and therefore the law of kinship will be that the child is of the mother's stock. And this being so, the rule of descent is unaffected whether the father comes and settles permanently with his wife's tribe, or whether the woman is only visited from time to time by one or more suitors.

These two sharply distinguished rules of kinship will correspond to two main types of marriage-relation, provided only that marriages are of a reasonably permanent character. But, even where a woman follows her husband to his tribe, a want of fixity in the marriage tie will favour a rule of female kinship or at least modify the law of male descent. We may suppose a state of things in which divorce is so frequent, and the average duration of a marriage so short, that a woman's family may at any one time embrace several children by different fathers, all too young to do without a mother's care. In that case the children will follow the mother, and when they grow up they may either return with her to her own tribe, or remain with one of her later husbands and be adopted into his tribe, or under special arrangement may go back to the tribe of their real father.

All these three types of marriage with the corresponding rules about the children can be shown to have existed in Arabia, but it was the first type which ultimately prevailed. And this is the explanation of the rule of male kinship, which follows of necessity from the prevalence of the first type of marriage in tribes that believed or feigned themselves to be of one blood. But there is evidence to show that the second type of marriage, or the modification of the first type due to instability in the marriage tie, was also far from uncommon in certain circles down to the later times of Arab heathenism, and thus again we are carried, from another point of view, to the conclusion that the establishment of male kinship as the normal rule is not of very ancient date.

In reviewing the evidence we may begin with the case in which the woman refuses, or is not permitted, to leave her own tribe. This practice has survived in certain cases down to the present day. Among the Bedouins generally it appears to be a rare thing for a woman to leave her tribe, while on the other hand a stranger is readily permitted to settle down and take a wife. One ought not perhaps to attach much weight to these modern instances, belonging as they do to a state of society considerably modified by Islam, and in which the husband is probably adopted into the tribe, so that the appearance of male kinship is preserved.

But we need not go back beyond the middle ages to find quite unambiguous evidence. Ibn Batūta in the 14th cent, of our era found that the women of Zebid were perfectly ready to marry strangers. The husband might depart when he pleased, but his wife in that case could never be induced to follow him. She bade him a friendly adieu and took upon herself the whole charge of any child of the marriage (Ibn Bat. 2 168). Going back to more ancient times we find that Shoraih ibn Hārith the Kindite, a famous jurist in the early days of Islam and Cādī of Cufa under 'Omar I., sustained a contract by which 'Adi ibn Artā had engaged not to withdraw his bride from the house of her kin (Ibn Khallikān, no. 289). This was not new law, for instances of the same kind turn up in the old traditions of the time before Islam. Thus in Freytag's *Arabum Proverbia*, 1 529 *sq.* (Maidānī, ed. Būlāc, 1284; 1 256), a story is told about Locman, in which a husband is introduced singing these words:

"My heart is towards the tribe (*hayy*), for my soul is held in hostage among them by the best of wives."

Taken by themselves such instances as these would not amount to a proof that among certain Arab tribes there was a fixed custom of the woman remaining with her own tribe. But there is more evidence to be adduced. In Aghānī, 16 106, in the story of Hātim and Māwīya, we read as follows. "The women in the Jāhillya, or some of them, had the right to dismiss their husbands, and the form of dismissal was this. If they lived in a tent they turned it round, so that if the door faced east it now faced west, and when the man saw this he knew that he was dismissed and did not enter." [4] The tent, therefore, belonged to the woman, the husband was received in her tent and at her good pleasure.

Marriage on these terms would plainly be out of the question if the woman did not remain with her own tribe. Yet Māwīya was a Tamīmite of Bahdala (*Hamāsa*, p. 729) while Hātim was of Tayyi. Here, therefore, we have the proof of a well-established custom of that kind of marriage which naturally goes with female kinship in the generation immediately before Islam, for 'Adī the son of Hātim and Māwīya lived to be a good Moslem.

The three features characteristic of the marriage of Māwīya are, that she was free to choose her husband, received him in her own tent, and dismissed him at pleasure. The same points come out, though less distinctly, more than two centuries earlier, in the brief notice of the marriage of the Saracens given by Ammianus, 14 4. According to Ammianus, marriage is a temporary contract for which the wife receives a price. After the fixed term she can depart if she so chooses, and "to give the union an appearance of marriage, the wife offers I her spouse a spear and a tent by way of dowry." [5] This account implies freedom of choice on the wife's part, and is distinct as to freedom of separation, subject to the fulfilment of a quite temporary contract. The tent and spear offered by way of dowry Wilken (*Matriarchaat,* p. 9) supposes to be a mistake; the Roman he thinks could not understand that it was only the man who made a present to the woman and not conversely. But by Roman law the *dos* returned to the wife on divorce, and doubtless Ammianus understood that, just as in the case of Māwīya, the wife kept the tent if she left, or rather dismissed, her husband. [6] The Roman and Arabian accounts are therefore in perfect unison, and as the woman could not go off by herself, with her tent, into the desert, we must suppose that among these Saracens the husband, if he was not his wife's tribesman, temporarily joined her tribe. As the wife gave her husband a spear it appears that as long as he remained with her he accompanied her people in war, as a *halīf* or *jār* would do. Conversely it appears from Arab sources that when a man sought protection

48

with a tribe it was natural for him to ask to be furnished with a wife, as Cais ibn Zohair did when he joined the Namir ibn Cāsit ('Icd, 3 273). And finally the detail that the husband took the wife on hire for a time, which does not appear in the story of Hatim, shows us that this kind of marriage was similar to the temporary alliances, known as *nikāh al-mot'a*, which were common in Arabia at the time of Mohammed, and were abolished with great difficulty, and only after much hesitation on the part of the prophet, if indeed it is not the better tradition that they were not finally condemned till the time of 'Omar. Full details as to these marriages, which are still recognised as legal by Shiites, are given by Wilken, *op. cit.*, from the collections of Snouck Hurgronje. The modern Persian practice will be familiar to most readers from Morier's *Hajji Baba*.

The characteristic mark of a *mot'a* marriage, as Moslem writers define it, is that the contract specifies how long the marriage shall hold. Strictly speaking, however, this can only have been a negative provision. The wife had received a gift from the husband as the price of her consent, and therefore it was natural that her right to dismiss him should not come into effect for a certain length of time. [7] It appears from Ammianus that if the parties chose the union might continue after the fixed term, and so it was in the time of the prophet also, for Bokhārī, 6 124, in a tradition showing that Mohammed sometimes allowed such marriages, makes him say "If a man and a woman agree together, their fellowship shall be for three nights; then if they choose to go on they may do so, or if they prefer it they may give up their relation." The contract for a certain period is, therefore, merely a limitation to absolute freedom of separation, and the real difference between *mot'a* marriages and such as Mohammedan law deems regular lies not in the temporary character of the union, but in the fact that in the one case both spouses have the right of divorce, while in the latter only the husband has it. Mohammedan husbands have always made the freest use of this right; Lane in his translation of the *Arabian Nights* (chap. iv. note 39, quoted by Wilken p. 18) records among other surprising instances that of a man who had married nine hundred women. It cannot, therefore, have been any sense of delicacy, any respect for the permanency of the marriage bond, that made *mot'a* marriages illegal in Islam, and apparently caused them to be viewed as somewhat irregular before that time. The explanation of this fact must rather be sought in another direction.

The *mot'a* marriage was a purely personal contract, founded on consent between a man and a woman, without any intervention on the part of the woman's kin. From the cases cited in the *hadīth* 'Nawawī (*apud* Wilken, p. 14) concludes that no witnesses were necessary to the contract, and that no *walī* (father or guardian of the woman) appeared. And that this is a correct view of the case is proved by *Agh.* 7 18, where, with reference to an actual case in the life of the Himyarite Sayyid, *mot'a* marriage is said to be a marriage that no one need know anything about. [8] Now, the fact that there was no contract with the woman's kin — such as was necessary when the wife left her own people and came under the authority of her husband — and that, indeed, her kin might know nothing about it, can have only one explanation: in mot' a marriage the woman did not leave her home, her people gave up no rights which they had over her, and the children of the marriage did not belong to the husband. *Mot'a* marriage, in short, is simply the last remains of that type of marriage which corresponds to a law of mother-kinship, and Islam condemns it and makes it "the sister of harlotry" (*Agh. ut supra*) because it does not give the husband a legitimate offspring, *i.e.*, an offspring that is reckoned to his own tribe and has rights of inheritance within it. And so, in fact, Nawawī says that no right of inheritance flows from a *mot'a* marriage.

An illustration of this kind of union as it was practised before Islam is given in the story of Salmā bint 'Āmr, one of the Najjār clan at Medina (Ibn Hishām, p. 88). Salma, we are told, on account of her noble birth (the reason given by Moslem historians in other cases also for a privilege they did not comprehend), would not marry any one except on condition that she should be her own mistress and separate from him when she pleased. [9] She was for a time the wife of Hāshim the Meccan, during a sojourn he made at Medina, and bore him a son, afterwards famous as 'Abd al-Mottalib, who remained with his mother's people. The story goes on to tell how the father's kin ultimately prevailed on the mother to give up the boy to them. But even after this, according to a tradition in Tabarī, 1 1086, the lad had to appeal to his mother's kin against injustice he had suffered from his father's people. The details of this story may probably enough be fabulous, but the social conditions presupposed cannot be imaginary. The same conditions underlie other legends of ancient Arabia, *e.g.* the story of Omm Khārija, who contracted marriages in more than twenty tribes, and is represented as living among her sons, who, therefore had not followed their respective fathers. In this legend the old form of marriage, applicable to such cases, appears to be preserved. All that was needed was that the man should say "suitor" (*khitb*), and that she should reply "I wed" (*nikh*), and the marriage was straightway accomplished without witnesses or *walī* (*Kāmīl*, 264 *sq.*; *Agh.* 7 is). In *Agh.* 13 123 1. 20 *sq.* there is a clear case at Medina where the woman stays at home but is regularly visited by her husband. On one of these visits the husband is waylaid and beaten, but whether by his wife's people is not clear. Again in *Agh.* 15 165 we have not only the wife in her father's house but her son there with her. She was of Khazraj and the husband of Aus (see Wellhausen *Skizzen*, 4 62 note).

From all this it is certain that there was a well-established custom of marriage in Arabia in which the woman remained with her kin and chose and dismissed her partner at will, the children belonging to the mother's kin and growing up under their protection. It is desirable to have a general name for this type of marriage. In Ceylon unions in which the husband goes to settle in his wife's village are called *beena* marriages, and J. F. McLennan has extended the use of this term to similar marriages among other races. We may follow this precedent whenever we have to do with regulated unions which really deserve the name of marriage; but among the Arabs *nikāh,* "marriage," is a very wide term indeed, and for the purpose before us we must even keep in view the large class of cases in which a woman only received occasional visits from the man on whom she had fixed her affections. This is the case which is so constantly described in Arabic poetry; the singer visits his beloved (who may often be a married woman) by stealth, and often she belongs to a hostile tribe. [10] It is usually assumed that such relations were simply illicit, and that the poets boast of them as in all ages poets have boasted of guilty amours. But it must be noted that though the lover ran a risk in seeking to approach his beloved the relation was generally matter of notoriety, openly celebrated in verse, and brought no disgrace or punishment on the woman. This sort of thing is not uncommon among savage tribes; often indeed the secrecy which a man is obliged to observe in approaching his mistress is a mere matter of etiquette, his visits being really quite well known. In point of fact the story of the Himyarite Sayyid already referred to (p. 84) shows that the kind of relation which the Arab poets are never weary of describing fell under the category of *mot'a*. The woman in this case was a Tamīmite by race and a Kharijite by religion, and her lover was of the hostile race of Yemen and of the Rāfidī sect. An open union was therefore out of the question, for the woman's people would not tolerate it, but she received the Sayyid under the form of a *mot'a* marriage. This is exactly the sort of thing that the poets describe, except that the Kharijites, unlike the old Arabs, will not allow of *mot'a* unions and threaten to kill the woman.

If *mot'a* connection is taken in this large sense it covers all relations between a man and woman in her own home which did not involve loss of character, or prevent the woman's tribe from recognising the children. But as usage limits the word to very temporary connections, in which the husband does not settle down with his wife, some term is wanted to cover both *beena* and *mot'a* arrangements. The choice of such a word, however, had better be deferred till we have looked by way of contrast at that type of marriage which in homogeneous tribes is associated with the rule of male descent — that namely in which the woman leaves her own tribe and follows her husband to his people.

Such a marriage might be constituted in two ways, (*a*) by capture, [11] and (*b*) by arrangement with the woman's kin.

Instances of marriage by capture might be accumulated to an indefinite extent from history and tradition. At the time of Mohammed the practice was universal. The immunity of women in time of war which prevails in Arabia now is a modern thing; in old warfare the procuring of captives both male and female was a main object of every expedition, and the Diwān of the Hodhail poets shows us that there was a regular slave trade in Mecca, supplied by the wars that went on among the surrounding tribes. [12] After the defeat of the Hawāzin — to cite but a single case — Mohammed, having agreed to restore the captives, was obliged to compensate many of his followers by promising them six camels from the next booty for every woman they gave up. Very commonly these captives at once became the wives or mistresses of their captors — a practice which Mohammed expressly recognised, though he sought to modify some of its more offensive features (Ibn Hishām, p. 759). [13] Such a connection does not appear to have been properly speaking concubinage, for in the time of the prophet when a woman became pregnant by her captor it was no longer proper that she should be sold in the market or ransomed by her people for money (Wellhausen, *Moh. in Med.* 179, *Sharh al-mowatta* [Cairo, 13 10], 3 78). This implies than the offspring would be freeborn and legitimate, unlike the sons of negro slave women, who were born slaves, as we see in the cases of 'Antara and 'Irār. A distinction, it would seem, was made between the sons of a foreign woman and those of a *horra* or freeborn tribeswoman. [14] According to Ibn 'Abd Rabbih (*'Icd,* 3 296) the *hajīn,* that is the son of an *'ajamīya,* or non-Arab woman, did not inherit in the Times of Ignorance; but there was no such disability as regarded the son of a captive, nay according to Arab tradition (*'Icd,* 3 290) the best and stoutest sons are born of reluctant wives. And so Hātim the Taite says (*'Icd,* 3 297):

"They did not give us Taites their daughters in marriage; but we wooed them against their will with our swords.

And with us captivity brought no abasement to them: and they neither toiled in making bread nor boiled the pot.

But we commingled them with our noblest women: and they bare us fine sons white of face [*i.e.* of pure descent].

How often shalt thou see among us the son of a captive bride: who staunchly thrusts through heroes when he meets them in the fight." [15]

The Sho'ūbiya reproach the Arabs saying: Their wives are captives carried behind men on camel's pillions, they are trodden upon (*watiya*) as a beaten path is trodden. Examples from the poets follow, and a story of Al-Hārith al-Kindi who tore to pieces by two horses his wife who had been captured and treated in the usual way. The laxity of Arab women is no doubt partly intelligible from the frequent captures (*'Icd,* 2 86, cited by Goldziher, *Muh. Stud.* 1 191 sq.).

There is then abundant evidence that the ancient Arabs practised marriage by capture. And we see that the type of marriage so constituted is altogether different from those unions of which the mofa is a survival, and kinship through women the necessary accompaniment. In the one case the woman chooses and dismisses her husband at will, in the other she has lost the right to dispose of her person and so the right of divorce lies only with the husband; in the one case the woman receives the husband in her own tent, among her own people, in the other she is brought home to his tent and people; in the one case the children are brought up under the protection of the mother's kin and are of her blood, in the other they remain with the father's kin and are of his blood.

All later Arabic marriages under the system of male kinship, whether constituted by capture or by contract, belong to the same type: in all cases, as we shall presently see in detail, the wife who follows her husband and bears children who are of his blood has lost the right freely to dispose of her person; her husband has authority over her and he alone has the right of divorce. Accordingly the husband in this kind of marriage is called, not in Arabia only, but also among the Hebrews and Aramaeans, the woman's "lord" or "owner" (ba'l, ba'al, bě'el — comp. Hosea, 2 16), [16] and wherever this name for husband is found we may be sure that marriage is of the second type, with male kinship, and the wife bound to her husband and following him to his home. It will be convenient to have a short name for the type of marriage in which these features are combined, and, as the name Baal is familiar to every one from the Old Testament, I propose to call it ba'al marriage or marriage of dominion, and to call the wife a be'ūlah or subject wife (Isaiah 62 4). For the contrasted type of connection, including mot'a and beena arrangements, we ought then to seek a name expressing the fact that the wife is not under her husband's authority but meets him on equal terms. Now it appears from Diw. Hodh. no. 19 that a woman who was visited by a man from time to time was called his sadīca or "female friend." [17] I apprehend that this term may have been technical; for a gift given to a wife by her husband on marriage is called sadāc. In Islam sadāc simply means a dowry and is synonymous with mahr. But originally the two words were quite distinct: sadāc is a gift to the wife, and mahr to the parents of the wife. The latter therefore belongs to marriage of dominion (as constituted by contract instead of capture), where the wife's people part with her and have to be compensated accordingly. And the presumption is that the sadāc originally belonged to the other sort of marriage, in which the woman disposes freely of her own favours, and is not different from the gift to a mot'a wife. But however this may be, the type of marriage which involves no subjection may very appropriately be called sadīca marriage, and the woman may be spoken of as a sadīca wife, while the husband is a sadīc husband. [18]

At the time of Mohammed, when mot'a unions were no longer looked upon as respectable, marriages in which the husband was the wife's lord were constituted by contract as well as by capture. But the subjection of the wife was quite as complete in the one case as in the other; practically speaking the contract brought the woman into the same condition as a captive wife. Of course there was a difference between a wife and a slave; the husband's lordship over his wife did not give him the right to dispose of her in the slave market; but this limitation, as we have seen, applied, by the usage of the prophet's time, in the case of a captive as well as in that of a woman obtained by agreement with her family. There is in the Kāmil, p. 270 sq. a very instructive passage as to the position of married women, which commences by quoting two lines spoken by a woman of the Banū 'Āmir ibn Sa'sa'a married among the Tayyi.

"Never let sister praise brother of hers: never let daughter bewail a father's death;
For *they* have brought her where she is no longer a free woman, and *they* have banished her to the farthest ends of the earth."

On these lines the author remarks, "'Aisha says 'Marriage is nothing but bondage, so a man should consider who receives his darling [*karīma*] as his bondservant.' Hence the phrases 'we were in the *possession* of such a one,' 'such a one *possessed* a woman,' 'her guardian gave her into his *possession*';" the words for possession in all these cases being forms of the root *malaka*, "to possess as a *mamlūk* (mameluke) or slave." "And so," Mobarrad continues, "the form of oath in which a man swears that, if he breaks his engagement, he will divorce his wife, belongs to the same region with those forms of asseveration in which one binds himself in case he proves false, to give up his goods or emancipate his slaves" — in point of fact the three are generally united in one form of oath (see De Sacy, *Chrest. Ar.* 1 47 *sq.*). "And the prophet says, 'I charge you with your women, for they are with you as captives (*'awānī*).' "According to the lexicons *'awānī* is actually used in the sense of married women generally, but this perhaps comes simply from the saying of the prophet just quoted. Mobarrad in his discursive fashion adds some further illustrations, but enough has been quoted to show how nearly the Arabs identified the position of the wife in the house of her husband with that of a captive slave.

And now the question arises: how were a woman's kinsfolk induced to give her up into this species of slavery? The answer cannot be doubtful: they did so — at least when the suitor was of an alien tribe — only in consideration of a price paid. Thus in the *'Icd,* 3 272, when Sa'sa'a ibn Mo'āwiya comes to 'Āmir ibn Al-Zarib to sue for his daughter's hand, the father says, "thou hast come to *buy* of me my liver [heart's blood]." In all the old stories of this kind it is perfectly plain that the dowry or *mahr* is paid by the husband to the bride's kin, and indeed the lexicographers, in explaining the old formula *hanīyan laka 'l-nāfija,* used to congratulate a father on the birth of a daughter, in the times before Islam, say that the daughter was welcomed as an addition to her father's wealth, because when he gave her in marriage he would be able to add to his flocks the camels paid to him as her *mahr* (*Tāj,* 2 109). It is only under Islam that this custom is abolished and the *mahr* becomes identical with the *sadāc* or present to the bride, which originally, as we have seen, must be held rather to belong to the *sadīca* marriage than to marriage of dominion. In fact marriage by purchase is found throughout the Semitic races wherever the husband is the wife's *ba'al* or lord. The Arabic *mahr* is the same word with the Hebrew *mōhar,* which is also paid to the damsel's father (Deut. 22 29), and the Syriac *mahrā,* which Bar 'Ali (ed. Hoffm. no. 5504) defines as "whatever the son-in-law gives to the parents of the bride." The etymological sense is simply "price." It is obvious that no Arab kin would have consented to give up its daughters without compensation, not so much because of the loss of the daughter's service in her father's house — for a fair woman, as we see from the verses of Hātim, was not allowed to spoil her beauty by hard work — as because if she remained in the tribe she might be the mother of gallant sons. The Arabs jealously watched over their women as their most valued trust, defended them with their lives and eagerly redeemed them when they were taken captive. When Mohammed asked the Hawāzin whether they would rather get back their goods or their women and children captured in war, they unhesitatingly chose the latter. It was a point of honour too not to give away a woman in an unequal match; "if you cannot find an equal match," says Cais ibn Zohair to the Namir (*'Icd,* 3 273), "the best marriage for them is the grave." The Arabs therefore were not disposed to make their daughters too cheap, much less to give them up without substantial compensation for the loss.

A woman then might leave her kin by capture or by purchase, but it is not to be supposed that the two methods are of equal antiquity.

That marriage by capture preceded marriage by contract seems probable *a priori*, for friendly relations between alien groups, which were never constituted except by a *casāma* or formal covenant, are surely a modification of an earlier state of universal hostility. And as the subjection of women to their husbands is regarded by the Arabs themselves as a virtual captivity, it is natural to think that this type of marriage first received its fixed character when all wives under the dominion of their husbands were in a state of real captivity. The very words used to express the relation — the derivatives of *malaka* — appear to imply that marriage originated in bondage; and in like manner the word *nazī'a,* which in actual usage means simply a woman married into an alien stock, denotes etymologically "one torn from her kin." The masculine *nazī'* according to the *Tāj,* continued to mean the son of a captive woman. J. F. M'Lennan has taught us to look to the preservation of the form of capture for the proof that in all parts of the world marriage by capture preceded marriage by contract, and in this connection he drew attention to the fact, attested by Burckhardt, that among the Bedouins of the Sinaitic peninsula, where marriage by contract is the rule, the form of capture, with a simulated resistance on the part of the bride, is still kept up. Whether the *zeffa,* or train, that in old Arabia escorted the bride to her bridegroom, assumed the semblance of a party returning from a successful raid and bearing the bride with them by force, I am unable to say; [19] and when we read of the girls of Medina surrounding the tent of Robayyi' on the night of her marriage, beating hand-drums and proclaiming the names of her fathers who had fallen at Badr (Bokhārī, 6 131 *sq.*), we cannot tell whether the object was to praise the bride as the daughter of martyrs, or to keep up an old custom, dating from days when a bride usually had the death of near relations to lament. But a trace of the form of capture seems to occur when the bride declares that she would be disgraced if she allowed her husband to enjoy her favours in the encampment of her father and her brothers (Rasmussen, *Addit.* p. 43, *Agh.* 9 150). The husband it appears must carry her off. [20]

Further indications of this sort are to be looked for, since it can hardly be thought that the form of marriage by capture described by Burckhardt has grown up, without any basis in ancient Arabian practice, in a country where the capture of women in war must have been extinct for centuries.

The conclusion to which we are thus led is as follows. Marriages of dominion were originally formed by capture and were still formed in this way down to the time of the prophet. Capture was afterwards supplemented by purchase, but the type of the marriage relation was not essentially changed by the introduction of this new method of procuring a *be'ūlah*-wife; in the days of Mohammed a woman who was under a husband was still one who had lost her personal freedom. This fact is expressed in the one-sided law of divorce, and the evidence quoted from the *Kāmil* shows that it was quite recognised that a married woman was in a sense her husband's property.

But at this point of the argument a difficulty arises. Before the time of Mohammed it had become very common for men to contract marriages of dominion with their near kinswomen, with a ward or with a *bint 'amm*, the daughter of a paternal uncle. [21] The origin of this practice cannot be explained till a later stage of our argument; it is enough to observe at present that in Medina, which as the scene of the prophet's legislation is the place about whose laws we are best informed, a man had a right to marry his ward if he pleased, and also, at least in certain cases, a right to the hand of his *bint 'amm*. [22] Now Professor Wilken maintains that with the rise of a custom of marrying near kinsmen, marriage by purchase would necessarily disappear; he believes therefore that before the time of the prophet the dowry had ceased to be a price paid to the father or guardian and become a gift to the spouse, and, in the absence of direct evidence to this effect, he urges that women in the time of the prophet enjoyed a position of social independence quite inconsistent with a custom of marriage by purchase. [23] These assertions amount to the thesis that the type of marriage by dominion, originally founded on capture, had already before the time of Mohammed undergone an entire transformation, at least among the more advanced Arabian communities. This view seems absolutely inconsistent with the language of the prophet and 'Aisha quoted in the *Kāmil,* but we must not reject it without examining the arguments on which the Leyden professor rests his case.

First then let us look at the argument that the purchase of brides would necessarily disappear when marriages with kinswomen became frequent. Prof. Wilken is of opinion that before the time of Mohammed marriages with aliens had practically ceased. But his only evidence for this is a passage of Shahrastānī which has been already discussed in a note and shown to contain an exaggeration. In point of fact, as the Arabs continued freely to practise marriage by capture, there is no reason why they should not have continued to marry by purchase. It is certain for example that the Coraish married the daughters of foreigners — Abū Sofyān had a Dausite wife (Ibn Hish. p. 275) — and allowed foreigners to marry their daughters under special contract. As regards the case of wards the right of the guardian to his ward's hand flows directly from the doctrine of purchase. He may take the girl to himself, without price, because he has the right to sell her hand to another; and so Loo the claim of a young man to his cousin's hand was of a special and oppressive character, and gave rise to similar complaints with the right of the heir to inherit the wives of the deceased. Wāhidī relates that when a widow called Kobaisha came to complain to the prophet that she had been taken to wife against her will by her deceased husband's heir, who would neither do a husband's part by her nor let her go free, "the women of Medina came to the apostle of God, saying, We are in the very same case as Kobaisha, except that we have not been taken in marriage by our step-sons but by our cousins on the father's side. [24] Marriage with near kinswomen, then, over whom the man had certain rights apart from special contract, could not tend to break down the system of purchase, as applied to women over whom the suitor had no rights.

I come now to the argument that the position of women in Arabia was too independent to allow them to be treated as chattels. As a matter of fact the married woman living under her husband, and without the power of divorce, was a sort of chattel and no better than a captive wife. Mohammed and 'Aisha say this of wives generally, and it is clear that wards married to their guardians and damsels married to their cousins were no better off than others. On the contrary the prophet, in Sūra, 4, found it necessary to make special provision against tyranny to wards, and the women of Medina, who had married cousins, felt their case to be peculiarly hard. What Prof. Wilken has to adduce against this turns on an entire confusion between marriages of dominion, in which the woman follows the husband home, and marriages of the *beena* type. In the latter the woman was free to dispose of her own favours as she pleased, because her father did not part with her, and her children remained with her own tribe. This kind of freedom necessarily disappeared wherever marriages of dominion became prevalent, as soon as the standard of chastity proper to such unions was extended to unmarried women. The fact that in many parts of Arabia unmarried women continued to enjoy considerable liberty, after married women were strictly under the dominion of their husbands, is simply an illustration of the common case of a different law of chastity for the married and the unmarried. Neglecting this distinction, Prof. Wilken contends broadly that women in general had a right to choose their own husbands. He cites the case of Khadija, who offered her hand to Mohammed; but if the traditional story is worthy of credit Khadija, had to obtain her father's consent, which she got by making him drunk. In Mohammedan law the guardian cannot dispose of his ward's hand without her consent, unless she is under age; but the traditions on this head (Bokhārī, 6 129 *sq.,* *Sharh al-mowatta'* 3 18 *sq.*) show quite plainly that this was an innovation, and indeed the whole law of the necessity of the woman's consent was long a matter of dispute among doctors. Hasan of Basra maintained that the father could dispose of his daughter's hand, whether she were a virgin or not, either with or against her will. So extreme a right was perhaps seldom enforced in old Arabia; but the mere fact of the father consulting his daughter's inclinations (*e.g.* Maidanī, 1 41; *Agh.* 9 149 *sq.*) does not change the essence of the marriage contract as a purchase by the suitor from the bride's father. [25]

The clearest light is thrown on the position of women and the nature of the marriage contract in Arabia at the time of the prophet by a point of ancient law already alluded to, of which we have fortunately full details.

The Coran (4 23) forbids men to "inherit women against their will," and verse 26 forbids them to have their step-mothers in marriage, "except what has passed "; *i.e.* marriages of this kind had been allowed before, and existing unions of the kind are not cancelled, but the thing is not to be done any more. Both passages, according to the commentators, refer to the same practice, and their explanation is certainly authentic, for they support it by numerous historical examples. From the mass of traditional accounts of the matter, I select as full and clear one of those preserved in Tabarī's great commentary (MS. of the Viceregal library in Cairo). [26]

"In the *Jāhilīya,* when a man's father or brother or son died and left a widow, the dead man's heir, if he came at once and threw his garment over her, had the right to marry her under the dowry (*mahr*) of [*i.e.* already paid by] her [deceased] lord (*sāhib*), or to give her in marriage and take her dowry. But if she anticipated him and went off to her own people, then the disposal of her hand belonged to herself."

The symbolical act here spoken of is the same that we find in the book of Ruth (3 9), where the young widow asks her husband's kinsman Boaz "to spread his skirt over his handmaid," and so claim her as his wife. [27]

The meaning of this usage is quite transparent; marital rights are rights of property which can be inherited, and which the heir can sell if he pleases. But the right of the heir lapses if the proper legal symbolism is not used to assert it, and in that case the woman can become free by placing herself under the protection of her own kin. [28] This can only be understood as meaning that marital rights over the woman had in the first instance been purchased from the kin, and indeed, in the tradition quoted, the word *mahr* is twice quite unambiguously used in the sense of "purchase-money." [29]

Prof. Wilken does not deny that, where the heir has a right to claim or dispose of the hand of a widow, marriage must be held to be an affair of purchase, but he maintains that the custom just described must have been confined to some few tribes, since there are, he says, many examples of women who were free to dispose of their own hands. I can only say that I have not been able to find these examples. There are instances of women offering

their hand to the prophet, or asking him to find a husband for them, but these cases are represented as justified only by the prophet's supreme authority
as universal *walī* (Bokh. 6 129), and the unenlightened thought such women
very immodest (*ibid.* p. 124, Sprenger, *Leb. Moh.* 3 84). Further, Prof. Wilken
appeals to the fact that later Arabic writers characterise the marriage of an
heir with the widow of the deceased as "the hateful marriage," and say that
"*daizan*" was an epithet of reproach applied to a man who had made such a
marriage. But no one who knows the sources can attach the least weight to
this; Arab authors are utterly unscrupulous in their attempts to minimise the
ungodly practices of their ancestors, and the term "hateful marriage" is simply borrowed from the words of the Coran. [30] In point of fact, though the
details of the evidence in the *hadīth* are derived from Medina, we know that
the custom referred to was very widespread in Arabia. In a list of cases of the
son marrying his father's wife, given by Ibn Cotaiba, p. 55 *sq.*, some are pre-
historic, and may be due to the ingenuity of the genealogists, who found that
an eponym was indifferently called Barra mother of Kinana and Barra mother of the sons of Kinana. But some of the cases are certainly historical, and
yet not Medinan. Thus Molaika, one of the wives of the Caliph 'AlI, had been
married to a Fazarite, and then to his son. Among the Meccans, Amina mother of Abū Moayyit was married first to Omayya ibn 'Abd Shams, and then to
his son Abū 'Āmr (comp. *Agh.* 1 9 *sq.*), and Nofail, grandfather of the Caliph
'Omar, left a Fahmite widow who was married by his son 'Āmr (comp. Ibn
Hish. 147 s). The practice therefore occurred in *both* the great branches of
the Arab race, and not only in Medina, but in the more advanced society of
Mecca. [31] Strabo knew it to exist in Yemen (xvi. 4 25), and there is little
question that at one time it was usual, not merely throughout Arabia, but in
all parts of the Semitic world, where the husband was the wife's *ba'al*. By it
must be explained, in the Old Testament, the conduct of Reuben with Bilhah,
[32] and the anger of Ishbosheth of Abner (2 Sam. 3 7) for an act that seemed
to encroach on his birthright. Absalom served himself heir to David by ap-
propriating his concubines (2 Sam. 16 22) without exciting any horror among
the Israelites, and Adonijah when he asked the hand of Abishag was in fact
claiming a part of the elder brother's inheritance (1 Kings 2 22, compared
with v. 15 *sq.*). Such unions were still common in Jerusalem in the time of
Ezekiel (22 10), but they were offensive to the higher morality of the prophetic religion, and form the subject of the only law of forbidden degrees in the
law-book of the prophetic party in the 7th cent. B.C., the original Deuteronomic code (Deut. 22 30). Yet even after the exile the Hebrew, like the Arab genealogists, seem to have used the marriage of a son with his father's wife as
one device for throwing the relations of clans and townships into genealogical form; in 1 Chron. 2 24, Wellhausen with the aid of the LXX. restores the
reading, "After the death of Hezron, Caleb came unto Ephrath the wife of
Hezron his father" (*De Gentibus,* etc. Gött. 1870,9. 14), And from the Syro-
Roman law-book edited by Bruns and Sachau (Leips. 1880), which appears

to have been written in Syria in the fifth century of our era, and contains many hints of customs divergent from Roman use which still lingered in these lands, we can infer that in spite of Western law, divers irregular unions, including that with a father's widow, were openly celebrated with a marriage feast and marriage gifts (§ 109 *sq.*, pp. 33 *sq.*, 280 *sq.*). We cannot therefore possibly think of the custom of Medina as isolated and exceptional. [33]

Once more, the fact that the heir could take the widow without *mahr*, or dispose of her to another and take the *mahr* (paid by the latter), is conclusive as to the fact that down to the time of the prophet *mahr* meant purchase-price. Under Islam the difference between *mahr* and *sadāc* — the price paid to the father and the gift given to the wife — disappeared, and so the traditionalists continually confuse the two and produce the impression that before as well as after Islam, the dowry was either a direct gift to the wife, or was settled by the father of the bride upon his daughter. But the real state of the case appears clearly enough in spite of this confusion, not only in the marriage of widows by the heir without dowry, but in another usage prohibited by Mohammed — the so-called *shighār,* in which two men who had marriageable wards gave each his own ward to the other without dowry. This usage is plainly inconsistent with the Mohammedan principle that the dowry is the wife's property, and therefore was abolished by the prophet (Bokh. 6 123, *Sharh al-mowatta'*, 3 17). And the fact that even in this case the traditionalists use the word *sadāc,* shows how carefully we must criticise all that they say on these matters.

Still another evidence of the real nature of the contract of marriage in ancient Arabia may be drawn from the law of divorce. Divorce among the Arabs was of various kinds, and in one type of marriage, as we have seen, either spouse could dissolve the union. But in *ba'al* marriage also there was, in the Time of Ignorance, as in Islam, a twofold method of divorce — *khol'* or "divestiture" and *talāc* or "dismissal." In Mohammedan law, the difference between the two is, that in ordinary divorce or dismissal the wife claims her dowry, while *khol'* is a divorce granted by the husband, at his wife's request, she undertaking either to give up her dowry, or to make some other payment, to induce him to set her free. In old times, on the other hand, *khol'* was a friendly arrangement between the husband and his wife's father, by which the latter repaid the dowry and got back his daughter (Freytag, *Ar. Prov.* 1 78). In the story related to explain the nature of this kind of separation, the spouses are said to have been cousins, from which it appears that even in such a case the daughter might be given in marriage by her father for a price.

Under the *khol'* the marriage contract was absolutely cancelled, because the material consideration paid by the husband in order to acquire marital rights was returned to him. But if a husband resolved to live no longer with his wife, and yet did not get back the *mahr*, it is plain that the woman would not be absolutely free under such a theory of the marriage contract as we have found to exist in Arabia. The husband had purchased the exclusive right to use the woman as a wife, and this right was of the nature of property, and did not revert to the woman or her kin simply because the owner declined to use it. Evidence that this was so may be found in the law of triple divorce, which still survives in Mohammedan law, and is proved to have been current in the Jāhilīya by a narrative and verses of the poet Al-A'shā (Shahrastanī, p. 441, Yācūt, 4 620). A divorce was extorted from Al-A'shā by the kin of his wife, who had other views for her, and to make her dismissal complete, he was forced to repeat the formula three times. Till the third divorce, the husband was still *ahaccu 'l-nasi bihā*, "had more right to her than any one else had," — the same phrase that is used to characterise the power of the kin over an unmarried woman or of the heir over a widow. In Islam, a man who has divorced his wife by a single repetition of the formula can take her again within three months without asking her consent; but there is a case in the *Hamāsa*, p. 191, where a man divorced his wife, and sent her back to her people, but was extremely angry to find that, under the new law of Islam, other suitors presented themselves to her at the end of a year. [34] On the other hand, while Moslem law forbade remarriage to a woman who was divorced in pregnancy, until after her delivery, we find that in old Arabia a pregnant divorced woman might be taken by another under agreement with her former husband (Maidanī, 1 160, Freytag, 1 321, *sq.*)j. One sees from all this, that marital rights were treated absolutely as the property of the husband, or failing him, of the husband's heirs. According to Shahrastānī the husband's heirs took up their claims over his divorced wife, just as they would have done upon his death. [35]

To complete this view of the dependent position of woman under the system of *ba'al* marriages which prevailed in Central Arabia, along with male kinship, at the time of the prophet, we must glance at the disabilities laid on women by the law of property and inheritance.

In a system of marriage with female kinship, there is no object to be served by excluding women from rights of property. The woman remains with her brothers, and her children are their natural heirs. But, on the other hand, where a woman leaves her own kin and goes abroad to bear children for an alien husband, there will always be a tendency to reduce her rights of property and inheritance as far as possible, because everything she gets is carried out of the tribe or out of the family. And so it was in ancient Arabia. The woman in Ammianus lives in her own tent and receives her husband in it. Māwīya, who receives Hātim in a similar marriage, has great wealth in herds, and the wife in Ammianus had also something to protect, for she gives her husband a lance to indicate the service he owes her. To this class of marriage, too, one may refer the form of divorce (Freytag, *Ar. Pr.* 1 498) in which the husband says to his wife "Begone, for I will no longer drive thy flocks to the pasture." Among the Tayyi, to whom Hātim belonged, women might own flocks down to the time of the prophet, as we know from the story of Zaid al-Khail (*Agh.* 15 51, Caussin de Perceval, 2 639). Zaid, during the life of his father Mohalhil, appears caring for cattle that belong to his sister, the daughter of Mohalhil, so that we have here a woman owning property while she lives in her father's *dār*. Is this a relic of such a distribution of property as goes with female kinship) It may be so, for there are undoubtedly traces of a law of descent through women in princely houses of Arabia, where old customs of inheritance naturally linger longest, cases where a man's heirs are his brother's and finally his sister's son (Abulfeda, *Hist. Anteisl.* pp. 118, 122). [36] But it is fair to remember that the Tayyi were by this time partly Christianised, and open to a good deal of foreign influence, so that they are not the best field for the observation of pure old Arabic law.

On the other hand, it is certain that where, as at Medina, marriage by purchase and male kinship were the rule, the position of women as regarded property was unfavourable. At Medina, as we are told by the commentators on Sūra 4, women could not inherit. So far as the widow of the deceased is concerned, this is almost self-evident; she could not inherit because she was herself — not indeed absolutely, but *quâ* wife — part of her husband's estate, whose freedom and hand were at the disposal of the heir, if he chose to claim them, while if he did not do so, she was thrown back on her own people. But further, there is an explicit statement, confirmed by the words of the Sūra (verse 126), that the men of Medina protested against the new rule, introduced by the prophet, which gave a share of inheritance to a sister or a daughter. We have seen above that this objection was based on the broad principle that none should inherit save warriors, and that this principle was applied in the most absolute way is made plain by the story of Cais ibn Al-Khatīm, who, when he went forth to avenge his father's death, provided for his mother by handing over to one of his kinsmen a palm-garden near Medina, which was to be his if Cais fell in his enterprise, subject to the condition that he would "nourish this old woman from it all her life." Where the mother of a man of substance could only be provided for in this roundabout way, the incapacity of women not only to inherit, but to hold property — at least lands — must have been absolute (*Aghānī,* 2 160).

Wilken, in accordance with his view that marriage was not a contract by purchase, questions the accuracy of the statement that at Medina daughters received no share of their father's estate, appealing to Wellhausen's abridgement of the Maghāzī (*Moh. in Med.* p. 147), where a widow complains to the prophet that, her husband having been slain at Ohod, his brother had seized the property and left his daughters penniless, "and girls cannot get married unless they have money." But the last clause is not found in other versions of this very familiar tradition, and it is only necessary to read the paragraph through and note the miraculous incidents it contains to see that it gives a late and dressed-up form of the story.

It would not, however, be reasonable to suppose that women could not possess private property of any kind, when even slaves were often allowed to keep their earnings, only paying a tribute (*kharāj*) to their masters

(Bokhārī, 4 219). The case of Cais is explicit only as to real estate, while the theory that women ought not to share in what they cannot defend would cover also flocks and herds, which are constantly exposed to raids, but certainly not personal ornaments, which a woman was in no risk of losing so long as she was safe herself (comp. Ibn Hishām, p. 581, where Hind presents her ornaments to the slayer of Hamza). And as eastern women generally wear their money strung as a necklace, it is tolerably certain that a woman might have money also. No legal principle can be pushed to its utmost limits, and it is therefore somewhat surprising that Prof. Wilken argues against the exclusion of women from inheritance, because certain women were able to make considerable presents to the prophet. In truth, though a woman could not inherit, there was no reason why she should not receive gifts from her father or husband — though one may guess from the arrangement made by Cais on behalf of his mother that her hold of these would not have been secure if she lost her natural protector. [37] It is even possible, and we shall see presently how such a custom might be introduced, that before Islam a custom had established itself by which the husband ordinarily made a gift — under the name of *sadāc* — to his wife upon marriage, or by which part of the *mahr* was customarily set aside for her use, and that thus the new law of Islam which made the dower a settlement on the wife was more easily established. There are old traditions of such a practice (*'Icd,* 3 272, *Agh.* 16 160), though the persistency with which the prophet insists on a present from the husband — be it only an iron ring or half his cloak, if the suitor has nothing else to give — seems to show that there was no absolute rule on the matter before his time. [38] What does appear to be possible is that the alleviations which the prophet introduced in the hard condition of married women were partly based on the more advanced laws of his own city of Mecca. In Mecca the influence of higher civilisations may have been felt, for the townsmen had large commercial dealings with Palestine and Persia, and some of them had lived in Roman cities like Gaza. And here accordingly we find that Khadija, though — if the traditions can be believed — she could not marry the prophet without her father's consent, led a perfectly independent life as a rich widow engaged in a lucrative caravan trade. Khadīja's estate included real property, for she presented to her daughter Zainab a house, which had a very interesting history and was ultimately purchased and rebuilt by Ja'far the Barmecide. From this it must be concluded that women at Mecca could hold property before Islam, and the sacrosanct character of the great holy city, which protected it from invasion, would certainly destroy the force of the argument used at Medina that no one ought to inherit who could not defend property. But we do not know how Khadīja came by her property; she may have received it through her former husbands by a *donatio inter vivos* or even by will — wills of some sort being already in use. We can only say that her case compared with that of Cais's mother seems to show that women were in a somewhat better position at Mecca than at Medina. [39] But at

Mecca, quite as much as at Medina, the husband became absolute possessor of the right to use a woman as a wife, and there is evidence to show that this right could be inherited and was not forfeited by simple divorce. Certainly Mecca made no exception to the rule that Arabian *ba'al* marriage was regarded as constituted by capture or by purchase, that the marital rights of the husband were a dominion over his wife, and that the disposal of her hand did not belong to the woman herself but to her guardian. For all this is true even under Islam; the theory of Moslem law is still that marriage is purchase, and the party from whom the husband buys is the father, though by a humane illogicality the price becomes the property of the woman, and the husband's rights are not transferable. And so, though Islam softened some of the harshest features of the old law, it yet has set a permanent seal of subjection on the female sex by stereotyping a system of marriage which at bottom is nothing else than the old marriage of dominion.

It is very remarkable that in spite of Mohammed's humane ordinances the place of woman in the family and in society has steadily declined under his law. In ancient Arabia we find, side by side with such instances of oppression as are recorded at Medina, many proofs that women moved more freely and asserted themselves more strongly than in the modern East. The reason of this lay partly no doubt in the conditions of nomad life, which make the strict seclusion of women impossible, and so allow a more independent development to the female character. But what chiefly operated to check marital tyranny and to preserve a certain sense of personal dignity under the humiliating conditions of marriage by purchase was the great weight attached to the bond of blood.

In Arabia a woman did not change her kin on marriage; she was not as at Rome adopted into her husband's stock, and she still continued to have a claim on the help and protection of her own people. The contract of marriage had conveyed to the husband a certain property which was absolutely his to enjoy, or to transfer by contract, and which could even be inherited by his heir; but strictly speaking the property was not in the woman herself but in the right to live with her and get children by her. The possession of such a right necessarily gave the husband a very full control over his spouse, but that control was limited by the fact that the woman's kin still recognised kindred obligations towards their sister, and were pretty sure to interfere if the husband was inordinately tyrannical. [40] The strength of the feelings of kinship bettered the wife's position, whether she were married in her own kin or to an alien, unless she were carried far out of the reach of her natural protectors: in *Agh.* 9 150, when the father comes to his daughter and says, "This is Hārith ibn 'Auf a chieftain of the Arabs who has come to ask thy hand, and I am willing to give thee him to wife, what sayest thou?" the reply is, "No! I am not fair of face and I have infirmities of temper, *and I am not his* bint 'amm (tribeswoman) so that he should respect my consanguinity with him, nor does he dwell in thy country so that he should have regard for thee; I fear then that he may not care for me and may divorce me, and so I shall be in an evil case." [41]

This may be illustrated by the story of Hind bint 'Otba when her first husband sent her back to her father on suspicion of unchastity. "Be frank with me, my daughter," says 'Otba; "if the man is speaking truth I will send someone to kill him and wipe out your shame, but if the charge is false we will make him refer the matter to a diviner" ('Icd, 3 273 sq.). [42] In the state of society which these words indicate, a woman's kin were her natural protectors after as well as before marriage; when Abū Salima left Mecca to emigrate to Medina his wife's clan kept her with them, though the husband's clan would not allow them to keep her little child (Sprenger, *Leb. Moh.* 2 535, cp. p. 130 below). And on the other hand in Wācidī, p. 178 we find that the Jews venture to insult an Arab woman married to a citizen of Medina because she is a *nazī'a, i.e.* of a strange kin. who has no one to protect her. Conversely it was quite understood that a woman would continue to take a special interest in her kinsfolk; in the 'Icd, 3 272 is a narrative, instructive in more than one way, where to a suitor proposing for a girl's hand the father says, "Yes, if I may give names to all her sons and give all her daughters in marriage." "Nay," says the suitor, "our sons we will name after our fathers and uncles, and our daughters we will give in marriage to chieftains of their own rank, but I will settle on your daughter estates in Kinda and promise to refuse her no request that she makes on behalf of her people." In this case we see quite clearly a sort of compromise between the system of marriage in which the children belonged to the mother's kin, and the system where the husband buys the right to have children born to himself of his wife. And as the husband looks on the last point as indispensable, he is willing in compensation to grant his wife a position of independence and honour such as naturally belongs rather to that type of marriage in which the husband follows the wife.

But indeed, to put the matter generally, when we observe that whatever independence and dignity the Arab wife enjoyed turns on the fact that she can count on her own kin, we must conclude *sadīca* marriage to have been originally vastly more common than it was at the time of Mohammed. If for many generations the prevalent feeling had been that girls were brought up only to be sold to husbands, the feeling of strong kinship obligation would have gradually ceased to be felt towards the women who left their home, and men could not but have felt that they had less obligation to stand by their sisters than by their brothers. But, in reality, the feeling was quite the other way; it is an old Arab sentiment, and not a Moslem one, that the women of the group are its most sacred trust, that an insult to them is the most unpardonable of insults. This feeling must have grown up under a system of female kinship; it was perfectly natural under such a marriage-system as Ammianus describes. Under such a system everyone in the tribe was interested to protect the women, who were not only their sisters but the mothers of the children of the tribe, and it was under this system, and not under that of *ba'al* marriage, that women could rise to such consideration as to be chosen queens like Māwīya of Ghassān (C. de Perceval, 2 218), or judges, as several women are said to have been. [43] The legendary character of most of these female judges shows that the Arabs themselves recognised that the position of woman had fallen; it could not but fall with the spread of *ba'al* marriages of the type we have described, and it continued still to fall under Islam, because the effect of Mohammed's legislation in favour of women was more than outweighed by the establishment of marriages of dominion as the one legitimate type, and by the gradual loosening of the principle that married women could count on their own kin to stand by them against their husbands. The last, no doubt, was the most powerful cause, and it was necessarily brought into play by the break-up of the tribal system, inseparable from the ordinances of Islam and the extension of the empire. But, apart from all external causes, there was an internal inconsistency between marriages of dominion and the freedom and independence of women. This comes out strongly in the case of marriages of the *ba'al* type between persons of the same *hayy*. No doubt in this case the woman might be more patient than an alien (*'Icd*, 3 290), and the man more forbearing in consideration of the tie of blood. But the cold prudence of the Semitic mind saw something unsatisfactory in such unions; "Do not marry in your own *hayy*," says 'Āmr ibn Kolthūm to his sons (*Agh.* 9 185), "for that leads to ugly family quarrels" — partly perhaps about money, since a dowry was often not paid up at once, but mainly because there was a real inconsistency in the position of a woman who was at once her husband's free kinswoman and his purchased wife. It was better to have a wife who had no claims of kin and no brethren near her to take her part.

Thus, *ba'al* marriage once introduced, it tended steadily to lower the position of woman. And it tended also, quite apart from Islam, gradually to supersede marriages of the older type.

So long as wives under dominion were exclusively captives, so long as they were at least always aliens, the two types of marriage might go on side by side, and even in the same tribe; Hātim for example contracts a *beena* marriage with Mawīya and yet boasts of the practice of marriage by capture as prevalent in his tribe. But the position of women under the two types of marriage was so diametrically opposite that they could not both continue permanently to go on together; and when it came about, in a way which we shall by and by be able to explain, that women were given as *be'ūlah-wives* within their own *hayy*, the other type of marriage was doomed. If the tradition about Salma is historical (p. 85), *beena* marriage, with kinship through the mother, was still possible in Medina in the time of the prophet's great-grandfather; but at the epoch of the Flight, *ba'al* marriage with male kinship was the universal rule, and the old type survived only in *mot'a* unions and other practices of a like kind, which were now viewed as irregular, at least in the more advanced urban communities. One can easily see how this came about. In the first place men wanted sons who should be theirs, and not belong to their wife's kin. And then also the idea of conjugal fidelity that is formed under a system in which marital rights are matter of purchase naturally produces in course of time a doctrine of chastity inconsistent with the freedom of women to take and dismiss their partners at will, and a young woman who entertained a *sadīc* husband would practically be regarded as a harlot. So we find that 'Āisha thinks it a shameful thing for a woman to offer herself to the prophet, and Hind the wife of Abū Sofyān says to Mohammed, when he recites to her the precept against fornication, "a freewoman, *horra, does not commit fornication.*" In this state of feeling, a woman who entertained a *mot'a* husband would sink in social estimation and not be regarded as a proper wife at all.

[1] Goldziher, *Lit. blatt,* p. 27*, adds *Nabigha,* Append. 5 2 (cp. Yācūt, I588 1. 18, *Hamāsa,* 766 4).

[2] The passage of Shahrastānī, 441, cited by Wilken to show that marriages with aliens were always disliked, is generalised in the usual reckless fashion of this author from the story of the marriage of Lacit b. Zorāra with the daughter of Cais Dhu 'l-jaddein, 'led, 8272 *sq.* (from Al-Shaibani; the form of the story in *Agh.* 19 131 does not, like that in the *'Icd,* contain the exact words used by Shahrastānī). In this case the girl was a very great match, whose hand Lacit would not have asked unless he had been very aspiring. Great chiefs, who in later times were given from motives of pride to kill their infant daughters, very probably disliked to sell them, but ordinary men had no such prejudices, and looked to the price of a daughter's hand as a valuable source of wealth (*Tāj,* 2 109). Wilken goes much too far in saying, mainly on the authority of this one passage, that marriage within the kin became the ordinary practice in Arabia "soon after the establishment of the system of male kinship." Marriage with women even of hostile clans must have been quite common, to judge from the numerous instances that meet us in all the sources — *e.g.* in the *Diwān* of the poets of Hodhail. What we do find is that the Arabs did not like to intermarry with and settle among people who had very different customs — *e.g.* who ate distasteful or forbidden food. Thus in *Diw. Hodh.* 57 2, 147 2, the poet is indignant at a proposal that he should marry and settle down among Himyarites "who do not circumcise their women, and who do not think it disgusting to eat locusts." In the same collection, no. 164, Taabbata Sharran's people are mocked for allowing their sister to marry into a kin accused of cannibalism. To this day Bedouin women are very reluctant to marry townsmen — mainly because they dislike the food of the towns, above all, green vegetables.

[3] The evidence for this will appear in the sequel, but it may be convenient to indicate some of it here, (1) The relation of husband and wife is expressed by the words *jār* and *jāra*. The *Tāj* cites two verses in which Al-A'shā calls his wife his *jāra,* 3 114 (see also Shahr. 441, *Agh.* 8 83 *sq.*), and the *Asās al-Balāgha* quotes "Ibn 'Abbās used to sleep بين جارتيه‎." This agrees with the fact that a relation of *jiwār* was constituted between two kins by intermarriage (at least in later times), but a woman still had a right to the protection of her own people, and often re-

turned to them, as she still tloes among the Bedouins. In the case of a widow, if the right of the husband and his kin lapsed, she returned to the circle of her own people. (2) *Kāmil,* 191, "A man of the Azd was making the circuit of the Ka'ba and praying for his father. One said to him, Dost thou not pray for thy mother? He answered. She is a Tamīmite." This is cited as an extreme instance of raceantagonism, and betrays exceptional feeling, but it is quite inconsistent with the incorporation of the wife in her husband's kin. (3) Another good evidence is that a wife who is not of her husband's kin does not scratch her face or shave her head for him, even if she loves him dearly (*Agh.* 19 131 1. 30, 132 6, Lacit's wife). [On the fleeting character of the relation expressed by the word *jāra* in old Arabian usage, see the *Diwān* of Hotai'a, p. 201 (note to 69 *v.* 6). — I. G.]

[4] [A milder form is: *darabat bainahu wa-bainahā hijāban* (*Agh.* 21 15 1. 19). On the above-mentioned incident cp. also Th. W. Juynboll, *Over het historische Verband tusschen de mohammedaansche bruidsgave,* etc., 26 *ff.* (Leyden, 1894). — I. G.]

[5] Among the Somāl the daughter brings as a dowry the moveable liut (*gourgui*), mats, household appurtenances, and a few cattle (Revoil, *Vallée du Darror,* p. 332, Paris, 1882). The husband at the marriage ceremony is received in his wife's tent. There is polygamy, but rarely, and only one wife under the same roof.

[6] Wellhausen's objections (*Ehe,* p. 445) do not seem important as they are there stated; on p. 466 he gives an example of a woman going off from her husband and taking her tent with her.

[7] The gift given to the woman is called *hulwān* (Lane, *s.v.,* p. 634).

[8] [Even in ancient times secret marriages (*nikāh al-sirr*) were distinguished from public marriages. The woman with whom a man entered into a marriage relation without the regular public contract seems to have been called *surrīya* (for *sirrīya,* from *sirr*), a name that in later times was used for women of still lower standing. See, further, "Ueber Geheimehen bei den Arabern," *Globus,* 68 32 ff. (1895).— I. G.]

[9] According to *Aghānī,* 13 124 1. 17 *sqq.,* Salma was previously married to the famous tribal chief of Medina, Ohayha. She fled from him when he purposed war against her own people and gave them warning.

[10] [All this, however, is doubled by Wellh. *Die Ehe bei den Arabern,* (*Nachrichten v. d. kgl. Gesellsch. d. Wissenschaften,* Göttingen, 1893, no. xi. p. 432).

[11] [For wives acquired thus cp. *Agh.* 10 48 1. 18: the mother of 'Alcama b. 'Ulāta was a *sabiya* (captured), that of his father a *mahira* (acquired by paying a *mahr*). Ibn Cais al-Rocayyāt boasts that his father is descended from Ātika al-mahīra (*Dīwān,* ed. Rhodokanakis, 14v. 15). See, on this, Mobarrad, 305. The children, even, are thus distinguished after the mother as *mu'alhaj* and *mahir* (Ibn Hish. 274 11). The plural of *mahīra* is *mahā'ir* (gloss. Tab.). I. G.]

[12] The first Moslem women who were treated as captives in Islam were of Hamdān in the time of Mo'awia (*Agh.* 4 132 I. 6).

[13] How very offensive these were we see from Farazdac, p. 235. (Boucher). For the practice of marriage by capture see also *ib.,* p. 202 1. 15, with the anecdote in *Agh.* 19 114. The suicide of a captive woman is mentioned in *Agh.* 13 3 1. 8. [See further Wellh. *Ehe,* 436, n. 1.]

[14] So Tarafa, 9 8. The frontier (farj) of the *hayy* is defended only by sons of a freeborn woman. [In Osd al-Ghāba, 4 43 (end), al-Wācidī and other genealogists and historians are cited for the fact that Ammār b. Yasir, whose father belonged to the S. Arabian tribe in Madhhij, and was attached to the tribe of Makhzūm because his mother had lived in this tribe as a slave before Yasir married her. Her son 'Ammār consequently became a *maulā* of the B. Makhzūm. This is cited to exemplify the circumstance that the son of a slave-woman is not incorporated into the tribe of his father, but into that from which his bond-mother was taken. — I. G.]

[15] Cp. also *Agh.* 13 3 last verse.

[16] [See *RS*, p. 108 *sq.*, n. 3.] On the associations of *ba'l*, see *Agh.* 8 43 I. 14 *sqq.*, where a virago is asked by Mohammed b. 'Alī (son of the Caliph): "hast thou a *ba'l* (husband)?" she answers, "I have a *ba'l* whose *ba'l* (lord) I am" [private communication from Nöldeke]. To the words that denote the husband's dominion belongs *'amlaka* with double accus. "to give a woman to a man as wife" (*e.g.*, B. *Hish.* 144 11.).

[17] I suspect, however, that a man's *sadīca* was very often another man's wife (*zauj*). Certainly it is so in Mof al-Dabbī, *Amthāl.*, p. 11 1. 7 from foot [cp. also 53, and Maidānī, 2 32, which go to show that the *sadīca* is considered, not in reference to any marriage contract, but from the point of view of harlotry (*zinā*). In Schol. Hodh. 61 1 there is a case where a man stands in the nadica relation to a mother and daughter. It is related in Tirmidhi, 2 202 (= Osd al-Ghāba, 4 345) that a public prostitute (*baghī*) was the *sadīca* of Marthad. In such cases as these the lover is called sadic, frequently also khalil (*e.g.* Maid. 1 350, where a woman has a zauj and a *khalil* at the same time, Kastal. 7 282 [above], Tafsir on 24 6) or *khill* (Maid. 2 38, in the proverb *cad calainā*). These words are quite synonymous, and therefore *sadic* and *sadīca* have nothing to do with *sadāc*, "dowry." — *I.e.*]

[18] [See, generally, Nöldeke's criticisms, *ZDMG* 40 154.]

[19] Wellhausen (*Ehe*, p. 443, n. 5), who doubts the *zeffa* being a form of capture, thinks this explanation possible with regard to the bridegroom grasping the bride by the forelock (*Agh.* 16 37 *sq.*).

[20] See, however, Wellh. *Ehe*, p. 442, n. 4.

[21] *Yā 'bna 'ammī* is the address of Chadīja in B. Hish. 154 8, *i.e.*, to a husband who is not a cousin the relation is closer and more endearing.

[22] [See Wellh. *Ehe*, 436 *sq.*']

[23] *Agh.* 19 131 1. 8 compared with '*Icd*, 3 372 1. 32 may seem to imply that the dowry was paid in the case of Lacīt's marriage to the wife, and by a special favour was provided by the father.

[24] Al-Wāhidī, *Asbāb nosūl al-Corān* (MS. of A.H. 627 [now Camb. Univ. Add. 3178]), on Sura, 423 [ed. Cairo, 131 5]. For Kabīsa, Tabarī, in his comm. on the verse, has more correctly Kobaisha bint Ma'n b. 'Āsim of the Aus. He gives the tradition from 'Ikrima in a shorter form and without the last part. The husband, whom Wāhidī calls Cais, Tabarī calls Abū Cais.

[25] In *Agh.* 9 II (cp. 13 136) Al-Khansā refuses the suit of Doraid, preferring her

نِسِيْ عَم to such an old man. But though her father says the choice lies with herself this is represented as exceptional.

حدثني محمد بن الحسين قال حدثنا احمد بن مفضل قال
حدثنا اسباط عن السدى اما قوله لا يحلّ لكم ان ترثوا النساء كرهًا فانّ
الرجل فى الجاهلية كان يموت ابوه او اخوه او ابنه فاذا مات وترك

[26] امرأة فان سبق وارث الميت فالقا عليها ثوبه فهو أحقّ بها ان ينكحها

بمهر صاحبها أو ينكحها فياخذ مهرها وان سبقته ذهبت إلى أهلها

[ed. Cairo, 1319.]

(read: فهم (فهى) أحقّ بنفسها

One of the traditions given by Tabarī goes so far as to say that the heir could even sell the woman into slavery; but this must be an exaggeration, probably due to a misapprehension of the heir's right to sell her as a wife for a *mahr* paid to himself.

[27] From this symbolic action we understand why words meaning garment, *libas, izār*, etc., are used to mean a spouse; cp. لبودثه, "his garment," "his wife," in Mai. 2 16. The symbolism of plucking off the shoe on declining to form a levirate marriage is similar, for *na'l*, "shoe," also means "wife," as وطأ means to use a woman as a wife. A Bedouin form of divorce is "she was my slipper and I have cast her off" (Burckhardt, *Bedouins*, 1 113).

[28] In *Agh.* 19 132 Lacīt's wife is free to return to her kin at his death, but in this case the husband had paid no *mahr*.

[29] The true understanding of the rights of the heir over a widow has been a little confused by the fact that in Sūra, 4 23, after the words "it is not lawful for you to inherit women against their will," the prophet adds, "nor prevent them from marrying that ye may go off with part of what ye have given them." This has led the commentators to add that sometimes the heir, instead of taking the woman to himself, simply confined her and kept her from marrying till she consented to free herself by giving up her dowry. If this applied to pre-Islamic times it would prove that the dowry was already a payment to the woman, her own absolute property. But we find in Tabarī express tradition that these two parts of the verse did not refer to the same thing. According to one account the first was revealed with reference to the practice of the Jāhilīya, and the second to that of Islam — where as we know the dowry was the wife's property; another account refers the second precept to the rights claimed by husbands in Mecca over their divorced wives.

[30] Shahrastānī, p. 440, says, "The Arabs observed some of the prohibitions of the Coran, for they did not marry mothers or daughters or aunts on either side, and the grossest thing they did was that a man took two sisters in marriage at the same time, or that the son succeeded to his father's wife." Out of this, by the change of a few words, Abulfeda makes "It was a most disgraceful thing in their eyes to marry two sisters at once, and they fixed ignomini on him who married bis father's wife, calling him *daizan*." *Daizan* cannot have been originally a name of contempt; it is a man's name (Nöld. *Gesch. d. Pers. u. Arab.* p. 35), it is said to be

the name of a god (Ibn Khall, no. 719), and in Tab. 1 756 1. 3 the two idols of

Jadiuma al-Abrash at Hira are called الضيزنان . It is certainly not in reproach that 'Antara and Tamīm b. Mocbil are called the Daizanān (*Asās al-Balagha, s.v.*). What the word means is very obscure; the native lexica give it a variety of senses but vary much from one another. The authority cited for the sense of the heir who takes possession of his father's widow is a verse of Aus b. Hajar which is very

variously quoted (Shahr. *ibid.*: the Sihāh gives instead والفارسية

for the last word there is a variant خلفت فيهم غير مكرة وكأهم لابيه ضيزن سلف ; see R. Geyer's ed., p. 67 [Vienna, 1S92]), but seems to refer rather to polyandry, where the son visits the father's wife, and so in fact Jauhari understands it. This is supported by other senses of the word. It is said to mean one who jostles his neighbours at a drinking-place, and also to mean a son, a domestic, a partner

generally. For the accusation باكت أمه as a proof that Ziyād al-'Ajami was of the Magian faith, see the verse of Ka'b al-Ashcarī (*Agh.* 13 62 1. 6).

[31] According to Wāhidī, on Sūr. 426, "this verse was revealed with reference to Hisn b. Abī Cais, who married Kabīsa [Kobaisha] bint Ma'n, his father's wife, and Al-Aswad b. Khalaf, who married his father's wife, and Hafwan b. Omayya b. Kha-

laf, who married his father's wife Fākhita (MS. وأختها), daughter of Al-Aswad b. 'Abd Al-Mottalib, and Manzūr b. Māzin, who married Molaika bint Khārija." Tabarl says, "with reference to Abū Cais b. Al-Aslat who succeeded to Omm 'Obaid bint Damra, who had been wife of his father Al-Aslat, and Al-Aswad b. Khalaf who succeeded to his father's wife the daughter of Abū Talha b. 'Abd al-Ozzā b. 'Othman b. 'Abd al-Dār, and Fākhita bint Al-Aswad b. Al-Mottalib b. Asad, who was successively the wife of Omayya b. Khalaf and of his son Safwān, and Manzūr b. Rayyān who succeeded to Molaika bint Khārija, who had been wife of his father Rayyān b. Yasar." For the ju'kdh al-mact, Goldziher (p. 21*) cites also *Agh.* 15 129 1. 28 (Haushab b. Yazīd al-Shaibanī). This is in Omayyad times and is made a reproach to him by Kumeit. He cites also *Agh.* 11 55 1. 27 *sqq.*, where the Fazārī Manzūr b. Zabbān (see his nisba, 1. 14) had made a *nikāh al-mact* (this name is put in Omar's mouth, p. 56 1. 2), and continued in it till Omar's Caliphate. He makes verses when forced to divorce her (cp. Nöldeke, Ghassān. *Fürsten*, p. 39). Finally, he cites Ibn Hajar, 4 303, 526, and the reference in Fihrist, 102 3 to Madā'inī's lost book on the subject.

[32] The incest of Reuben is twice mentioned, Gen. 35 22, 49 4. The incident, like that in Gen. 49 5, 6, must have an historical basis in the history of the tribe. The tribes of Bilhah are Dan and Naphtali, and the most natural supposition is, that Reuben in early times endeavoured to assert over these an authority which Israel declined to sanction. It is noteworthy that the Blessing of Jacob, which condemns Reuben's act, lays weight on the place of Dan as an autonomous tribe and on Naphtali's unrestrained freedom. The words פחז כמים do not imply lust, but must be taken according to the standing sense of the figure of boiling water in Arabic poetry. In *Diw. Hodh.* 197 2, warriors eager for the fray are likened to boiling cauldrons, and so Al-Farazdac, in a verse cited at p. 251, speaks of the seething cauldrons of war. פחז is closely parallel to יתר, see Prov. 17 7. The sense is,

"Thou art my first-born, my strength and the first-fruits (*i.e.* the best part) of my vigour; overweening in pride and overweening in might, ardent in battle as boiling water — yet thou shalt not make good thy pre-eminence because, etc." For עלה at the end of the verse the easiest correction seems to be עלי (Gen. 48 7), expressing that the act was an injury or a grief to Israel.

[33] In Ex. 21 1 *sqq.* a man who buys a slave-girl and is not pleased with her must (1) offer her father the privilege of redeeming her, or (2) offer her to his son with a suitable provision (כמשפט הבנות), or (3) retaining her and taking another wife, not curtail her rights. Failing all these she goes out free. Now, for יָעָדָה, (לוֹ Keri) לֹא Budde (ZATW 11 103 [1891]) would read יְדָעָהּ לֹא. But the context requires יְדָעָהּ without לֹא or לוֹ. That the father could transfer his concubine to his son was shocking to the later age, and two corrections were made and ultimately fused. Targ. Jon. has neither לֹא nor לוֹ, and takes יָעֵד to mean "purchase." On the trouble the passage gave to the Jews, see Geiger, *Urschrift,* 189. [See further *ZATW* 12 162 *sq.* (1892).]

[34] In the story of Hind bint 'Otba and her first husband Al-Fakih, the husband attempts a reconciliation, but she refuses to have anything to do with him, and ultimately he is forced to divorce her. He had previously turned her out of his house and sent her to her own people.

[35] This is confirmed by what Tabarī quotes from Yūnus b. 'Abd al-A'lā in explanation of the second half of Sūr. 4 23. Yūnus says:

أخبرنا ابن وهب قال قال ابن زيد كان الفضل في

قريش بمكة ينكح الرجل المرأة الشريفة فلعلها لا نوافقه

فيفارقها على أن لا تتزوج ألا باذنه فيأتي بالشهود فيكتب

ذلك عليها ويشهد فاذا خطبها خاطب فان أعطاه وأرضاه

أذن لها وإلا عضلها.

Everything that the Moslems tell about the pre-Islamic prerogatives of the Coraish is suspicious, but Yūnus's authority cannot have imagined out of his own head that before Islam a husband could prevent his divorced wife from remarrying, and could drive a bargain for his consent to the application of a suitor.

[36] [For striking parallels among the African Massūfa see Ibn Batūta, *Voyages,* 4 388 (Paris, 1858), and for the Malabar custom of inheritance through the sister's son, *ib.* 76. — I. G.]

[37] Among the Tamīm when a man makes a present of camels to his wife to induce her to say nothing of an injury she had received from his son by another wife, the camels are branded with her *brother's* brand. This shows that there was a difficulty about a woman holding property in her own name (Mofaddal al-Dabbi, *Amthal al-'Arab*).

[38] Sūra, 43, and various passages in which "their hire" (ojūr) is spoken of, though most of these seem rather to be really a permission of mot'a marriage; traditions in Bokh. 6 132, etc.

[39] See *Additional Note* B.

[40] How far is (and was) a Bedouin's wife liable to be beaten or otherwise badly treated? In Doughty, *Ar. Des.* 1 232, to beat one's wife is *'aib*, but it is done. In Ibn al-Sarrāj's Masāri' al-'Oššāc, p. 326, there is a bad case of wife-beating among the B. Hilāl. This story is again referred to at p. 333 with a reference to the author of the *Aghānī* where it may probably be found. In *Agh.* 16 38 1. 11 the wife's mother herself intervenes. This is in Islam.

[41] Cp. B. Hish. 62 11, for the counsel not to marry women into an unlucky lot among strangers. The desert-woman desires to marry her cousin and not live in a town. See the pretty speech of such a woman, *'Icd* 2 119 1. 1 *sqq.*

[42] Cp. al-Rāghib, *Mohadarat,* 1 191, *Agh.* 8 50.

[43] Māwīya is said to have been a Roman by race, a captive who pleased the king of the Saracens by her beauty and so became queen (Theophanes, p. 101). Two [North] Arabian queens are named on inscriptions of Tiglath-Pileser III. (Schrader, KAT (2) 253,255 sq., (3) 57 150). For a list of female judges see Freytag, *Ar. Prov.* 1 56 n. The best known is the daughter of 'Āmir b. Al-Zarib, who assisted her father in his old age in giving judgment (cp. *Agh.* 4 119).

Chapter Four - Paternity

We have had occasion, in the course of last chapter, to observe that in ancient Arabia a contract of marriage conveyed to the husband certain rights over the wife which were so far of the nature of property that they could be transferred by him to another and passed with the rest of a man's property to his heirs. At the same time the woman was not a slave — though her condition often resembled slavery in its practical effects; and on enquiring wherein the wife differed from a bondwoman we found the answer to be that the slave has no free kinsmen to take her part, while the freeborn Arab wife does not cease to have claims on the protection and aid of her kin. In the desert no one is really free who is without helpers — a man cannot live alone, and so even the emancipated slave necessarily remains the client of his master. The Arab wife has helpers in the men of her tribe, and therefore she does not lose the sense of personal dignity as a freewoman in spite of the extraordinary powers which the husband has over her as a wife. Of course this advantage practically disappears if the husband carries his wife into a remote region; there indeed, as the unhappy wife in the *Kāmil* complains, "she is no longer a free woman." This no doubt is the reason why, as we have seen, contracts were sometimes made which prevented husbands from carrying their wives away to strange places; sometimes indeed this condition appears to have been tacitly taken for granted, for when Abū Salima migrates to Medina he is unable to prevent his wife's kin from detaining her. But they have no power to detain her little child; he, as the husband's kin maintain and make good, belongs to their people and not to hers (see Ch. 3, above).

This last point gives us an insight into the real nature of the right conveyed to the husband by his contract with the wife's kin; what he purchases is the right to have children by her and to have these children belong to his own kin.

That this is so comes out very clearly in the case already quoted (Ch. 3., above) from the *'Icd*, 3 272, where the haggling between a father and a suitor as to the terms of the contract is set before us. The father would like to retain the children of his daughter, for he proposes that he should give names to the sons and give the daughters in marriage. But this is the very thing to which the suitor cannot consent; he is ready to grant anything but that; his wife shall have estates and influence, but he must have her children to himself, give his own daughters in marriage as he sees fit and name his sons after his fathers and uncles. The naming is a more significant point than we might imagine: [1] in *Agh.* 4 129 Sa'sa'a, a man rejected by his kindred, betakes himself to Sa'd ibn Al-Zarib, who gives him his niece in marriage; and here, where the father (or rather, as the story goes, the putative father) has no kin, the child is named 'Āmir after his maternal grandfather, 'Āmir ibn Al-Zarib. Wherever the child is named after the mother's father it belongs to the mother's kin, and the father is a *sadīc* husband or a *jār*. Just so in the story of Joseph, who entered Egypt as a captive cut off from his family, his children Ephraim and Manasseh are naturally regarded as Egyptians, and their right to be reckoned as Israelites seems to be based on a formal adoption by Jacob — "thy two sons which were born to thee in the land of Egypt before I came to thee into Egypt are mine, as Reuben and as Simeon, so Ephraim and Manasseh shall be mine" (Gen. 48 5).

I now proceed to show that the Arab idea of paternity is strictly correlated to the conception just developed of the nature of the contract in marriage by purchase. A man is father of all the children of the woman by whom he has purchased the right to have offspring that shall be reckoned to his own kin. This, as is well known, is the fundamental doctrine of Mohammedan law — *al-walad li 'l-firāsh* — the son is reckoned to the bed on which he is born. But in old Arab law this doctrine is developed with a logical thoroughness at which our views of propriety stand aghast.

Among the Arab customs of the times of heathenism recorded by Bokharl (6 127), in a passage the importance of which has been signalised by Goldziher and after him by Wilken, we find a usage known as *nikāh al-istibdā'*. When a man desired a goodly seed he might call upon his wife to cohabit with another man till she became pregnant by him. The child, as in the similar case in Hindu law, was the husband's son. [3]

In Mohammedan law the principle that the child belongs to the bed is limited by the rule that a woman who is pregnant when her husband dies or divorces her cannot remarry till after her delivery. But in old Arabia there was no such restriction, and "the well-known Arabic 'āda," as it is called in Tāj. 5 461, "that the son is reckoned to the stock of his mother's husband," held good for the remarriage of a pregnant woman. So fully was this recognised that one of the staple artifices of the genealogists for reconciling discrepant opinions as to the origin of tribes is to say that the mother of the tribe conceived by one husband and was delivered on the bed of another. Coda a, for example, was said by those who reckoned him to Himyar to have been begotten by Malik the Himyarite, but to have been born after his mother married Ma'add, and so to have passed as son of Ma'add in ancient times. There are many cases of this kind, from among which I select one which throws light on the relations of the important tribe of 'Āmir ibn Sa'sa'a, a branch of the great confederation called Hawāzin, which corresponded to the modern 'Otaiba. The Hawāzin are reckoned to the Caisites, and, as usual, the fact that they were properly a nation made up of various stocks is disguised by a genealogy in which Hawāzin is one of the posterity of Cais-'Ailān through his wife (or son) Khasafa. 'Āmir again is son of Sa'sa'a son of Mo'āwiya a grandson of Hawāzin. [4] But as a matter of fact our earliest authentic information as to the relations of the Banū 'Āmir is to the effect that they were originally a fraction of the Sa'd, one of the great branches of Tamīm, who had left their kin and joined the Caisites (Kāmil, 659); and hence at the battle of Shi'b Jabala, the Sa'd refused to take part with the rest of Tamīm against the Banū 'Āmir (Agh. 10 36), alleging that they were children of Sa'd. The Kāmil cites a line in which 'Āmir is called son of Sa'd (658 16). The genealogists, using the principle already explained, get over this by saying that Sa'sa'a was begotten by Mo'awiya but born after his mother's marriage with Sa'd; and in Agh. 4 129 we are further told that on Sa'd's death, when his sons divided his inheritance, they excluded Sa'sa'a, saying, "Thou art the son of Mo'āwiya." This of course is a lie with circumstance, for the history shows us that the Sa'd acknowledged the Banū 'Āmir ibn Sa'sa'a long after they had separated. And in fact the genealogist himself carries through his fiction in a half-hearted manner: Sa'sa'a, he tells us, now betook himself to the sons of Mo'āwiya, who "acknowledged that he was of their stock but excluded him from inheritance." Next he goes to a quite different branch of Cais, the 'Adwān, and as we saw above marries a wife who gives his son the name of 'Āmir after her own father. This is only another way of making the Banū 'Āmir Caisites, for the child who took his maternal grandfather's name was of his stock (cp. p. 124). And to make it doubly sure that Sad and 'Āmir have no stock connection we are told that Sa'sa'a was not even the physical father of the son born on his bed, since the mother was pregnant by a former marriage when she was given to Sa'sa'a. One sees from this what a tissue of fiction might be woven to disguise a single historical fact. But the fiction would have been impossible unless it had been well known that it was a new thing to attach weight to physical paternity and that in old time the mother's husband was the father. [5]

But further it appears that young children whom a woman carried with her to the house of a husband and whom he brought up were often incorporated with his stock. This at least was usual where these children were not the offspring of a previous *ba'al* marriage and therefore belonged to their mother. Thus the tribe of 'Anbar, though usually reckoned as son of 'Āmr ibn Tamīm by Omm Khārija, is said by others to be really a branch of Bahrā adopted into Tamīm. The story is that when 'Āmr married Omm Khārija she was living as her own mistress with her sons about her, and that when he took her home the young 'Anbar, whose real father was Bahra, followed her and so became Tamīmite (*Kāmil,* 264 *sq.*). There is another good example in Tebrīzī on *Ham.* p. 190 where Morra ibn 'Auf of the Dhobyān courts a woman of Balī, named Harcafa. She is her own mistress and already has a Balawite son who follows her to her new home. In process of time the lad has a quarrel with a man of Ball and cuts off his nose, and the tribesmen pursue him and claim to have him given up to them as having shed the blood of his own kin. Morra however er rescues the boy by swearing that he is no longer of Balī: — no doubt, having acknowledged the offender as his son, he would have to pay a fine for his offence, but he was not bound to give him up as an impious doer. [6]

Both these stories seem to be genealogical fictions to explain how certain groups had come into tribes to which they did not originally belong, and in both the kindred of the wife's second husband are the later political associates of the group, whereas in cases where the son is represented as born after the second marriage the group to which he originally belongs is that of the second husband. Properly speaking, therefore, the marriage contract does not by old Arabic law give an absolute right to any children that are not born on the husband's bed, and of course, if the first marriage as well as the second was of contract, conveying the children to the father and his kin, the wife would have no right to take even young children with her when she remarried. But in this case she had also no right to marry except with the consent of the first husband or his heirs (unless of course in a case of triple divorce, or if she had succeeded in escaping to her own people before the heir cast his garment on her and claimed her). In general, therefore, when she got leave from her first husband's people to marry into another kin, it would be matter of contract whether she should take her children with her; but an infant could not conveniently be separated from its mother, and would therefore be usually brought up "in the lap" of the second husband. So Samora ibn Jondob of Fazāra was brought up by his mother's second husband at Medina (Nawawī, p. 303). When the child grew up he might either return to his father's kin or be incorporated in his step-father's stock, according to arrangement. The examples I have found seem to show that the arrangement varied, but that very often he became a member of his step-father's tribe: thus 'Auf ibn Loayy became a Fazarite (Tabarī, 1 1101) though by his father he was of Coraish. Instances like this are pretty common, and though often unhistorical are doubtless framed to accord with old custom. There is in fact a proverb in Maidānī 1 48 (Freyt. 1 89), "If thou dost not beget sons, sons are begotten for thee," which is said to be applied to a man who marries a widow with children.

The husband of a be'ūlah-wife, as he had the right to send her to live for a time with another man and reserve the child or children to himself, might also, if he chose, transfer his wife to another, giving him the right to the children. This in fact was what happened under divorce not triple. In such a case the whole affair was arranged between the two men, though probably the woman's consent would often be obtained to prevent trouble with her kin, A case of such a contract has already been cited from Maidānī but without the details, which are more appropriate here. 'Ijl son of Lojaim, marrying a pregnant woman by arrangement with her former husband, promises that he will bring up the child and ultimately restore it to its real father. 'Ijl fulfils his contract, but his kin, among whom the lad had grown up, are most indignant; "has the boy," they said to 'Ijl, "any other father than thyself." and they proceed to recover him by force. The true father gets little help from his own people, and after being soundly beaten gives in, exclaiming, "He who has drunk thy morning draught is thy undoubted son."

We see then that though the marriage of a divorced woman took place under contract with her former husband, custom and feeling would not sanction so atrocious a proposal as that physical paternity should override the claims of the stock in which a child had been actually born and brought up. And it is most important to observe that the right to the boy belongs not so much to the husband of the woman as to his kindred as a whole; 'Ijl's abnormal contract is repudiated by his brethren and they carry their point. The significance of this fact will appear presently.

First, however, let us observe that the facts already cited, and many others of the same kind which it may suffice to mention very summarily, make it quite certain that in Arabia paternity did not originally mean what it does with us. With us the very foundation of the notion of fatherhood is procreation, and the presumption of law that the husband is father of all his wife's children rests on a well-established custom of conjugal fidelity, and on the certainty that the husband will object to have spurious children palmed off on him. But in old Arabia the husband was so indifferent to his wife's fidelity, that he might send her to cohabit with another man to get himself a goodly seed; or might lend her to a guest, as the 'Asir did up to the time of the Wahhabites (Burckhardt, *Travels in Arabia*, 8vo ed. ii. 378), and as the people of Dhahabān must once have done according to Ibn Al-Mojāwir's account (ca. A.D. 630); [7] or going on a journey might find a friend to supply his place, as the Yam did in the time of Burckhardt (*op. cit.* ii. 386); or might enter into a partnership of conjugal rights with another man, in return for his service as a shepherd, as we read in the *Fotūh al-Shām*, p. 238 *sq.* (Calc. ed.). It is incredible that a state of society like this, in which, nevertheless, the mother's husband (*ba'l*) was father of all her children, can have been preceded by a state in which fatherhood really implied procreation.

In point of fact *ab* (*abu*), the Semitic word for father, is not only used in a wide range of senses, but in all the dialects is used in senses quite inconsistent with the idea that procreator is the radical meaning of the word, from which the metaphorical senses are derived by analogy. [8] In such phrases, still current in Arabic,' as "father of mustachios," "father of blue spectacles," "father of dots" (*abū nocat, i.e.* a Maria Theresa dollar with the authentic number of stars on the diadem), "father of cannon" (a Spanish pillar dollar), or in the Ethiopic "father (*i.e.* owner) of an ox," the northern Semites would say not *ab* but *ba'al,* the word for "lord" or "owner" which also means "husband with marital dominion." This alternation in the same phrases between the word for father and the word for husband is not an accident, for both in North and South Semitic, the husband can be called the "father" of his wife. The Arabic philologists recorded with amazement a usage so foreign to later thought (Lane, *s.v.*), plainly not taking the phrase in the sentimental sense in which the '*Icd* 3 272 says that a good husband is a father in room of the natural father. [9] The expression is not a mere rhetorical phrase, but rests on old Semitic usage, for in Jer. 3 4, in a passage which speaks of Israel as Jehovah's spouse, "my father" is synonymous with "the companion of my youth," that is "my husband" (Prov. 2 17). To find the ideas "possessor," "husband," "father" united in one word would not be surprising if the ancient Semites had had *patria potestas*, but of *patria potestas* there is not a trace in anything we know of their institutions, as Messrs J. F. and D. McLennan have well shown after Locke. So far as the Arabs are concerned it is plain that the wife never came into the *patria potestas* of her husband, since she was not even taken into his stock. The various senses of *ab* cannot then have come from that of "progenitor"; but they might very well come from that of "nurturer," which is common enough in the actual usage of the Semitic languages, and would give in the most natural way such a doctrine of fatherhood as we have found in Arabia. Of course the Semites were not without a word for procreation, and the various dialects are able to designate the father as procreator by using a participial form of the root *w-l-d*; but languages which have to use a participle to designate a physical father must beyond all question have been developed in a condition of life in which physical fatherhood was not the basis of any important social relation.

In ancient Arabia, therefore, fatherhood does not necessarily imply procreation, and the family of which the father is the head is held together, not by the principle of physical paternity, but by the rule that the husband is father of all the children born on his bed. Since now it was never necessary that the family should be all of the father's blood, the genealogists cannot possibly be right in holding that the tribe, of which unity of blood is the recognised formula, is merely an extension of the patriarchal family. A tribe developed out of such a family as we have been examining could never have come to believe that it was all of one blood — much less to hold unity of blood to be so essential that it was necessary, when a member was taken in from an alien group, to feign that he was of the tribal blood and even devise a ceremony which gave this fiction the air of reality. The doctrine of the one tribal blood must have sprung up in groups that were not patriarchal families. We have seen that there were such groups in Arabia, groups of mother-kinship, where the daughters of the tribe remained with their brothers and bore children which were reckoned to the mother's tribe; in such groups the doctrine of the unity of tribal blood corresponded with actual fact, while in groups of male kinship it never did so until, at quite a late date, and in many parts of Arabia only through the influence of Islam, practices like the nikāh al-istibdāʿ were given up. And hence it suggests itself as a reasonable hypothesis that the doctrine of unity of blood as the principle that binds men into a permanent social unity was formed under a system of mother-kinship, and subsequently modified to correspond with a new rule of male kinship. We shall see that this hypothesis can be verified, but for the present we must still confine our attention to groups with male kinship.

What we have hitherto learned, not as hypothesis but as matter of fact, is that among the Arabs the idea of stocks of male descent was firmly established before fathers thought it at all necessary to beget their own children. And from this we can infer, that before fatherhood came to mean what it does with us, before anyone cared who was the individual who had begotten a child, the relations of the sexes were regulated in such a way that it could ordinarily be taken for granted that the child of a purchased or captured wife, born and brought up in a kindred group, was of their blood, even though his mother was an alien. This was so much the case that ultimately, if a child was born in the tribe of a woman brought in by contract of marriage, it was reckoned to the tribal stock as a matter of course, without enquiry as to its actual procreator. This was not done because it was a legitimate presumption that the mother's husband was the procreator — such a presumption would not have been legitimate in a state of society in which the husband could lend his wife if he pleased and keep the children. The rule must have arisen at a time when though the individual father was uncertain it could be fairly presumed that he was of a certain stock. In short, the doctrine that the child is ot the blood of his mother's husband does not in Arabia stand on an independent basis, but is simply a corollary from an earlier rule that the child of a wife who has been brought into any stock for the purpose of bearing children is of their blood. This being so we have two things to explain.

We have (1) to consider the nature of unions between the two sexes in a state of society in which alien women are brought into a kinship tribe to bear children, which are to be reckoned to the tribal kin, but which are not yet assigned to a particular father. And (2) we have to show that out of this state of society such an idea of fatherhood as was actually current in Arabia could and would naturally arise. If we can furnish a satisfactory elucidation of the-se two points we may fairly claim to have explained the origin of the Arabian tribes of male descent.

To any one who is familiar with recent researches on the origin of the fami-ly, and especially with the epoch-making enquiries of J. F. McLennan, the type of society of which we are in search is not far to seek. It is that of which the best known form occurs in Tibet and which McLennan has therefore named Tibetan polyandry.

Polyandry, or the marriage law under which a woman receives more than one man as her husband, presents, it may be explained, two main types. In the one type, called by McLennan Nair polyandry, [10] the woman remains with her own kin but entertains at will such suitors as she pleases. She is of-ten prevented from so receiving men of her own kin (who are to her as brothers), but her husbands may be of various kins, and therefore, when a child is born, neither its actual father nor the kin to which he belongs can be determined with certainty. The infant is therefore reckoned to its mother and kinship descends in the female line. The type of marriage which we have already found in Arabia along with female kinship, in which unions are of a very temporary character and the wife dismisses her husband at will, is only a development of Nair polyandry.

In Tibetan polyandry on the other hand a group of kinsmen — in Tibet a group of brothers — bring a wife home, who is their common wife and bears children for them. In this case also it cannot be known which of several men is the child's father; but, as all the husbands are of one kin, the child's kin is known in the male as well as in the female line, and, as the joint fathers are all bound by natural ties to the children which grew up in their midst, a law of male descent readily establishes itself *before* the rise of the idea that the child belongs to one father. As society advances, however, it is natural that the woman brought into the kin from outside should by and by come to be specially under the protection of one man. If the common spouse is originally the property of a considerable group, living in different tents or houses, she will come to live regularly in one tent or house and to be specially the wife of its inmates. Thus in Tibet a family of brothers living together have one wife. But again, the eldest brother, who in this state of society is the natural head of the house, will also be in a special sense the husband of the woman and the protector and nurturer of the children. In Tibet he is regarded as the fa-ther of the children, though the wife is really the wife of all the brothers. And thus the idea of individual fatherhood has its rise, just as we find to be the case in Arabia, *before* the idea that it belongs to a true marriage that the hus-band should keep his wife strictly to himself. When this stage has been reached, further progress is comparatively easy. The eldest brother or head of the polyandrous group will begin to desire to have his wife to himself; to ensure this he must find another wife for his younger brothers, and so gradually the principle of individual marriage and fatherhood must be established.

Here then we have a condition of things, not imaginary, and not even uncommon in primitive societies, which supplies exactly what we want for the explanation of the origin of Arabian tribes of male descent. And I think it is safe to say, that no other known form of marriage-custom will account for the circumstance that we find in Arabia a recognition of blood-kinship in the male line among groups which had no notion that a man should keep his wife strictly to himself. Thus the view that the Arabs passed through a stage of polyandry, of the type in which a woman had several members of one kin as her husbands, meets all the conditions of a legitimate hypothesis. And to raise the hypothesis to a certainty it is only necessary to show that the conditions under which such polyandry arises were actually present in Arabia.

The first condition for a custom of polyandry under which the joint husbands are of one kin, is of course the absence of our ideas of chastity and fidelity, and of all feeling of repugnance to share a wife with others. That this condition was present in ancient Arabia has been abundantly proved in the preceding pages, and there is only one remark that need be added here in order to dispose of a common but futile objection. It is by no means necessary to suppose a state in which a man was never so much in love with a woman that he would rather have had no rivals. All that is necessary is that his feelings should not be so refined that he would rather give her up altogether than admit a rival. This then being so, the next condition for polyandry of the Tibetan, as distinguished from the Nair type, is the presence among a group of kinsfolk living together, of women who are not free to choose their own lovers. This condition is satisfied by the practice of marriage by capture or contract. In either case the woman loses the right of freely disposing of her favours and comes under the control of her capturers or purchasers. If these form a kindred group, all the conditions for polyandry of the Tibetan type are present, and such polyandry must necessarily arise if it is not possible or not convenient that every member of the group should have a wife to himself. To show, then, that such polyandry must have existed in Arabia we have only to show (1) that women procured by capture or contract would generally fall in the first instance not into the hands of an individual but into the hands of a group of kinsmen, and (2) that these kinsmen, who certainly were not restrained from sharing their women by any feelings of delicacy, must often have been in circumstances where the idea of reserving one wife for each man would be out of the question. In looking into these points more closely it is desirable to have a somewhat wider designation for the kind of polyandry in question than the adjective Tibetan. The Tibetan practice is, strictly speaking, polyandry of a tolerably advanced kind in which all the husbands are brothers. But for our argument it is only necessary that all the husbands should be of one blood, and should have control over the wife's person. In default of a better term, I shall call this *ba'al* polyandry, because in it the polyandrous husbands have jointly the same sort of control over the woman's person that the individual husband has in *ba'al* marriage. It is true that the term proposed might cover cases in which the captors or purchasers were not of one kin, but such arrangements could hardly occur in practice in the society with which we are dealing, where every group that permanently lived and acted together was or feigned itself to be of one blood.

Proceeding now to inquire further whether the conditions that would necessarily lead to the rise of such polyandry were actually present in Arabia, let us for simplicity's sake begin with the case of capture. By old Arabian law booty taken in war was the common property of the captors, which, as we see from the wars of the prophet, was divided at the close of the campaign. The group that made war in common was always a kindred group, or a confederation of such groups, and the division of the prey that ensued was a division among the warriors of the *hayy*, as we have seen above (Ch. 2). Now after a great success there might be "one woman or two for every warrior," as Sisera's mother expected in Judges 5 30. [11] But often the claims would exceed the supply, the division could not be effected without dissatisfying some one, and as partnership in a wife presented nothing repugnant to the feelings of the time, while savages well know the danger of quarrels within the tribe and are extremely accommodating towards their fellow-tribesmen, polyandrous arrangements would naturally occur. In truth we may go further than this; for we have seen in chap. 2. (*ut supra*) very clear indications that personal property of any sort is quite a secondary thing in Arabia. In very early times, when the kindred groups must necessarily have been very small and continually struggling for existence, no sharply defined ideas of personal property could have arisen; even in historical times, in the hard life of the desert, it is not so much a virtue as a duty for the man who has to impart freely to him who has not, and the poor asks help from the rich not as a favour but as a right. All this points to a state of things in which property was undivided, and leads us to think that division began only as the groups became larger, and their substance accumulated. If women were captured in these early times they would not be assigned to individuals at all. The first steps upwards from the absolute promiscuity which this involves would naturally accompany the development of the idea of property. Before individual property and individual marriages were thought of there would be small sub-groups having property and wives in common as in Tibetan polyandry.

What has been said of women procured by capture applies with little modification to the case of contract. Our whole evidence goes to show that the prices asked for women in ancient Arabia under the name of *mahr* were often very high, and in the time of Mohammed, as among the Bedouins at the present day, there were many men who could not afford a wife. Such men, intolerant of celibacy as all Arabs are, usually took refuge in what the prophet called *zinā*, "fornication"; but, as we shall see in the next chapter that there was no stain of illegitimacy attached to the child of a harlot, even after male kinship and paternity were fully recognised, *zinā,* before Islam, was only a kind of Nair polyandry in which the number of the husbands was not defined. But we know also that more exactly regulated partnerships in women often took place; Bokhārī, 6 127, speaks of a practice by which ten men at most had one woman to wife between them. This was in later times, when the doctrine of individual paternity was fully established, and the woman had the right to fix on any one of the men as father of her child, so that we must regard the institution not as *ba'al* marriage, but as a modification of *mot'a* marriage under the influence of the rule of male kinship. Where such things happened there was no reason why several kinsmen should not unite to purchase a wife in common. And in this case, as in that of capture, we have only to transplant ourselves to the earlier stage of society in which property was communal to see that if wives were then purchased at all, they must have been procured by a group, and that individual men could not have had an exclusive right to them. But as marriage by capture is no doubt older than marriage by purchase, the presumption is that the customary position of an alien wife in the tribe was fixed by the practice of capture, which, as we have seen, led in the most natural way to *ba'al* polyandry. Whether the origin of male kinship is older than marriage by contract is another question, for *ba'al* polyandry must have gone on for some time before it affected the rule of kinship. [12]

The extent to which a custom of polyandry would spread under such favourable conditions would, one must suppose, depend on the scarcity of marriageable women, and McLennan has taught us to look on the practice of killing female children as one great cause of such scarcity in savage peoples. That certain Arab tribes, especially the Tamīm, practised female infanticide is well known; but as the point is of considerable interest, and the current accounts of the matter from Pococke (*Specimen,* p. 322 *sq.*) down to Wilken (*op. cit.* p. 36 *sq.*) admit of supplement, I will enter into some details in a note. [13] Wilken doubts whether among the Arabs the practice was carried to such an extent as to do more than keep the sexes balanced — men being more exposed than women to violent death; but there is evidence that, at any rate in some places and at some times, there was a strong pressure of public opinion against sparing any daughter, even though she were the only child of her parents. If we take along with this the fact that wealthy and powerful men had often several wives, there can I think be no question that, at least in some parts of the country, wives must have been so scarce that the mass of the tribesmen were often driven to practise polyandry. It is true that our evidence as to all this is drawn from comparatively recent times, and that our authorities themselves seem to represent the practice of infanticide as having taken a new development not very long before the time of Mohammed, but there is no reason whatever to think that at an earlier date the Arabs, as a whole, had more refined practices and higher views about the relations of the sexes, and the chief motive to infanticide was the scarcity of food which must always have been felt in the desert.

[1] In the Old Testament patriarchal legends the child generally gets its name from the mother [so at least in the older narratives, J and E, as contrasted with P and Jubilees, where it is always the father (cp. Nöld. *ZDMG* 40 150, Wellh. *Ehe,* 487 n., *Oxf. Hex.* 2 24, on Gen. 16 11, and others). Gen. 38 3 is no exception, the Sam., Sept., and Targ. read "she called." On the other hand, the father names the child in the early passages, Gen. 4 26 (contrast *v.* 25), 5 29, 41 51 *sq.* For passages outside Genesis, where the name is given by the mother, see Judg. 13 24, 1 S. 1 20, 4 21, 2 S. 12 24 (Kĕrī), Ex. 2 10 (but contrast V. 22), also Is. 7 14 (but contrast 8 3), and Ruth 4 17 (the name given by the women in attendance)].

[2] This, of course, is a fictitious story, and quite another account of the marriage of Sa'sa'a to the daughter of 'Āmir is given in the *'Icd,* 3 272. But all such stories, usually, the offspring of tribal vanity or the fictions of rival clans, are framed on the actual usage of old Arab society.

[3] This and other forms of marriage in the Jāhilīya are referred to in Albērūnī's *India* (Ar. text pp. 52 ult., 53), and compared with the parallel Indian customs. There is a detail in the tradition, as recorded by Bokhārī, which deserves notice, as the explanation of it is also the explanation of a vexed passage of the Old Testament, The moment chosen for uniting the woman with her husband's substitute is ابذا طهرت من طمثها, "when she is cleansed from her impurity." Now comparing *Agh.* 16 27 1. 31, and the verse in the following page, 1. 8, with the note on it in *Hamāsa,* p. 447, we see that this was the time when the Arabs expected to beget a goodly offspring and were wont to visit their wives (cp. also Mof al-Dabbi, p. 18 1. 10). Hence, in 2 S. 11 4, we are to take והיא מתקדשת מטמאתה, as the accents take it, as a circumstantial clause to וישכב עמה, "he lay with her when (just after) she had purified herself"; compare for the tense indicated by the participle i K. 14 5 [cp. the commentaries of Driver, H. I'. Smith, Thenius-Löhr, Budde].

[4] On this question of kinship see also Mofaddal al-Dabbl, *Amthāl,* p. 21, who says that the thing is often referred to by the poets of Tamini and 'Āmir. Yet another account follows on p. 22. Al-Dabbī is particularly strong in Tamīmite legends.

[5] Goldziher (*Lit. bl.* p. 21*) cites, as a survival of these relations, Ya'kūbī, ed. Houtsma, 2 348. The question here is whether Saht was really son of 'Abdallāh b. 'Abbās. It arose because his brother 'Ali slew him. When charged he said it was his slave not his brother he had killed. The father, it is related, said, "I know he is not my son but I will not disinherit him." The circumstances are too obscure to build on.

[6] The text of this story in Freytag's edition requires at least one correction. In 190 23 the words ابنها البلوى must be transposed to stand immediately after خصيلة.

[7] According to Ibn al-Mojāwir, guests at Dhahabān were invited to kiss and embrace the host's wife, but were threatened with the poniard if they went be-

yond these liberties (Sprenger, *Post Routen*, p. 132 *sq.*). [Cp. de Goeje, *Actes du XIe Congr. internat. d. Orientalistes*, Paris, 1897, sect. iii. p. 29. — I. G.] This usage resembles that recorded of Mirbāt by Yācūt, 4 482, where an ancient custom allowed men and women to meet every night outside the town and talk and sport together in a way that would have excited deadly jealousy in ordinary Eastern countries under Islam. Here also, as at Dhahabān, the theory seems to have been that the flirtations had a limit; but neither custom can well be separated from an earlier polyandry: indeed Ibn Al-Mojāwir speaks of a tribe in the same district where the wife of the host was put entirely at the disposal of his guest. For another indication of ancient polyandry at Mirbāt see Ch. Five. A similar absence of jealousy on the part of husbands is recorded by Ibn Batūta, 2 228, among the people of 'Oman. Add also Goldziher's remark (*Lit. bl.* p. 21*), who refers to Ibn Khallikān, No. 430, where it is said that manliness and jealousy should prevent this. Cp. also Volney, *Voyage en Syrie*, 2 149 (Paris, 1787).

[8] [Cp. Nöldeke's remarks, ZDMG 40 71 *sq.*'l

[9] Grimm (*Deutsche Rechlsalt.* (4) p. 579) makes Goth, *aba*, maritus = *afi* grandfather or father. But see Vigfusson, *s.v.* 'Afi.'

[10] [See M. J. Rowlandson, *Tohfut-ul-Mujahideen*, pp. 61 *sqq.* (Oriental Translation Fund, London, 1833); J. F. McLennan, *Studies*, 1st series (1886), pp. 100 *sqq.*, 2nd series (1896), pp. 49, 63; Élie Reclus, *Primitive Folk*, pp. i 56 *sqq.*]

[11] Cp. pp. 89, n. 3, 169, n. 1.

[12] It will appear more clearly in the sequel that kinship through women must have been fully established before male kinship began to be regarded at all. Tibetan polyandry was preceded by Nair polyandry, and the group of kinsfolk that had a wife in common was originally a group of mother-kin. Accordingly when Tibetan polyandry was introduced, all that it would do at first would be to make it possible to observe the fact of kinship in the male as well as in the female line. At first the mother's blood would still determine the stock to which a boy was to be reckoned and the stock-name he was to bear, and it would be only by a deliberate act that the fathers, feeling that he was as much of their blood as of his mother's blood, and desiring to have him as their own, could annex the child to their own stock. If the mother was a captive, they might perhaps do this of their own authority; but if she had been procured by friendly contract, it would at first be matter of special arrangement that the children should follow the father's and not the mother's stock. But there were so many reasons why a woman's husbands should wish to have her children as their own, and such an arrangement went so naturally with the subject position of the mother, that we may be sure that the new system, when it was once thought of, would spread fast, and that by and by no explicit contract would be needed to secure the children to their mother's husbands' stock.

In the abstract it is quite conceivable that through contract a change of kinship might have been effected without the aid of Tibetan polyandry at all. Nair polyandry might have given way to monandry while kinship was still reckoned only in the female line, and then the individual husband might have begun to stipulate that the children which he knew to be his own by procreation should also be reckoned to his stock — be his heirs and lake up his blood-feud. (That the right of the father to the child rested mainly on contract — at least in some cases —

seems to appear clearly in the [fabulous] story of Tasm and Jadīs [*Agh.* 10 48], where the right to the child on divorce is the subject of a law-suit. The father's argument is: "I paid her her full dowry and have no return except the child" [1. 15].) What shows that this was not the course of development in Arabia — apart from the actual evidence of Tibetan polyandry given in ch. 5. — is that stocks of male descent were fully recognised before husbands were at all concerned about their wives' fidelity. It is true that a man might wish to have children to be his heirs and discharge various social duties towards him before he was concerned that these children should be actually begotten of his body. And in Arabia this must actually have been the case, for the Arab father had no scruple about acknowledging sons whom he knew that he had not begotten. But the fiction which regards such children as real children could not establish itself, without entirely breaking down the principle that the strongest bond is a bond of blood, until it was certain that in an overwhelming majority of cases the putative son was a real son. And it seems quite plain that in the rude state of society which existed when the change of kinship began to take place, this certainty could not arise. But if the woman lived, on the Tibetan system, amidst a group of kinsmen, there could and would be a reasonable certainty that one or other of them was father of all her children. Tibetan polyandry allowed the change of kinship to begin in a much ruder state of society than would have been otherwise possible.

[13] See *Additional Note* C.

Chapter Five - Paternity, Polyandry with Male Kinship, and with Kinship through Women

We have seen that the conception of paternity current in Arabia before Islam is inconsistent with the idea that the Arabs originally regarded the bond of kinship as a system of links, each one of which connected a father with a son begotten of his body; on the contrary the son of an alien woman born in the tribe must have come to be regarded as having a share of the tribal blood in his veins before it was thought at all important to know who was the tribesman who begot him; and if an individual father was assigned to him this father was not necessarily his procreator, but only the protector and lord of the mother, the guardian and nurturer of the child. This apparently anomalous state of things, we have farther seen, is such as can naturally arise where there is a custom of Tibetan polyandry, and finally it has been shown that the conditions of life and moral sentiment in ancient Arabia were such that women procured by capture or contract would in many cases be more naturally the common wives of a group of kinsmen than reserved to a single man, while in some cases the scarcity of women made polyandry inevitable. The view that the Arabic doctrine of paternity arose under Tibetan polyandry appears therefore to satisfy the conditions of a legitimate hypothesis. It explains the facts and it postulates the operation of no cause that cannot be shown to have existed. It is true that we have as yet only found reason to believe that polyandrous groups of the Tibetan type must have existed; we have not found evidence that the practice of such polyandry was so widespread as must necessarily have been the case if the whole doctrine of paternity is founded on it. But this is always the case in investigation by means of hypothesis; the very object of hypothesis is to enquire whether a real cause (*vera causa*) has not had a wider operation than there is any direct evidence for, the necessary and sufficient proof that this is so being the wide prevalence of effects which the cause is adequate to produce. The hypothesis that polyandry was once generally prevalent in Arabia is sufficiently established if we can show on the one hand that it sometimes existed, and on the other hand that the effects which it would necessarily produce are found all over Arabia in later times. At the same time it appears possible to show in a more direct manner, that in point of fact *ba'al* polyandry must have prevailed in Arabia to a great extent, and indeed that at one time polyandry was no exceptional phenomenon, but the rule.

The oldest and most direct evidence is that of Strabo (xvi. 4 25), and refers to Arabia Felix or Yemen. As the passage presents some obscure features, I quote it nearly at full length.

"Brothers have precedence over children; the kingship also and other offices of authority are filled by members of the stock (γένος) in order of seniority. All the kindred have their property in common, the eldest being lord; all have one wife and it is first come first served, the man who enters to her leaving at the door the stick which it is usual for every one to carry; but the night she spends with the eldest. Hence all are brothers of all (within the stock of συγγενεῖς); they have also conjugal intercourse with mothers; an adulterer is punished with death; and adulterer means a man of another stock. A daughter of a certain king who had fifteen brothers all much in love with her "tried to keep her room to herself by getting sticks like her husbands' to put at the door. One of the brothers found a stick at the door when he knew that the whole family were in the market place, and suspecting the presence of an adulterer, he runs to the father, who comes up, and it is found that the man has falsely accused his sister."

Wilken (p. 8) sees in this narrative endogamy combined with absolute promiscuity within the tribal group, not "a regulated polyandry." But surely this is quite impossible. The stock (γένος) in Strabo's account is a small group, rather a family than a tribe, living together under the headship of the eldest of the group (called indifferently eldest brother or father), who is the special guardian of the chastity of the common wife, and is her companion by night. These features with their accompaniments — the community of property and the succession of the next eldest to the seat of authority — embrace all the most characteristic marks of Tibetan polyandry and indicate not an unregulated promiscuity, but a very exactly ordered marriage-system. And the wife is manifestly a wife under dominion, for she has no right to withhold her favours from any of the kinsfolk or brothers, and adultery, that is intercourse with her on the part of anyone else, is a criminal offence. There is only one point that occasions difficulty, *viz.*, that the woman is called the sister of her husbands. It is scarcely credible that such a small polyandrous group as Strabo speaks of could have been, as this seems to imply, strictly endogamous, and that they always had a sister (and only one sister) to be their wife. The true explanation I apprehend is this. The eldest brother was called the "father" — a designation that cannot surprise us after what has come before us in the last chapter. He was also "father" of the wife, who was under his special charge, as we have seen that the Arabs sometimes call a husband his wife's father, and thus Strabo or his informant came to conclude that she was his daughter and the sister of the junior members of the group.

A proof almost equally direct of the prevalence of Tibetan polyandry in Arabia, is supplied by Bokhārī, 6 114, who relates that when the prophet made 'Abd al-Rahmān ibn 'Auf and Sa'd ibn Rabī'a take each other as brothers, the latter, who had two wives, proposed that they should go halves in his goods and his women. [1] 'Abd al-Rahmān therefore got one of Sa'd's wives. A state of things in which this seemed a natural consequence of brotherhood can most naturally be regarded as a relic of Tibetan polyandry, similar to what Strabo describes, in which goods and wives were the common property of the brothers. Compacts of brotherhood implying fellowship in women and goods were actually known in other parts of the Semitic world, for in the SyroRoman law-book of the fifth century, the various forms of which have been collected and illustrated by Sachau and Bruns, we find the following paragraph (§ 86, p. 24):—

If a man desires to write a compact of brotherhood with another man that they shall be as brothers and have all things in common that they possess or may acquire, then the law forbids them and annuls their compact; for their wives are not common and their children cannot be common.

On this Bruns observes (p. 254) that the law seems to suggest that attempts were actually made to form compacts of brotherhood in which wives as well as goods were common. The observation is doubtless just, and as the law-book took shape in Syria it is there where we must look for such attempts — the same region in which down to the time of Constantine unbridled licence was given to wives and daughters at the temple of Astarte at Baalbek (Euseb. *Vit. Con.* 3 58, comp. Barhebraeus, *Chron. Syr.* p. 65, who generalises this into a common practice of polyandry in the town). [2]

Once more, a tolerably distinct trace of the early prevalence of *ba'al* polyandry in Arabia is preserved in the word *kanna*, which usually means the wife of a son or a brother, but in the *Hamāsa*, p. 252, is used by Jahdar, a poet of Dobai'a, to designate his own wife. [3] So too in Hebrew *kallah* means both "daughter-in-law" and "spouse," and in Aramaic the same word usually means a bride but also apparently a sister-in-law (*Thes. Syr., s.v.*). That the same words can have these three meanings is naturally to be explained as the relic of a time when a man's wife was also the wife of his brother and of his son. The etymological sense is that of covering, so that the word belongs to the same sphere of metaphor as the symbolic action of the heir in casting his garment over the widow whom he desires to inherit or the common expression that a be'ūlah-wife is under (taht) her husband. The correlative of kanna is ham, i.e. one who has the duty of protecting the kanna against those outside (comp. Freyt. Ar. Pr. 2 529). But according to the whole usage of the root h-m-y the kind of protection meant is protection from encroachment; the husband's brother, father or other kinsman is called her ham because they together make up the group which reserves the woman to themselves.

The testimony of Strabo, the surrender of a wife to an adopted brother, and the use of the word kanna, are all more or less direct evidence of a widespread custom of ba'al polyandry, rather than verifications of the hypothesis that it was from the prevalence of such a custom that the Arabian doctrine of paternity and the system of individual ba'al marriage were developed. But verifications in the usual sense of the word — such verification as the hypothesis of universal gravitation receives, let us say, from the phenomena of tides or from planetary perturbations — may be obtained from certain peculiar features of the later marriage -law which become plain to us only when we recognise that marriage as practised at the time of the prophet rested on an earlier custom of kinsmen combining to procure a wife in common. We have already seen that the right of the heirs to inherit the widow of the deceased involves the conception that, a contract of marriage having been effected by purchase, marital rights were of the nature of heritable estate. But this does not fully explain how, as Shahrastānī tells us, the heirs had a right to take the woman if her husband divorced her. That implies that the kin had an interest in the woman's marriage even while her husband lived, and that their interest became active as soon as he divested himself of his special claims on his wife. In short the right of the heir is a modification of the older right of kinsmen to share each other's marriages; and as soon as the exclusive right conferred on the husband by more modern law ceases and determines, whether by marriage or divorce, the older right of the kin revives.

Now if in this way the kinsmen had a sort of common property in the wife, they would also have a common property in the children. So we saw in the case of 'Ijl that they refused to surrender a boy whom his mother's husband was willing to give up. By following up this principle we may, I think, reach the explanation of one of the most widespread rules of Arabian law, viz. that a man has the first claim to the hand of his cousin on the father's side. In modern Arabian custom the father cannot give his daughter to another if his brother's son asks for her, and the cousin can have her "cheaper," as it was put to me at Tāif, than any other wife. This is just what would arise under the system of Tibetan polyandry, provided only that the law of forbidden degrees allowed the marriage of paternal cousins. We know from Sūra 4 and the relative traditions that such marriages were allowed, for in the case of orphan daughters the father's male kinsfolk not only annexed his property but married his daughters whether they would or not (*e.g.* Bokh. 6 113, 128). The father's kin therefore were heirs to his daughters' hands as well as to his estate, and on the general principle that heirship is a modification of a right of common possession, the paternal cousin would also have the first claim to a girl's hand in her father's lifetime. That this is the correct explanation of a young man's right to the hand of his *bint 'amm* is proved by the tradition cited above (Ch. 3) from Wāhidī's *Asbāb* on Sur. 4 23. According to this tradition the right of the cousin to his *bint 'amm* is on all fours with the right of the heir to the widow of the deceased. [4]

Further verification of the hypothesis that Arabian *ba'al* marriage with male kinship was developed out of a system of polyandry may be obtained by comparing the hypothesis with recorded facts as to the chastity and fidelity of women and conditions of legitimate sonship.

As *ba'al* marriage in Arabia existed side by side with *sadīca* marriage, so of course Tibetan polyandry must have existed side by side with Nair polyandry. Women who, bearing children for their own tribe, were free to choose their own husbands and dismiss them at will, could hardly have been confined to one husband at a time, when women brought under dominion by conquest or capture had several spouses. For such women in short the idea of unchastity could not exist; their children were all full tribesmen, because the mother was a tribeswoman, and there was no distinction between legitimate and illegitimate offspring in our sense of the word, though, as in cases of Nair polyandry in other parts of the world, there was possibly a law of incest which forbade a woman to bear children to certain men (men of her own kin). [5]

But with the higher polyandry, where the group of husbands reserves the wife to its own members, a certain idea of conjugal fidelity naturally arises; and as soon as it is established doctrine that the children are of the blood of the mother's husbands, there is room for the rise of a doctrine of legitimacy and illegitimacy; for if the husbands find that the wife has formed relations beyond the circle of her lords, they may naturally refuse to acknowledge the offspring. This however in the first instance will be entirely their own affair; so long as the wife does nothing that they forbid, no one has a right to interfere. But now polyandry gradually begins to yield to a practice of individual marriage. Chiefs in the first instance, who have their fourth part of all booty, can plainly have wives to themselves if they wish it, and they are sure soon to wish it; thus Agatharchides and Artemidorus describing the polyandry of the Troglodytes say that the "tyrant" alone had a wife of his own, adultery with whom was punished by the fine of a sheep (*Geog. Gr. Min.* ed. Muller, 1 153, Strabo, xvi. 4 17). Once introduced, monandry must necessarily spread in proportion as life becomes easier; for a man to have a wife to himself must be the respectable thing, and with this there will go a corresponding progress towards civilised ideas of conjugal fidelity. Still, however, it will be the husband's affair to decide who shall actually beget his wife's children; and so we find it in Arabia — a proof that monandry is not the result of refined feeling, but has its origin in a gross state of society, and then operates to produce more refined ideas as to the proper relations of the sexes.

But again, on this view of the development, we cannot suppose that chastity on the part of women who are their own mistresses will be insisted on as early as fidelity on the part of a subject wife. And for a time at least, as we may see in the case of Morra's Balawite wife, a man will no more object to take a woman to wife who already has children by a *mot'a* or other similar connection, than a modern Englishman objects to marry a widow. Thus, the old licence of girls, divorced women, and widows will still go on side by side with a common practice of *ba'al* marriage, and so we can understand how *mot'a* marriages, as well as more orderly *beena* marriages, subsisted down to the time of Mohammed. But unions of this sort had gradually come to be viewed as discreditable, and the women who practised them seem to have generally been found in inferior classes or less influential tribes. We have already seen from the answer of Hind to Mohammed, that a Meccan woman of good birth piqued herself on her chastity; the restraint which was originally imposed on captive women by their lords had come to be accepted by the wife herself as a point of honour. And how this came about we can judge from the narrative in *Agh.* 16 22, where, a Fazarite having seized Fatima, wife of Ziyād, by surprise and bearing her off, she casts herself from her camel and so dies, rather than that any shame should touch her sons on her account. If the relation of the Arabian wife to her lord was in many ways a humiliating one, and men could not greatly trust their wives' affection — as indeed they have never done in the East — the mother was bound to her children by the strongest tie, and fidelity to the husband was felt to be a sacred duty when it involved the position and honour of the children. Now, all men who were really desirable matches sought to contract *ba'al* marriages, and they could make their alliance acceptable to the fathers of daughters not only by gifts, but because a daughter in the house of a powerful or wealthy chief was a pledge of his help in trouble. For the wife's father stands to the husband in the relation of *jār*, and so has a claim on his son-in-law to help him or to avenge his death. In Ibn Hishām, p. 275, Hassān ibn Thābit bitterly reproaches Abū Sofyān for leaving the death of his *jār, i.e.* his Dausite father-in-law, unavenged, and the accompanying narrative shows that the conduct of the Omayyad chief, who abstained from taking up the quarrel, that he might not bring disunion among the Coraish, was really unusual. [6] When such advantages were to be gained by giving a daughter in *ba'al* marriage to an equal match (*kaf*), it gradually came about that all the fairest women became *be'ūlah*-wives in honourable households, and the standard of constancy established among them became that of all honourable women.

Women who still adhered to the old laxity now formed — at least in cities like Mecca and Tāif — a separate class of prostitutes, generally freedwomen or slaves, whose houses were marked by a flag hung over the door. But there was still no idea that a man was disgraced by visiting such houses. Nay, paternity being now everywhere regarded, men were not unwilling to claim the fatherhood of a prostitute's child, [7] and there was actually a class of wise men (*cāif,* pl. *cāfa*) whose business it was to discern the bodily marks by which a child could be recognised as a particular man's son, and assigned to him. [8] Bokhārī will have it that a man was compelled to acknowledge a prostitute's son when the *cāif* declared it to be his; but the details of the famous case of Ziyād "son of his father," whom Mo'āwiya recognised, after a very extraordinary legal process, as the son of Abū Sofyān and a legitimate member of the Omayyad house, seem to show that this is an exaggeration. To the men of later time it seemed strange that a man should acknowledge a harlot's child except on compulsion, and Mo'awiya gave great scandal to all good Moslems by parading the fact that his father had a base-born son. [9] But his conduct was defended by others, as corresponding to sound old Arabian law. And in fact the other main branch of the Omayyads, the house of Abu 'l-'Āsī, which took the Caliphate in the person of Merwān I., had for their ancestress a certain Zarcā, of whom their enemies never forgot that she was one of "those who hung out a Hag" (Ibn al-Athīr, Būlāc ed. 4 81).

One sees from this how very lax, even at a late date, was the idea of chastity, at least as applied to other women than *be'ūlah*-wives, and how very slowly those ideas of paternity and legitimacy made their way which prevail in the modern world and imply that there is some reasonable certainty who is the begetter of a child.

On a general view of all that has come before us in this and the preceding chapter it does not seem too much to say that the hypothesis that the Arabian system of sonship was developed with the aid of *ba'al* or Tibetan polyandry has been made out. The fundamental facts about Arabian sonship are such as must suggest the hypothesis; the kind of polyandry suggested was such as would naturally and even necessarily arise in the conditions of Arabian society; we have evidence that it did exist, and exist largely; and we have found that a great variety of outlying facts are satisfactorily explained by the hypothesis, just as the outlying facts of the motions of the solar system are explained by the hypothesis of gravitation. I do not see what stronger proof can be offered in favour of any hypothesis, in a field where exact numerical evaluation of phenomena is impossible.

But now let it be observed that we have not yet reduced the phenomena of the Arabian system of kinship to ultimate unity. Starting with the fact that, in the first ages of Islam, *ba'al* marriage, with individual fatherhood and sons of the stock of the father, was the only type of relation between the sexes regarded as legitimate, we have found that before Mohammed put the seal of his authority on what was no doubt already the current view of the more advanced Arabian societies, there were two types of marriage and two types of kinship in the peninsula. We have seen how thorough in every respect was the contrast between the two; *ba'al* and *sadīca* marriage not only lead to different laws of kinship but they imply fundamental differences in the position of women and so in the whole structure of the social relations. But now again we have found that, going still farther back, we reach a point where the contrast is not between two types of marriage, but between two types of polyandry — polyandry in which the woman is under dominion, and cannot refuse her favours to the circle that has brought her into their dominion in order to bear children for them and for their tribe, and polyandry in which the woman lives among her own kin and, bearing children for them and not for outsiders, is free to distribute her favours at will. What is common to the two systems is that in each case the children belong in virtue of their birth to a certain group, and are held to pertain to this group in no artificial way but because the blood of the group flows in their veins. But on the system of *ba'al* polyandry with male kinship the blood of the group is transmitted through the begetter and the mother's blood is disregarded; on the other system the child is always of its mother's blood and the blood of the father is of no account. Now it is quite true that these opposite rules are justified by one and the same practical necessity; in each case the object was to unite the child by the most sacred ties to the kindred group in which it was born and nurtured. But the Arabs do not content themselves with saying that the child born and brought up in the tribe is a member of the tribe, bound to it by a religious tie; they say that the tie is one of blood, and they say so equally whether the child comes into the group through his mother (with *beena* marriage or Nair polyandry), or through his mother's husband or husbands (with *ba'al* marriage or polyandry). If these two quite distinct ways of counting blood-kinship had both gone on from the beginning, it is not conceivable that tribal unity could ever have been identified with blood-unity, for that would involve that a man could be of two tribes or kindred groups, which is inconsistent with the whole system. When the idea became dominant that in every quarrel a man must side with those of his own blood, the transmission of blood must everywhere have been understood as following a single unambiguous principle. That is, if blood depended on parentage, only one parent can have been taken into account and that parent must necessarily have been the mother. For that a child is of his mother's blood is a fact that at once forces itself on the observer when he begins to think at all; [10] and in a society where the mother remains with her own people and entertains any man she pleases, where, even, as we have seen to be the case in Arabia, it is often not known who visits her, observation of parentage cannot go beyond the mother. A rule therefore which reckons blood-kinship only through the mother is simply the natural and necessary expression of the kind of relations between the sexes which were universal in old Arabia wherever women did not leave their people to follow a husband abroad. On the other hand, the rule that makes a son of the blood of his father cannot be primitive; for we have seen that individual fatherhood is a comparatively modern notion, and that men were

93

reckoned to the stock of their mother's lords before they were one man's children. But this conception of a group of men conveying their common blood to a child has a visibly secondary character; it implies a process of reasoning, such as men could only be led to by the desire to take the child away from the mother's stock. Before the child can be made of the blood of the mother's husbands it must already be settled that these husbands are themselves of one blood: that principle, therefore, is older than the first beginnings of a rule of kinship through males. In short, we need an older system of kinship through the mother alone to supply the conditions for the rise of male kinship through *ba'al* polyandry.

This argument, I think, is conclusive if blood originally depended on parentage at all; but to guard it on all sides it is necessary to inquire whether perhaps at one time people could reckon themselves of one blood for some other reason than that of parentage. There are some facts which seem at first sight to make it conceivable that they could.

Unity of blood, as we saw in the symbolic act of drinking blood in order to create brotherhood, is to the thinking of early man no metaphor but a physical fact. The members of one kin regard themselves as parts of a physical unity; the *hayy* or kin is, so to speak, one living whole. Unity of blood is merely a synecdochic expression for this; strictly speaking, the kindred are not only of one blood but of one flesh. Thus we have seen from Hamdānī that in certain parts of Arabia *lahm*, "flesh," means a clan (*batn*); and generally in Arabic *lohma* means kinship or kindred, just as in Hebrew "thou art our bone and our flesh" means "thou art our kinsman," and in Lev. 25 49 "flesh" is explained by the synonym *mišpāhāh*, or "clan." Now there is at least one way in which community of flesh and blood may be established after birth in a way not merely symbolical, viz. by fosterage. The suckling draws his nourishment directly from his nurse, and in fact the Arabs sometimes call milk "flesh"

(*Asās al-balāgha*, s.v. لحم). [11] In this way there is a real unity of flesh and blood between foster-mother and foster-child, or between foster-brothers; and so we find among the Arabs a feeling about milk-kinship so well established that Mohammed's law of forbidden degrees gives it all the effects of blood-relationship as a bar to marriage. We see, however, that the recognition of milk-kinship rather makes for than against the position that all kinship was originally through women; generally speaking the mother and the nurse are one, and the bond of birth is confirmed by the continued dependence of the suckling on the nourishment that it draws from the mother's body.

Quite apart from this, however, the Arabs attached the greatest importance to the bond created between men by eating together. [12] "There was a *casāma* (sworn alliance) between the Libyān and the Mostalic, they ate and drank with one another" (*Diw. Hodh.* 87). "O enemy of God, wilt thou slay this Jew? Much of the fat on thy paunch is of his substance" (Ibn Hishām, p. 553 sq.). The bond created by eating of a man's food is not simply one of gratitude, for it is reciprocal: Zaid al-Khail refuses to slay the thief who had surreptitiously drunk from his father's milk-bowl the night before (*Agh.* 16 51). It seems rather to be due to a connection thought to exist between common nourishment and common life. [13]

At the same time we can hardly look on this idea as equally primitive with the idea that those who are born of the same womb and have sucked the same breast share the same life derived from the mother; and at any rate the fact that *rahim,* womb, is the most general Arabic word for kinship shows clearly enough that the argument which has led us to regard kinship through the mother as the earliest and universal type of blood-relation is not false. When, therefore, we find such a maxim as "Thy true son is he who drinks thy morning draught," we must regard this as a secondary principle, not older than the rise of relationship through the father, and really confirming the view that mother-kinship is older than fatherhood. The share of the begetter in his son's blood is so little considered that the mere act of procreation does not make a bond between the father and the child to whom he has never given the morning draught, but the mother both bears and feeds the child of her own blood. The father's morning draught given to his boy acquires the same significance in constituting kinship as mother's milk had formerly done, after the weight formerly given to the bond of motherhood is transferred to fatherhood. Procreation and nurture together make fatherhood, but the first is too weak without the second.

The general result of this argument then is that kinship through the mother alone was originally the universal rule of Arabia, and that kinship through males sprang up in polyandrous groups of kinsmen which brought in wives from outside but desired to keep the children of these alien women to themselves. Now if this be so we must expect to find some traces of the older rule surviving among communities which have begun to regard a child as of his father's stock, and in such survivals we should look for a confirmation of the correctness of our reasoning. The expectation is not unfounded, for it can be shown that among the Arabs bars to marriage were constituted down to the time of the prophet by female kinship only. This observation is of such importance and has connections so far-reaching that I only mention it now, reserving the proof to a fresh chapter; but there are some other things of the same kind, less striking or less certain, yet not without weight, that may be adduced now,

A change of the rule of kindred such as we have found reason to suppose cannot have been accomplished all at once. Before it was an understood thing that all sons are of the father's stock, or rather of the stock of their mother's husbands, there must have been a transition period in which individual fathers or polyandrous groups arranged to have their children to themselves and to make them of their own stock by a definite rite, just as a foreigner could be grafted into the stock by a covenant of blood - brotherhood. From the analogy of other races, and indeed from the nature of the case, we may conclude that a necessary feature of such a rite would be consecration to the stock-god. Now in this connection it is remarkable that a ceremony of consecration or dedication was actually practised on infants by the heathen Arabs in connection with a sacrifice called 'acīca. [14] Mohammed, though he made some modifications on the ritual and preferred that the 'acīca should be called nasīka, that is simply "a sacrifice," recommended the continuance of the practice, and the traditions on the subject give us pretty full details as to its character and that of certain other customs observed at the birth of a child (Bokhārī, 6 205 sq., Sharh al-mowatta, 2 363 sq.). The animal chosen for sacrifice was usually a sheep; at the same time the child's head was shaved and daubed with the blood of the victim. [15] Shaving or polling the hair was an act of worship commonly performed when a man visited a holy place (comp. Krehl, p. 13 sq.) or on discharging a vow (as in the ritual of the Hebrew Nazarites). At Tāif when a man returned from a journey his first duty was to visit the Rabba and poll his hair. The hair in these cases was an offering to the deity, and as such was sometimes mingled with a meal offering. So it must have been also with the hair of the babe, for Mohammed's daughter Fātima gave the example of bestowing in alms the weight of the hair in silver. The alms must in older times have been a payment to the sanctuary, as in the similar ceremony observed in Egypt on behalf of children recovered from sickness (Herod. 2 65, Diod. 1 83 — compare also 2 Sam. 14 26), and the sacrifice is meant, as the prophet himself says, "to avert evil from the child by shedding blood on his behalf." This is more exactly brought out in the old usage — discontinued in Moslem times — of daubing the child's head with blood, [16] or the sprinkling of the blood on the doorposts at the Hebrew passover. The blood which ensures protection by the god is, as in the ritual of blood-brotherhood, blood that unites protector and protected, and in this as in all other ancient Arabian sacrifices was doubtless applied also to the sacred stone that represented the deity. The prophet offered a sheep indifferently for the birth of a boy or a girl, but in earlier times the sacrifice seems to have been only for boys. Some authorities (in Lane, s.v.) say that the ceremony fell on the seventh day after birth, but this is hardly correct; [17] for when there was no 'acīca offered the child was named and its gums rubbed with masticated dates on the morning after birth. The Arabs were accustomed to hide a newborn child under a cauldron till the morning light (Reiske, Abulf. 1 7 note 3); apparently it was not thought safe till it had been put under the protection of the deity. I presume that in general the sacrifice, the naming, and the symbolical application of the most important article of food to the child's mouth all fell together and marked his reception into partnership in the sacra and means of life of his father's group. At Medina Mohammed was often called in to give the name and rub the child's gums — probably because in heathenism this was done by the priest. Such a ceremony as this would greatly facilitate the change of the child's kin; it was only necessary to dedicate it to the father's instead of the mother's god. But indeed the name 'acīca, which is applied both to the hair cut off and to the victim, seems to imply a renunciation of the original mother-kinship; for the verb 'acca, "to sever," is not the one that would naturally be used either of shaving hair or cutting the throat of a victim, while it is the verb that is used of dissolving the bond of kindred, cither with or without the addition of *al-rahim.* If this is the meaning of the ceremony, it is noteworthy that it was not performed on girls, and of this the words of the traditions hardly admit a doubt. The exclusion of women from inheritance, and especially the connection which is made between this and the practice of female infanticide in the passages quoted below in *Additional Note* C, would be easily understood if we could think that at one time daughters were not made of their father's kin. That certainly has been the case in some parts of the world: see McLennan, *Patriarchal Theory,* p. 240.

While the rule of kinship was changing, and the old principle had not yet thoroughly conquered the new, we should further expect to find that when a boy grew up he would sometimes attach himself to his mother's rather than to his father's people. The famous poet Zohair is a case in point, and the Arabian antiquarians appear to have known that such cases were not uncommon: thus Bakrī, p. 19, in describing the dispersion of Codā'a says that "Codā'a broke up into four divisions, each division containing some groups taken from the others, when a man followed his wife's or his mother's kin." Mothers, we can suppose, would generally prefer their children to remain attached to their "maternal uncles," especially if like Jalīla wife of Kolaib they thought and openly declared that their brothers were nobler and more magnanimous than their husbands (C. de Percival, 2 277). This was still the temper of wives taken from a proud house even when male kinship was so thoroughly established that the son of Jalīla by Kolaib avenged his father's death on his maternal uncle and father-in-law Jassas, though he had lived from the day of his birth among his mother's kin and did not know his father's name till he was grown up and married (C. de Percival, 2 336, *Agh.* 4 150 *sq.*). And so De Goeje has quoted a line of Al-Farazdac which makes it the mark of a bad mother that she "transplants" her son. In Al-Farazdac's time this meant only that the son reproduced the bad family characteristics of the mother; at an earlier date the expression must have meant literally that she withdrew him from his father's kin.

One effect of this struggle between two systems of kinship was that, where the rule of male descent had been established, there was an increasing tendency on the part of men who were not confident of the superiority of their own clan to marry within their paternal kin and so avoid the risk of their sons being drawn away from them. Another was that rich and powerful men, though they freely adopted marriage by capture or contract to provide wives for themselves — being confident that the son would not be tempted to leave a noble and wealthy house — were yet unwilling to give their daughters to aliens, preferring to keep them at home to bear children for their own kin by men who were not their husbands in the new sense, *i.e.* their lords. Hence we easily understand how marriages of the *beena* type occurring in historical times are generally said to be made with rich and noble women. The highest mark of the superiority of a kin was that in giving its daughters in marriage it was able to insist on keeping the children, and this was what suitors were most unwilling to concede. It is recorded, I know not with what truth, that the Coraish used to stipulate that the sons of their daughters should belong to the religious community of their mothers, the so-called Homs (Azracī, p. 123). Religion and tribesmanship were so closely connected that if this be true it can only be taken as a surviving protest against the more modern principle formulated by the poet quoted by Tebrīzī (*Hamāsa* 260 3), "Our sons' sons are our sons, but the sons of our daughters are sons of foreigners."

The supposition to which our argument has led us, that before female was wholly superseded by male kinship there was a period of conflict between the two systems, seems to supply the natural explanation of a class of Semitic proper names which has always been a puzzle and of which the biblical Ahab, אחאב, "father's brother," is the best known example. [18] These names are commonest among the Aramaeans, and examples taken from them — "sister of her father," "brother of his father," "brother of his mother" — are collected in the notes to plate 63 of the Palaeographical Society's *Oriental Series*; [19] see also Barhebraeus, *Chron. Eccl.* 3 24, where the not very tenable explanation is given that a man was called "his father's brother" from his great likeness to his father. It is much easier to suppose that such names came into vogue when it was still matter of arrangement whether the son was to be "brother" or kinsman of his father or of his mother. The Arabic Omm Abīhā, "mother of her father," belongs perhaps to the same class, implying that her son was named after his maternal grandfather.

So long as fatherhood was uncertain or disregarded there could not arise any ambiguity or conflict of kindred ties. But when male kinship began to be acknowledged, the ties of mother's blood could not be at once forgotten, and even when it came to be understood that a man belonged to his father's *hayy* and to it alone, his mother's people could not be to him as mere aliens. There are many instances to show that even where a man did not leave his father's kin and attach himself definitely to his *akhwāl* or maternal uncles, he had duties of blood towards them and claims upon them. [20] In the time immediately before Islam, it was understood that when a woman became a man's wife by contract, a relation of *jiwār* or guest-friendship was established between his people and hers. The wife is her husband's *jāra* (see note to p. 77) and her father is his *jār*. [21]

Intermarriages on a friendly footing, by agreement not by capture, would of course take place most naturally between tribes united "by guestfriendship and treaty" (*Diw. Hodh.* no. 128, introd,.), or would even be contracted to seal a treaty, but the bond of mother's blood was often strong even between members of hostile tribes. In this case of course it was not inviolable; Hodhaifa in attacking his mother's tribe in a matter of blood-revenge deems it sufficient to direct that her house shall be spared (*Diw. Hodh.* no. 103), but on the other hand (*ibid.* no. 143) 'Abd Manāf the Hodhalite bewails the death of his sister's son Dobayya, though he was sprung on the father's side from So-laim, the bitterest enemies of Hodhail, and had met his death while treacher-ously taking advantage of the friendship of his mother's kin to bring the So-laim upon them by surprise. "Though his father and he alike put on the gar-ment of faithlessness to kindred bonds, though his perfidy admits of no de-fence, I would have saved the life of my sister's son." [22] Similar language in a like case is used in no. 182. In both poems the technical term *'acca,* sever-ance of the blood-bond, is used, so that it can only be a later theory which tries to get rid of the difficulty of a man having two blood-bonds by the doc-trine of guest -friendship constituted by affinity.

The relationship between a man and his maternal uncles and aunts has always in Arabia been regarded as both close and tender; Wilken has shown at length, mainly from Wetzstein's observations at Damascus, that it is so at the present day. That indeed by itself would not prove much, as Islam is en-tirely founded on the system of kinship by degrees in both lines and not on that of stocks or kindred groups; but the old history also shows many exam-ples of the duty of blood-revenge being undertaken by the mother's kin or sister's children, and from Freytag, *Ar. Prov.* 2 310, we learn that it was dis-graceful for a man to make a foray and take women of his mother's kin cap-tive. [23] Thus even in old time the tribal system, when it came to be based on paternity, had often to give way to the persistency of the ancient kindred law. [24]

To maintain the system of stocks or kindred groups in perfect working or-der as the fundamental principle of society it is absolutely necessary that kindred should be reckoned in one line only. The Romans long preserved their gentile system because they had agnation and paid no regard to a man's female ancestry as determining any social duty or right. But the Arabs never had agnation and therefore the tribal system began to break down as soon as kinship through the father was established. [25] It has already been re-marked that before the time of Mohammed the old notion of an absolute blood-bond binding the whole group together had been greatly relaxed. Fam-ily feeling was stronger than gentile or tribal feeling, and the mark of this is the numerous fratricidal wars that raged all over Arabia just before Islam. This decay of tribal feeling was, we cannot fail to see, connected with the rise of male kinship and paternity. The double system of kinship weakened the tribal blood-bond by creating conflicting obligations on the part of individual tribesmen, and the growth of a real family system inevitably led men to count the bond of kinship by degrees and not to feel it so strong towards re-mote kinsmen as towards nearer ones. One of the chief signs of this was the relaxation of the rule that made homicide within the kin an inexpiable of-fence. We find in many cases that the near kinsmen of the slayer would not deliver him to justice, and ultimately it seems to have become quite common to accept a blood-wit even in such a case rather than break up the harmony of the tribe. The formula of consulting heaven for leave to accept the blood-wit by shooting an arrow towards the sky seems properly to belong to the case of murder within the kin; if the god insisted on blood for blood, the arrow, it was believed, would return stained with gore; but this we are told never happened, and so it was always permitted to settle the matter amicably (Lane, p. 2095 [cp. 2946 c]). The arrow was called 'acīca, apparently because the act cancelled the kindred-obligation to take vengeance.

[1] See also Bokhārī, 7 87, where this detail is not given, but a feast is said to be necessary.
[2] See *Additional Note*, D.
[3] Other examples of this are cited by de Goeje *ZDMG* 44 708 (1890).
[4] The right of the cousin to take his *bint 'amm* to wife is, it need hardly be said, altogether different from the provision in the Hebrew Priestly Code (Numb. 36), by which heiresses were compelled to marry within their father's stock, so that the estate might not — on the law of male descent — be carried into another tribe or clan. Laws of this sort are found elsewhere; *e.g.* the Athenian law as to the marriage of an ἐπίκληρος, and that at Gortyna in Crete for the marriage of a πατρῳῶχος. In the Greek cases the law fixed on a particular kinsman who had a right to marry the heiress, in the law of the Priestly Code her choice was free within a certain circle. But, in any shape, a law applying only to heiresses, and directed to keep the estate in the same line of male descent, is altogether different from the Arab law, which is part of a system in which women do not inherit, or at any rate is not confined to heiresses.
[5] Examples of polyandry, where the woman is free to admit any suitor, are generally represented by Moslem writers as fornication. But where the children are not bastards, and the mothers are not disgraced or punished for their unchastity, this term is plainly inappropriate. A relic of this kind of polyandry survived in 'Oman in the fourteenth century, where any woman who pleased could receive from the Sultan licence to entertain lovers at will without her kin daring to interfere (Ibn Batūta, 2 230). In Arabia and elsewhere in the Semitic world, as we shall see by and by, unrestricted prostitution of married and unmarried women was practised at the temples, and defended on the analogy of the licence allowed to herself by the unmarried mother-goddess. Cp. pp. 161, 211, 297.
[6] In this case the murderer was a Makhzūmite, that is a member of the Coraish, but of a house tolerably remote from that of Abū Sofyān. But the incident occurred after the battle of Badr, when the Meccans, deeply engaged in the struggle with Mohammed, could not afford to be divided among themselves. Abū Sofyān, therefore, thought he did enough in offering to pay the blood-money, which, as we have seen at p. 50 *sq.*, was a recognition of the duty of *jiwār* in the very highest sense of the word.
[7] Even the Antar romance (Beirut ed.) tells that all the captors of his mother claimed each that the boy was her son, and "it is said that the 'ashira had been partners in coitus with the handmaid, and that this was the source of the contro-

versy" (i. 7 16 *sq.*) which was decided by the Cādi al-'Arab either on the ground of 'Antara's resemblance to Shaddad, or, according to another version, in a more sentimental way.

[8] On the recognition of the children of prostitutes by the man to whom the *cāif* assigned them, see Bokh. 6 124, from whose account Shahrastānī, p. 442, draws. Maidanī (Fr. *Ar. Pr.* 1 171) says with more probability that a man was not obliged to recognise the child. The case of Ziyād, whom Abū Sofyān would have gladly acknowledged, had he not been afraid of the strict Caliph 'Omar, shows that men were often willing to have a child fathered on them; and no doubt it was usually the putative father who went to the *cāif,* or to the sacred lot (Rasm. *Addit.* p. 61), to make sure that the child was his own.

In Tebrīzī's notes on the *Hamāsa,* p. 504, it is said that the cāif judged by resemblances between the child's members and those of the father, and from a verse there given it appears that *cafa* were also used to trace stray camels. For this original sense of *tracker* see what is said of the *ciyāfa* of Locmān (al-Dabbī, *Amthal,* 75). From Freytag's *Chrestom.* p. 31, cited by Dozy, we learn that the art of the *cāif* was hereditary in the B. Modlij; as a physiognomist he could read the future of a child as well as tell its kin. [For *ciyāfa* and the B. Modlij, cp. Goldziher, *Muh. Stud.* 1 84 *sq.*; in modern times the B. Fahm are reputed *cāifs,* so Doughty, *Ar. Des.* 2 525.] So he comes to be a sort of wise man in general: in Hoffmann's *Bar 'Alī,* 4385, القافة is one rendering of the Syriac *yaddū'ē.* But the Arabs in general observed small personal peculiarities with great exactness. In Ibn Hishām, p. 564 *sq.,* Wahshī recognises a man because he had seen his feet once, when he lifted him as a babe to his mother's lap as she rode on her camel; and in *Agh.* ii. 1618 Khirāsh (Khidāsh) sees the foot of Cais (who was a perfect stranger to him) and recognises its likeness to the foot of the father of Cais who had been his old friend. A tribesman could often be told by his looks (see for example *Agh.* 16 55), and men were willing to recognise kinship with distant tribes if confirmed by similarity of physical type (Ham. p. 162). The function of the *cāif* is not therefore so surprising as it seems at first sight. On the *ciyāfa* see also al-Rāghib, al-Isfahāni, *Mohadarāt, al-Odabā,* vol. 1. p. go *sq.* The *foot* is here, also, the special thing observed. [From a story related by Maid. 1 297 it appears that genealogical indications were sometimes inferred from the flight of birds. — I. G.]

The adoption of Ziyād, "son of his father," *i.e.* son of an uncertain father, into the reigning house of Damascus, is in all the histories; there are some interesting remarks on the law of the case in *Fakhri,* p. 135. See also *'Icd* 3 298 *sq.*

[9] Cp. with Goldziher, *'Antara* 5 4. The woman is said by the collector to be of Bajila, one of the tribes noted for laxity. A quite similar instance is that of 'Auf b. Jāriya (Mofaddal al-Dabbi, *Amthāl,* p. 18).

[10] According to Goldziher (*Lit. blatt.,* p. 27*) this is so far modified by facts in Legouvé, *Hist. morale des Femmes* (3) pp. 217 *sqq.*

[11] Goldziher (*loc. cit.*) refers to *Agh.* xix. 159 26, a verse where we have the phrase اطعميا اللحم of a mare, with notes by Al 'Asma'i and Ibn al-A'rābī. The former understands milk which was called *ahad al-lahmain,* the latter dry flesh pounded and given to horses in lieu of fodder.

[12] [See generally RS, pp. 269 *sqq.*]

[13] The privilege of the guest as such is temporary. According to Mohammed, three days' hospitality and a viaticum. Lane, *s.v. ja'iza,* Harīrī, ed. de Sacy, (2) p. 177; Sharishi, *Sharh Macamat al-Har.* (Būlāc, 1300), 1 242. The oath probably is needed to give the relation durability (see, however, Burckhardt, *Bed. u. wah.* 179).

[14] [On the *'acīca* see *RS*, 329, n. 1.]

[15] According to Asās al-balāgha, *s.v. haid,* children's heads were rubbed with the *haid* of the samora, the gum of this tree being regarded as its menstruous blood.

[16] [According to Kremer, *Studien,* 1 45 *sq.* n. 5, the sprinkling of the blood in *M. in M.* p. 42 (*Maghāzī,* ed. Kremer, p. 28), is only an omen from a camel which was badly sacrificed.]

[17] From Imraulc. 3 i *sq.* it would seem that it was contemptible for a man to grow up with his *'acīca* or first hair; or perhaps that it was not cut off till he emerged from childhood. On the root see in general *Kamil,* 405 *sq.*

[18] Is this simply "Antipater"? Cp. *CIS,* i, no. 115 [where Ἀντίπατρος apparently corresponds to the Phoen. (—) שׁם]. As another example Moab is suggested by a reviewer in the *Athenaeum,* July 1886, p. 75 [cp. LXX Gen. 1937: ἐκ τοῦ πατρός μου; Halevy, too, Rev. *Ét. Juiv.,* 6 6 (1885) explains Moab as "father's mother"].

[19] [אחתבו on an Aramaic inscription from Memphis (CIS 2 no., 122), cp. Ass. *Ahat-abišu, Beit. z. Assyr.* 4 47 72, etc.; אחדרבו, *Bābā Bathra,* f. 9b, etc. (Chajes, *Beiträge,* 8 [Vienna, 1900]; cp. Syr. ܐܚܕܐܒܝ ܐܚܐ) and ܡܚܕܒ); and ܐܡܚܕܘܐ, ܐܡܚܕܘܐ, *Achudemes,* cp. אחמה (*i.e.* אמה אח on an Aramaic gem, Vogüé, *Mél. D' Archéol. Orient,* pl. v. no. 9, and p. 112); the Hebrew אחיאם (for אחיאם, "mother's brother") and אחומי (for אחי אם, "my mother's brother") are doubtful (G. B. Gray, *Heb. Proper Names,* 83 n. 2). To these add Sabaean אחתמהו "sister of his mother" (*ZDMG* 19 273), Palmyrene בתחי, according to Nöldeke, for בת אחוה "daughter of her brother" (Mordtmann, *Palmyrenisches,* p. 8; Lidzbarski, *Ephemeris,* 1 77), Talmud. אבימי "father of his mother" (Rev. *Ét Juiv.* 6 6), and possibly Hebrew אחאבן "brother" (for אחיבן). See Nöldeke, *Vienna Or. Journal,* 6 311 *sq.* (1892), and *Ency. Bib.* col. 3296 *sq.,* § 65; Clermont-Ganneau, *Rec. d'Archéol. Orient.* 4 145, and Gray, *l.c.*]

[20] In *Agh.* ix. 7 7 *sqq.* it is suggested to Doraid by his mother that if he is not able to avenge his brother's death himself he may ask help from his khdl (her brother). Doraid is offended at the suggestion. This makes it quite clear that the legal obligation to revenge lies on the father's kin; what the akhivdl may do is an act of grace.

[21] So a man's sister's son has a right to *jiwār* (Ibn Hish. 244 16).

[22] [See Wellh. *Ehe,* p. 477, who compares Abimelech, Judg. 9 2.]

[23] Yet (*Kāmil,* 191) a man will not pray for his alien mother.

[24] [See the case of the pre-Islamic poet 'Abdallāh ibn 'Anama, who was among the Banū Shaibān when they made a raid upon his own tribe, the Banū Dabba (Ibn-al-Athīr 1 461). The narrative contained in the Oxford MS. of the Nacā'id of Jarīr and al-Farazdac has here a fuller text, which rests on the authority of Abū

'Obaida, and explains the conduct of the poet as follows (fol. 54 *b*): — -"He was devotedly attached to the Banū Shaibān because they were his kinsmen on his mother's side, and he was wont to accompany them on their raids, and on that day (*i.e.* on the day of the battle of Naca-al-Hasan) he was with Bistam (the leader of the Banū Shaibān)." — A. A. B.]

[25] The following example from *Aghānī,* 4 136, is too instructive to be omitted. Zohair b. 'Āmir the Coshairite met Kharrāsh b. Zohair the Bakaite, and they laid a wager of a hundred camels as to which of them was the nobler and greater man. The dispute was referred to an umpire, who decided that the victory lay with whichever was nearer in descent (*nasab*) to 'Abdallāh b. Ja'da. Kharrāsh said, "I am the nearer, for the mother of 'Abdallāh was my paternal aunt (*i.e.* my kinswoman in the father's line), and thou art nearer to him than I am only by a father" (*i.e.* by male descent Zohair was descended from 'Abdallāh's grandfather, and Kharrāsh only from his great-grandfather — see Wüstenfeld, Table D). The dispute therefore went on.

The Arabs, as is well known, always lay weight on nobility of descent in both lines, and this is old (*e.g. Diw. Hodh.* no. 64). But the Arabs are a practical people and cannot have been guided by mere sentiment in such a matter. In point of fact they held very strongly that physical qualities were inherited from the mother's stock as well as the father's, and also they knew that a man's mother's brethren owed him a kinsman's duty. Apart from these very practical reasons there cannot in early times have been any great weight laid on unmixed Arab blood, for the sons even of foreign slaves were adopted without hesitation if they proved themselves gallant men. Arabian national pride, as distinct from tribal pride, is hardly in its first beginnings older than the victory of Dhū Cār. Up to that time no Arab thought himself better than a Persian. The reason why sons of non-Arab slave women were not as a rule acknowledged by their fathers, while sons of Arab captives were so, seems to be purely one of practical prudence. The negro bondwoman's son had no kindred, while the captive's son, if he were not made of his father's blood, would grow up as the member of a hostile clan, and so would be in danger in the midst of his father's people.

Chapter Six - Female Kinship and Marriage Bars

I have reserved for a fresh chapter the difficult and important subject of prohibited degrees, from which, as every student of early society knows, the most useful light is often thrown on problems of early kinship.

Where there is kinship only through women, bars to marriage can of course arise only on this side; and not seldom it is found that, after fatherhood has begun to be recognised, a relic of the old law of kinship subsists in the law of prohibited degrees, which still continues to depend on motherkinship. Thus at Athens we find marriage with a half-sister not uterine occurring in quite late times, and side by side with this we find an ancient tradition that before Cecrops there was a general practice of polyandry, and consequently kinship only through mothers. The same survival appears in various parts of the Semitic field; thus Abraham married his half-sister Sarah, Tamar might have been legally married to her half-brother Amnon (2 Sam. 13 13), and such unions were still known in Judah at the time of Ezekiel (22 11). Among the Phoenicians, king Tabnīth marries his father's daughter Em'ashtoreth, as we learn from the sepulchral inscription of their son Eshmun'azar, and indeed at Tyre a man might marry his father's daughter down to the time of Achilles Tatius (1 3). Now the same thing appears at Mecca; 'Auf, the father of the famous Companion 'Abd al-Rahmān, married his paternal sister Al-Shafā (Nawawī, p. 385). [1] A trace of this kind of marriage has survived to modern times: Seetzen relates that a man could marry his sister — doubtless only his half-sister — at Mirbāt (Knobel on Lev. 18 6). And when marriage with a half-sister is allowed, we cannot possibly suppose that there is any bar to marriage in the male line, unless probably that a man cannot marry his own daughter. In point of fact, we know from the commentators and traditions on Sūr. 4 that guardians claimed the hands of their wards, *i.e.* of their paternal nieces or cousins. It is safe therefore to say that there was no bar to marriage in the male line.

As regards relations on the mother's side the question is more difficult. But on the one hand we know that a man could not marry his own mother, for the most solemn form of divorce was to say "Thou art to me as the back of my mother" (Sur. 33 4, with the commentaries), [2] after which it was as illegal for him ever to touch her as if she had been his real mother. [3] On the other hand, cousins, the children of sisters, were free to marry, for Zainab, daughter of Mohammed by Khadīja, 'married Abu 'l 'Āsī, son of Khadīja's uterine sister, before the Flight (Nawawī, p. 736). The only degrees between these which fall to be considered are uterine sister, and mother's sister and sister's daughter. That a man could not marry his uterine sister seems pretty certain, for had he been allowed to do so, the paternal cousin could not well have acquired so established a claim on the hand of his *bint 'amm*. [4] And, indeed, a woman's brother always appears as her natural protector in a way hardly consistent with the idea that marriage could be superinduced on this relation. The cases of a nephew marrying his aunt, or an uncle his niece, cannot be decided with certainty from any evidence that I know of, but there is some reason to think that these were forbidden degrees. Shahrastānī (p. 440) says that, before Mohammed, marriage with mothers, daughters, and sisters, either of the father or the mother, was forbidden, and Yācūt (4 620) says that the Meccans, who, unlike the uncultured Bedouins their allies, observed many parts of the religion of Abraham, avoided marriage with daughters or granddaughters, sisters or sisters' daughters, disliking and shunning the Magian (Persian) usage. Now these statements cannot be quite correct; marriage with a sister not uterine was allowed, and marriage with a father's sister can therefore hardly have been forbidden. But a Moslem writer, whose own law made no difference between kinship through the father and through the mother, might easily overlook the distinction between the two lines of descent, and it seems more reasonable to suppose that the statements have been falsely generalised, by being extended to both lines, than that they are altogether fictitious. With this it agrees that in historical times there was more natural affection between children and their maternal uncles and aunts than between them and the brothers and sisters of their father (Freyt. *Ar. Prov.* 1 44, 224), [5] and that according to the lexicons "the two mothers means the mother and her sister. And if we assume that this is really the case, and that on the mother's side all relations nearer than cousinship barred marriage, Mohammed's own law of prohibited degrees of consanguinity is at once explained; for he simply places the father's and mother's lines on the same footing, and forbids marriage between relations nearer than cousins on either side. That this is the real explanation of the rule in Sūr. 4 27 is made more probable by his prohibitions within certain degrees of affinity. Putting aside the rule that a man could not marry two sisters at once — which is not a real rule of prohibited degrees, since a deceased wife's sister was a lawful wife — the prohibited degrees of affinity are these: a father's wife, the wife of the son of the man's loins (as distinguished from a mere adopted son), [6] the mother of a wife, and the daughter of a wife who is "in the lap of," *i.e.* nourished and protected by, her mother's husband. The heathen Arabs did not recognise the two of these four bars to marriage which are on the man's side, for the heir took his father's or son's wife. But we learn from *Diw. Hodh.* 61, that it was reprehensible to court a woman and her daughter at the same time. That commerce with a mother-in-law is objectionable, is in truth a feeling that arises in all parts of the world in a very rude state of society; many tribes forbid a man even to look at his wife's mother (McLennan). [7] Now Mohammed's addition to the bars of affinity lies in this, that he forbids the wife to marry her father-in-law or step-son, as well as the husband to marry his mother-in-law or stepdaughter. [8] This explanation of Mohammed's law of prohibited degrees has to contend with the current idea that the law was borrowed from the Jews, with whose ordinances in fact the law about veiling, Sur. 24 31, agrees, as Michaelis showed. But the Jews allowed marriage with a niece, and Mohammed forbids this. So, though the general principle of prohibitions in the male line may have come from Judaism, the details did not, and in precise agreement with our theory Yācūt declares that the daughter of a sister was not taken in marriage in heathen Mecca, but is silent as to the daughter of a brother.

This seems a reasonable account of the law of forbidden degrees at the time of the prophet, and it is such as follows naturally from the priority of female kinship. If it be asked why natural feeling did not before Mohammed's time correct the law of incest so as to fit the new kinship through males, the answer must be, that old rules do not readily change except under practical pressure, and that the children of the same father by different mothers are not brought into such close contact as the children of one mother. Under the *beena* system of marriage, as we know, the wife received her husband in her own tent, and this tent plays quite a significant part both in marriage (Ammianus) and in divorce (Hātim and Māwīya). This feature was retained in *ba'al* marriage in a form which throws interesting sidelights on the subject of our inquiry and may therefore justify a digression.

The common old Arabic phrase for the consummation of marriage *is banā 'alaihā,* [9] "he built [a tent] over his wife." This is synonymous with "he went in unto her" (*dakhala,* and Heb. בא אליה), and is explained by the native authorities by saying that the husband erected and furnished a new tent for his wife (Misbak, Baicl. on Siir. 2 20, etc.). This explanation must have been drawn from life, for though the wife of a nomad has not usually a separate tent to live in, a special hut or tent is still erected for her on the first night of marriage, (*ZDMG* 6 215; 22 153). In Northern Arabia this is now the man's tent, and the woman is brought to him (Burckhardt, *Bedouins,* 1 107. Comp. *Agh.* ix. 150 11, *odkhilat ilaihi;* Psalm 45 15 [EV. 14]). But it was related to me in the Hijāz as a peculiarity of Yemen that there the *dokhla* or "going in" takes place in the bride's house, and that the bridegroom if home-born must stay some nights in the bride's house, or if a foreigner must settle with them. This Yemenite custom, which obviously descends from an old prevalence of *beena* marriage or Nair polyandry, must once have been universal among all Semites, otherwise we should not find that alike in Arabic, Syriac and Hebrew the husband is said to "go in" to the bride, when as a matter of fact she is brought in to him. [10] And with the Hebrews the tent plays the same part in marriage ceremonial as with the Arabs. Thus, in 2 Sam. 16 22, "they pitched for Absalom on the roof" not a tent, as our version has it, but "the tent" proper to the consummation of marriage, identical with the nDn, *huppāh,* or bridal pavilion of Ps. 19 6 (EV. 5), Joel 2 16. So bii?, *'éres,* the covered bridal bed (Cant. 1 16), is primarily a booth, Arabic *'arsh.* [11] In all these cases the bridal bed with its canopy is simply the survival of the wife's tent; and originally the tent belonged to the wife and her children, just as it did among the Saracens, for Isaac brings Rebekah into his mother Sarah's tent (Gen. 24 67), and in like manner in Judges 4 17 the Kenite tent to which Sisera flees is Jael's, not Heber's. The traditions about Abraham, which are the only part of the patriarchal legend that have a distinct colour of nomad life, belong to the district of Hebron, which was long occupied by the same race as the nomad Kenites, so that these two examples must be taken together. Returning now to the Arabs, we observe further that significance was attached not only to the bridegroom's going in, but to his coming forth again to his expectant friends (*Agh.* 9 150); Mohammed changed the name of his wife Barra to Jowairiya that it might not be said that "he had gone forth from the house of Barra" — Barra meaning righteousness, so that the phrase might be taken to mean that he had apostatised (*Moh. in Med.* 178; comp. with Wellhausen, Ps. 19 6 [EV. 5], "as a bridegroom coming forth from the nuptial pavilion "). We note that in Mohammed's time the tent or house is called the bride's; in fact we see from Bokh. 6 131 *sq.* that the prophet's wives, who had huts of their own, continued to lodge each in the hut erected for the consummation of her marriage. Thus every wife with her own family formed a little separate group; even now in Arabia where a man has more wives than one, they usually live apart each with her own children. Under these conditions it is easy to see that the old law of incest— or certain parts of it — might long survive the change of the rule of kinship that followed after the establishment of *ba'al* polyandry; for whatever is the origin of bars to marriage they certainly are early associated with the feeling that it is indecent for housemates to intermarry. But it will not do to turn this argument round and say that the pre-Islamic law of bars to marriage may have arisen under the system of *ba'al* marriage and male kinship, in virtue of a custom that every wife and her children shall have their own tent. For in the first place that custom itself cannot be separated from the existence of an earlier custom of *beena* marriage, or Nair polyandry, in which the tent was the wife's and after her death passed to her children, so that her husband had no right to bring a new wife into it. And in the second place the bars by affinity recognised before the time of Mohammed imply that when a woman was married her daughter and probably also her mother continued to be her housemates. Even Mohammed's law seems to imply that down to his day the daughter generally followed her mother, for when he forbids a man to marry his step-daughter, he does so on the ground that she lives under his charge. If the rule of male kinship had been primitive the daughter as soon as she was old enough to leave her mother would have gone back to her real father.

If now throughout the Semitic area the tent was originally the woman's and not her husband's, the use of *bait,* house or tent, and *ahl,* equivalent to the Heb. *ōhel,* tent, in the sense of family or kindred group is itself an independent confirmation of an old law of female kinship. And with this I think one may venture to connect a further argument. In Arabia *bait* has the further sense of a princely house: the princely houses (*buyūtāt*) of the Arabs in the Time of Ignorance were three; the princely house of Tamīm was the Banū 'Abdallah ibn Dārim and its *markaz* (literally, the place where the lance was struck into the ground, as the sign that the chief was to be found there; comp, i Sam. 26 7) was the Banū Zorara; the princely house of Cais was the Banū Fazāra and its *markaz* the Banū Badr; finally that of Bakr ibn Wail was the Banū Shaibān with the Banū Dhi 'l-Jaddain as *markaz* (*Kāmil,* p. 35). Now in Bakrī, p. 34, we find that a tent, *cobba,* was pitched "over" the chief of a great tribe or confederation — indeed the marks of the authority of his house were the possession of this tent and of the tribal idol. [12] Take this along with the *markaz,* and we see that the tent and the lance are the marks of the chief. But these are just what the woman brings to her husband in the system of female kinship, and thus we seem to have an indication that sovereignty descended in the female line. And that this is not mere fancy appears in the many traditions about queens and female judges from the queen of Sheba downwards, in the fact that Zenobia certainly exercised over the Arabs of the Syrian desert an authority which was wholly incomprehensible to the Roman historians, and in express testimonies as to the succession in kingly houses first to brothers and then to a sister's son. With these facts before us we can no longer have any difficulty in understanding the derivation of tribes from female eponyms, or of groups of tribes from a common mother, *Omm alcabāil* (Ibn Cotaiba, 47 5).

Let us now see what is the net result of this enquiry. At the time of the prophet there was inside the Arab tribal system a family system in which the centre of the family was a paterfamilias — not a Roman father with despotic authority with his wife and children *in manu*, but still a male head who by contract or capture had the right to have all his wives' children as his own sons. But we now see that before this state of things there must have been one in which there was indeed a family system, but a system in which the centre of the family was a materfamilias. The house and the children were hers; succession was through mothers, and the husband came to the wife, not the wife to the husband. In Central Arabia this state of things was not so remote but that it still regulated the law of forbidden degrees and had left many other visible traces on the structure of society. Such is the conclusion to which we are led by argument, and it is still possible to verify it historically in the case of Medina. The settlement of the Aus and Khazraj in the date lands of Yathrib was not formed many generations before the Flight, and each of these divisions of the Banū Caila formed but a single *hayy* united in blood -revenge and war. Yet in the genealogical tables we find among them divers metronymic groups like the Banū Hodaila and the Banū Maghāla. The former had a castle of their own in Medina, the Casr Banī Hodaila, said to have been built by their mother's husband Mo'āwiya, [13] and owned also the place called Mos'at (Bakri, 555), so that we have here a mother's kin holding family property. It is not certain that Hodaila is an historical personage, for there are traces of the same clan in Yemen (Yācūt, *ut supra*); but the inference for the late survival of tribal subdivisions by motherhood is hardly affected by this doubt.

We have then two systems of what may be called marriage, because they involve a certain regularity in the union of the sexes, preceding the establishment of the ordinary *ba'al* marriage with male kinship in Arabia. Of the two systems that which lies nearest to *ba'al* marriage, and out of which the modern marriage-system of the East sprang, is *ba'al* or Tibetan polyandry, the existence of which in the incense country is attested by Strabo. At the same date many of the Northern Arabs, who had come most in contact with Aramaean civilisation, seem already to have had the usual *ba'al* marriage of the Northern Semites, and some of them even, as we see from Palmyrene inscriptions, had clans of male descent (פחד =*fakhidh,* See Ch. 1 above); but for centuries later many of the nomad tribes practised *sadīca* marriage with female kinship. That the latter kind of marriage took a tolerably regular form, that women did not live in absolute promiscuity, but had, for a time at least, one recognised husband, appears in the account of Ammianus and otherwise — indeed the bars to marriage depending on affinity cannot well be explained either from the system of *ba'al* marriage or from one of absolute promiscuity. But behind both these systems there must have lain a practice of polyandry in a form so rude that one can hardly speak even of a temporary husband. The natural condition for the origin of polyandry is a state of morality in which no weight is laid even on temporary fidelity to one man, where there is no form of marriage with one husband at all, but every woman freely receives any suitor she pleases. We have had evidence before us that forms of polyandry much grosser than Tibetan — to our view indeed no better than prostitution — went on down to the time of the prophet, and that legitimate sons were born of them. These indeed are the unions which Mohammed called fornication, for it is certain that he did not always, and very doubtful if he ever did, include even the very lax *mot'a* contracts under this name. In some parts of the country this quite unregulated polyandry seems to have had great vogue; it was long remembered against the Hodhail that at their conversion they asked the prophet to permit fornication (*Kāmil*, p. 288 *sq.*). [14] "Fornication" was the resource of the poor after their betters had a more orderly marriage system, and it was so in various parts of Arabia, as we see from the laws about fornication framed for Nejrān under the Abyssinian rule by the Christian bishop Gregentius. "Many," says this law-book, "say, I am poor and cannot have a wife" (Boissonade, *Anecdota Graeca*, 5 80). That the very grossest forms of polyandry once prevailed over all the Semitic area seems to be proved by the fact that absolute licence continued to be a feature of certain religious rites among the Canaanites, the Aramaeans, and the heathen Hebrews; and as regards Arabia no other condition of things can be supposed as the antecedent alike of *beena* and *mot'a* marriage, of *ba'al* polyandry, and of the continued licence of the poorer classes. [15]

Our evidence seems to show that, when something like regular marriage began and a free tribeswoman had one husband or one definite group of husbands at a time, the husbands at first came to her and she did not go to them. For both the use of the tent in the marriage ceremony and the prohibited degrees — at least in affinity — are seemingly borrowed from *beena* marriage or Nair polyandry.

As the ceremony of the tent is common to all the Semites, the kind of marriage to which it points must have begun very early, and with this it agrees that among the Hebrews, as Mr. McLennan [16] has pointed out, there are many relics not only of female kinship but of an established usage of *beena* marriage. In Gen. 2 24 marriage is defined as implying that a man leaves his father and mother and cleaves to his wife and they become one flesh. These expressions seem even to imply that the husband is conceived as adopted into his wife's kin — at any rate he goes to live with her people. This is quite in accordance with what we find in other parts of the patriarchal story. Mr. McLennan has cited the *beena* marriages of Jacob, in which Laban plainly has law on his side in saying that Jacob had no right to carry off his wives and their children; and also the fact that when Abraham seeks a wife for Isaac, his servant thinks that the condition will probably be made that Isaac shall come and settle with her people. He might have added other things of the same kind; the Shechemites must be circumcised, *i.e.* Hebraised, before they can marry the daughters of Israel; Joseph's children by his Egyptian wife become Israelite only by adoption; and so in Judges 15 Samson's Philistine wife remains with her people and he visits her there. All these things illustrate what is presented in Gen. 2 24 as the primitive type of marriage; but perhaps a still more convincing proof that the passage is based on a doctrine of *beena* marriage and mother-kinship lies in the name חַוָּה, *hawwāh,* Eve (Gen. 3 20). For, in virtue of the permutability of ו and י, *Hawwah* is simply a phonetic variation of *hayy* with a feminine termination, and in fact the author explains that Eve or Hawwa is so called because she is the mother of all living, or more literally of every *hayy*. We know that the Arabic *hayy* meant originally a group of female kinship; is it not plain, then, that our author understood this, and that to him therefore Eve is simply the great mother, the universal eponyma, to whom all kinship groups must be traced back? Eve is the personification of the bond of kinship (conceived as exclusively mother-kinship), just as Adam is simply "man," *i.e.* the personification of mankind.

The Hebrews, then, looked on *beena* marriage as the oldest type of lawful union of the sexes, and as the tent plays the same part in their marriage ceremonies as in Arabia, we cannot doubt that the wife received her husband in her own tent before the separation of the Arabs and the Hebrews. But Arabia, stagnant within its desert barriers, retained this type for many centuries after the Hebrews had passed on to *ba'al* marriage, and not only so, but had stripped off the features in such marriage that were humiliating to woman to a degree which the Arabs have never attained to, because the Coran with its inflexible precepts has made progress impossible beyond these reforms of Mohammed which, real as they were, were too dearly bought when the price of them was that they should be accepted as final.

Whether the beginnings of *ba'al* polyandry in Arabia are also older than the Semitic separation is not quite so clear, but the words *ham* and *kanna* seem to favour the idea that they are, since these cannot well be loan words. [17] We should therefore have to suppose a very early practice of marriage by capture, which indeed is perfectly consistent not only with general analogy but with the view now constantly gaining ground that the Hebrews and Aramaeans emerged as armed hordes of nomads from Arabia. Such an emigration would necessarily be preceded by wars and capture of women. Regulations for marriage by capture seem to be part of the old Hebrew law of war; in the observances prescribed in Deut. 21 12, 13, the paring of the nails corresponds to one of the acts by which an Arab widow dissolved her widowhood and became free to marry again (Lane, p. 2409). The conquests of the Hebrews may even have tended to give a rapid extension to *ba'al* marriage and to hasten the adoption of male kinship. For the law of Deuteronomy supposes, and the early history confirms it, that wars in which captives were taken would be wars of extermination (Deut. 20 13 *sq.*), so that nothing remained for the children of captives but incorporation with the Hebrews, unless they were treated as slaves. But to this point we must return later.

Finally, I think it may be concluded with probability that individual *ba'al* marriage was not known before the Semitic dispersion. Ba'l seems to be a loan word in Arabia. [18] For among the Northern Semites the institution of *ba'al* marriage goes hand in hand with the conception that the supreme deities are husband and wife, Baal and Ashtoreth. But, except among the Himyarites, who were early influenced by the civilisation of the Euphrates and Tigris valley, Baal is not an Arabian deity or divine title; and except the comparatively modern Isāf and Nāila in the sanctuary at Mecca, where there are traditions of Syrian influence, I am not aware that the Arabs had pairs of gods represented as man and wife. In the time of Mohammed the female deities, such as Al-Lāt, were regarded as daughters of the supreme male god (Sūr. 37 149, 53 21). But the older conception, as we see from a Nabataean inscription, is that Al-Lāt is "mother of the gods." [19] At Petra the mother-goddess and her son were worshipped together, and there are sufficient traces of the same thing elsewhere to lead us to regard this as having been the general rule when a god and a goddess were worshipped in one sanctuary. As the details are interesting but take some space to develop, I reserve them for a note. [20] At present let us observe that this is the kind of association of a male and female deity which is natural with polyandry — indeed at Petra the mother is expressly represented as a virgin, *i.e.* as unmarried, and the worship of the Arabian "Venus" or "Aphrodite," as the Westerns call her is associated with the same sexual irregularities of a polyandrous kind as go with the worship of a mother-goddess in other parts of the Semitic world. At Mecca the mother-goddess was changed to a daughter — an accommodation to later kinship-law which produced the absurdity, signalised by Mohammed, that gods had no sons but only daughters, though men desired not daughters but sons. Thus the god-name Baal and the conception of a divine husband are not old in Arabia; moreover *ba'l* in Arabia is certainly a loan word in its application to land watered without irrigation, [21] and it has not, as in Northern Semitic, the general sense of "lord" or "owner," from which that of "husband" would naturally arise. Hence it would seem that monandry of the *ba'al* type began among the Northern Semites after they separated from the Arabs, and that the Arabs borrowed the name, if not the idea, of individual *ba'al* marriage in later times of renewed contact with their northern kinsmen.

It seems hardly probable that we can get beyond these results by observations or arguments drawn from the Semitic races alone, without comparison of the course of social development in savage races generally; for when we talk of things older than the Semitic dispersion we are far beyond the range of authentic tradition. Moreover the origin of an institution so fundamental

as the system of kinship must lie in a stage of the evolution of society so remote that the special characteristics of individual races, like the Semites,
cannot be thought to have been developed; and therefore, if the earliest steps
in the history of kinship can be explained at all, they can be so only on general principles, based on a wide induction far exceeding the limits of such a
special research as the present. But there still remains behind all that we
have reached a series of questions of the highest interest to the student of
primitive society in general, and of these one at least is too important to be
left quite untouched — indeed to pass it over altogether would be to leave
our whole argument incomplete in a very essential point.

We have seen that Arab tradition, and indeed Semitic tradition as a whole,
knows no more primitive state of society than that in which all social obligations of an absolute and permanent kind are based on the bond of blood. As
social obligations are meaningless unless the persons whom they unite are
within reach of one another, this constitution of society necessarily involves
that kinsmen were gathered together in groups, or at least could be called
together on an emergency to defend the common interests of the kin. And so,
as we have seen, in historical times, the local group and the kindred group
were identical, or at least the kernel and permanent element in every local
group was a body of kinsfolk, dependents and allies not of the kin occupying
a secondary position or being so loosely connected that they might break off
at any moment. This being so, the stability and strength of the group was in
precise proportion to its homogeneity, and the object of every *hayy* was to
recruit itself by the birth in its midst of children of its own blood. This object
was attained by *ba'al* marriage with male kinship; it was also attained without departing from the older system of female kinship wherever women did
not leave their own kin to follow husbands abroad. And thus it is easily understood that long after the children of *ba'al* marriages, founded on capture
or contract, were reckoned to the kin of the mother's husband, traces of the
persistence of a law of female kinship may still be observed wherever there
is a survival of *beena* or *mot'a* marriage. But now we have seen that these
two systems of marriage and kinship cannot have gone on side by side from
the first. Originally, there was no kinship except in the female line, and the
introduction of male kinship was a kind of social revolution which modified
society to its very roots. And this being so, it follows that there must have
been a time when the children born in any circle of kinsfolk must often have
been of an alien kin. Let us suppose, by way of hypothesis, that a body of
kinsfolk, with female kinship as their rule, lived together. Such a group would
continue homogeneous if it never brought in women from outside, or if the
children of women who happened to be brought in were either killed or sent
back to their mother's kin. But one can see that it is extremely doubtful
whether these conditions could be fulfilled, while the number of full tribesmen was yet kept up; they could not possibly be fulfilled if marriage by capture was common and if there were no friendly relations with neighbouring

stocks. I will not pursue this subject in detail, as it has been fully worked out in McLennan's *Primitive Marriage*, to which the reader may refer; it is enough to say that if captive women were brought into a kin in any considerable numbers, the local group in the second generation would contain representatives not only of the original stock but of all the stocks from which captives had been made. But indeed, so far as our knowledge goes, among most primitive races the operation of the forces that tend to render a group heterogeneous has been intensified by a law of exogamy, under which it is incest for a man to marry in his own kin, the usual results of this law being that every local group contains within it representatives of a number of stocks and that precisely the same stocks are found in every local group within a somewhat wide district. In such rude societies a man's stock is not determined by counting degrees, but each kin has its stock-name and its stock-emblem or totem, which in tribes of female kinship descends from mother to child. By aid of the totem a man knows what persons in each group are united to him by blood-ties and what persons he may not marry. Totemism has religious as well as social aspects, but its primary importance for the student of early society is that it supplied the necessary machinery for working a law of exogamy and enabling a man to fulfil the obligations of kindred in the complicated state of things which has been described. For among savages like the Australians the blood-feud is still an affair between stock and stock, not between one and another group of neighbours, and so at any moment the outburst of a blood-feud war may break up the local groups of a district, the several stocks rallying together in forgetfulness of all those home-ties which to our ideas are much more sacred than the blood, or totem, bond.

Now whether the Arabs were originally exogamous is a question which can hardly be answered by direct evidence. The extremely narrow range of forbidden degrees in historical times makes it probable that if they (or rather their remote ancestors) ever were so, exogamy must have broken down comparatively early. But at any rate it is quite certain that at one time their marriage customs were such as would necessarily introduce heterogeneity. The change from female to male kinship, which we have learned to connect with the practice of a small group of kinsmen having an alien wife in common, could not take place in a moment. The motive of the change was to retain for the paternal stock children that by the old rule would have been aliens, and before the change was made there must have been practical experience of the inconveniences which the new rule was designed to remove. At one time, therefore, in Arabia as in other parts of the world, there must have been a certain amount of heterogeneity in the local groups. The heterogeneity was ultimately overcome, for the groups before Mohammed's time were again homogeneous; but it is clear that this heterogeneity — a factor in the problem which in our backward course from the known to the unknown meets us now for the first time — must be taken account of, before we can feel confidence in the results of our investigation. But to do this to any purpose we must begin by searching for such traces of an earlier heterogeneity as may have survived down to historical times, and for this purpose we must ask whether the old stock-groups of Arabia took the form of totem tribes. If they did so, the distribution throughout the peninsula of tribes that can still be recognised as of totem origin may render us substantial help in realising the extent to which heterogeneity had gone and the way in which it ultimately disappeared. I propose therefore to devote a chapter to the subject of totemism.

[1] Similarly Locaim is son of Locmān by his sister Maidanī, 2 288 *sq.*, but this may be a story like that of Lot and his daughters, for it was done by deceit. See also al-Dabbi, *Amthāl,* p. 69.

[2] Cp. the wording in the *Masāri 'al-Oššāc* of Ja'far ibn Alimad, p. 368, 1. 7 from foot (in a story of the Jāhilīya with an *isnād*).

[3] It appears from the passage of the Coran, taken with the explanations of the commentators, that the wife to whom the husband said "thou art to me as the back of my mother," was invested with all the legal attributes of motherhood, and was in fact as much the man's real mother as in old law an adopted son was a real son. When we remember how highly Arab sons esteemed their mothers — the phrase "thou art my father and my mother" expresses the warmest devotion — we must conclude that this form of divorce was meant not to hurt but to benefit the wife. Even in Medina a man thought it a duty to provide for his mother, and when the people of that city protested against Mohammed giving a share of inheritance to sisters and daughters, they raised no objection to the mother's share (Baidāwī on Sur. 4 126). The husband would therefore still be called on to provide for the wife who had become to him as a mother. And if she had all the rights of a mother she would not fall by divorce into the hands of his brothers. For just as any man had a right to grant his protection to a stranger, who then became the *jār* of the whole kin — this was so in the time of Herodotus (3 8), and was still so down to the time of Mohammed (Wellh. *Moh. in Med.* p. 324) — the man's adopted mother would be mother of all his brethren.

[4] In *Agh.* 12 127 *sq.* Burj, in a drunken fit, violates his sister. As he is a great warrior the tribe overlooks the fault, but he enjoins on them that no one should know the thing, and when "he is exposed" he leaves his people and rides off alone to the land of Rome. That the sister was uterine is implied in the last of the verses which Hosain utters against him, and is actually stated in 128 1. 2.

[5] Freytag has misunderstood both passages, as may be seen by comparing the Arabic text of Maidanī. In the explanation of the former proverb it is the maternal aunts that make the child laugh, the paternal aunts that make it cry; and the explanation ought to run that the paternal aunt is better because more severe. [See Wellh. *Ehe,* p. 475 *sq.*, and compare also the Talmudic rule: רֹב בָּנִים דּוֹמִין לַאֲחִי הָאֵם, "children on the whole resemble the brothers of the mother" (*Bab. Talm., Bābā Bathrā,* 110 a). — I. G.]

[6] Perhaps there is also an allusion to, or inclusion of fosterage, for Ibn 'Abbās forbids the marriage of a boy and girl who have been suckled together because

the *licāh* (*semen genitale*) is one: the mother's milk being regarded as due to the father's *semen* (see Lane, s.v. p. 2668, and under *rada'a,* iv., p. 1097).

[7] [Cp. Lubbock, *Orig. of Civiliz.* (5) 12 *sqq.*; Frazer, *Golden Bough,* (2) 1 288 *sq.*]

[8] Mohammedan law draws a distinction between marrying the daughter first and then the mother — which is forbidden even when the marriage with the woman has been followed by divorce before consummation — and marrying the mother first and then the daughter. The latter is allowed if the marriage with the mother has never been consummated. This distinction is based on the text of Sūr. 4 27, "the mothers of your wives and your step-daughters that are in your bosoms (*i.e.* that are your wards) through wives of yours to whom you have come in; but the restriction does not apply if you have not come in to them" (*i.e.* to the mothers). The point here seems to be that the daughter of a wife "to whom you have come in" is a sort of adopted daughter; which certainly is inconsistent with the doctrine that adoption makes no real blood, and therefore cannot be the source of an impediment to marriage. But this view of adoption was given out only to legitimise Mohammed's own marriage with the wife of his adopted son, so that one cannot expect consistency. What is clear is, that the prohibition of marrying the mother first and then the daughter is not so absolute, and therefore seemingly not so deeply founded in a traditional sense of propriety, as the converse rule that a mother cannot be taken after her daughter. This is most easily understood by supposing that the feeling against a man's marrying his own mother was stronger than that against his marrying his own daughter, which in a state of things ultimately sprung from polyandry with female kinship would naturally be the case.

[9] [Or *banā bihā,* Ibn al-Sikkit, 399 1; cp. also Wellh. Ehe, 444. - I. G.]

[10] The phrases בא and ܠܠ in this connection are generally taken to mean "inivit feminam," and sometimes this wider sense does occur. But it is not the usual or original sense — see especially Gen. 38 8, Deut. 22 13, and the explicit phrase, "come in to my wife into her chamber," Judges 15 i. In Syriac there seems to be a distinction between ܥܠܠܬ ܠܠ used of the bridegroom (Pesh. *passim,* Bernstein, *Chrest.* p. 90, last line), and ܥܠܘܬܗ ܠܠ used of sexual intercourse in general (Gen. 30 16, 38 16; 2 Sam. 12 24).

[11] Wetzstein, *ZDMG* 22 153, tells us that instead of عليها بْنى the Syrian nomads say عليها عَرَّس. The roots عرس and عرش not clearly distinguished, for side by side with *'arsh,* a booth, we have *'irris,* a thicket, perhaps through Aramaic influence, as thickets are hardly a feature in Arabian landscape. Thus *'arrasa* is simply "he made a booth," עֲרָי, and *'arās,* "bride, or bridegroom," is derived from this. This is also *'ars* "tent pole," which is primitive. But Nöldeke (*ib.* 40 737) makes *'arsh* primarily a wooden frame or trestle.

[12] *Cobba,* which is the word used for the princely tent, seems also to be a word specially employed of the bridal pavilion. Compare the verse of Aus b. Hajar in Shahrastānī, p. 440, with the use of the same word in Hebrew, Numb. 25 8. [On the meaning of *cobba* in ancient Arabia, see the note to *Diw. Hot.,* no. 65; *cobba* as an asylum also *Agh.* x. 145 i, xix. 79. — I. G.]

[13] Bakrī, p. 271, Yācūt, 2 227, where for ﻧﺼﺮ read ﻗﺼﻴﺮ.

[14] [Reference is made to this in the satirical poem of Hassān b. Thabit in Ibn Hish. 0464 *sqq.*, cp. Sībawaihi, ed. Derenbourg, ii. 122 9, 175 11.— I. G.]

[15] Cp. *Additional Note*, D.

[16] [*Studies in Ancient History*, second series, pp. 169 *sqq.*]

[17] *Kanna* stands to North Semitic *kallah* as *sanam* (an idol) does to *selem*. In the latter case, the form with *n* seems to be a loan word. But *kanna*, on the other hand, is immediately connected with the verb ﻛﻦ "to cover," just as *kallah* is with ﻛﻠﺄ, "to close in," and apparently also "to cover or protect," Ezek. 27 4, n. On the Assyrian forms and for the sense "crowned" compare the very speculative remarks of Jensen in the *Vienna Oriental Journal,* 6 210 (1892). [The precise meaning is doubtful. Muss-Arnolt (*Dict. Ass.*) gives to Ass. *kallātu* the original meaning "bridal-chamber," then "bride" and "daughter-in-law." See the literature there cited. Nöldeke (*ZDMG* 37 737) ventures upon no explanation.]

[18] [See RS 100 *sq.*]

[19] Vogüé, *La Syrie Centrale,* p. 119 [*CIS* 2 no. 185].

[20] See *Additional Note* E.

[21] This, however, is denied by Wellh. (*Heid.* (1) 170 *sq., Heid.* (2) 146).

Chapter Seven - Totemism

The subject of totemism in its relation to the problems of early society is the creation of the late J. F. McLennan, to whose essays, readers not already familiar with the subject must be referred for many details that cannot find place here. [1] A few general explanations must, however, be given before we can take up the question of the evidence for totemism among the Arabs.

A totem tribe — which is not necessarily a local unity, but may be distributed through a number of local groups over a considerable region — is one in which the belief that all members of the tribe are of one blood is associated with a conviction, more or less religious in character, that the life of the tribe is in some mysterious way derived from an animal, a plant, or more rarely some other natural object. If the totem is a bear, the tribe is the bear tribe, and all its members not only call themselves bears but believe that actual bears are their brothers, and refuse to eat their flesh (unless perhaps on solemn occasions by way of sacrament). The totem animal is sacred and is often invested with the character of a god. In that case the tribesmen are children of their god. Again the totem supplies a stock-name, and the mark of any person belonging to the stock is that he or she bears that name; so that by this test two persons know at once whether they are under kindred obligations to one another, and whether, if there is a law of exogamy, they are or are not forbidden to form sexual connections. There is reason to think that in early times totem tribesmen generally bore on their bodies a mark of their totem, and that this is the true explanation not only of tattooing but of the

116

many strange deformations of the teeth, skull, and the like, which savages inflict on themselves or their children. Totemism is generally found in connection with exogamy, but must, as J. F. McLennan concluded, be older than exogamy in all cases; indeed it is easy to see that exogamy necessarily presupposes the existence of a system of kinship which took no account of degrees but only of participation in a common stock. Such an idea as this could not be conceived by savages in an abstract form; it must necessarily have had a concrete expression, or rather must have been thought under a concrete and tangible form, and that form seems to have been always supplied by totemism. The origin of this curious system, lying as it does behind exogamy, is yet more obscure than the origin of the latter.

In inquiring whether the Arabs were once divided into totem-stocks, we cannot expect to meet with any evidence more direct than the occurrence of such relics of the system as are found in other races which have passed through but ultimately emerged from the totem stage.

The complete proof of early totemism in any race involves the following points: (1) the existence of stocks named after plants and animals; (2) the prevalence of the conception that the members of the stock are of the blood of the eponym animal, or are sprung from a plant of the species chosen as totem; (3) the ascription to the totem of a sacred character, which may result in its being regarded as the god of the stock, but at any rate makes it to be regarded with veneration, so that, for example, a totem animal is not used as ordinary food. If we can find all these things together in the same tribe the proof of totemism is complete; but, even where this cannot be done, the proof may be morally complete if all the three marks of totemism are found well developed within the same race. In many cases, however, we can hardly expect to fmd all the marks of totemism in its primitive form; the totem for example may have become first an animal god, and then an anthropomorphic god with animal attributes or associations merely. In that case it may require considerable accumulation and sifting of evidence to satisfy us that the phenomena are really a survival of totemism and not due to some other source.

The existence among the Arabs of tribes with animal names has already been referred to at p. 18 *sq.*, in discussing the theory that tribes are named after a patriarch or hero eponymus. [2] It was there pointed out how violent is the supposition that a group of tribesmen who called themselves "panthers" or "sons of panthers" derived their name, as the genealogists imagine, from an individual ancestor named "panthers" in the plural. We can now go a great deal farther, and say that the history of paternity among the Arabs makes it quite certain that ancient stock-names were not derived from fathers; for the system of stocks was in existence, and the stocks must have had names, long before fatherhood was thought of After fatherhood was established, and after the family came to be regarded as the fundamental type of all kindred unities, and then of all hereditary societies whatsoever, groups named after a common father or a chief doubtless arose; and then, if the father or chief had an animal name, these new groups would to outward appearance be exactly like the old animal tribes. This observation enjoins caution in dealing with tribal names that are not certainly ancient, but it does not impair the force of the observation that many of the most ancient tribal names are taken from animals. Some of these names go back far beyond the establishment of the doctrine of male kinship, and are equal if not superior in antiquity to the class of tribal names derived from such deities as Cais or Manāt — deities that certainly are not mere ancestors exalted to godhead in the sense of the ancient or modern Euhemerists.

And here it is to be noted that though plural names like Panthers, Spotted Snakes, and the like, present the most exact and striking analogy to the totem tribe-names of the Americans or Australians, there is no real difference between these and tribal names that are in the singular number. We know that if a tribe was called Nomair or "Little Panther" the tribesmen called themselves indifferently "Sons of the Little Panther" or "Little Panthers" (al-Nomairuna: see page 19, note i, and that every man in the tribe was supposed to have a right to call himself Little Panther in the singular. Thus when we find one tribe that calls itself Banū Kalb, "sons of a dog," and another that calls itself Banū Kilāb, "sons of dogs," the two names are really one and the same; on the patriarchal eponym theory the one is sprung from a hero named Kalb, the other from a man named Kilāb, but in reality both are simply dog-tribes. An individual member of a dog -tribe was entitled to call himself "Dog" or "Son of a Dog" or "brother of Dogs" or "son of Dogs" at pleasure, and it was a mere question of the prevalent mode of expression in any particular dog -tribe whether the eponym, when an eponym was thought of, was taken to be Kalb or Kilāb. The fact that every member of the Nomair tribe had a right to call himself Nomair, as Mobarrad attests, is itself a very clear proof that these names are in their origin stock-names and not personal; it would be absurd to say that every descendant of John has a right to the name of John. No one has a right to a personal name other than his own, and the Arabs in conferring personal names on children chose not that of the father but that of the grandfather or uncle.

I now proceed to give a list, which does not by any means claim to be exhaustive, of ancient Arab stock-names derived from animals. There are also certain tribal names derived from plants; but these are comparatively few, and I have not thought it necessary to include them in the list. [3] As the old genealogies contain many merely "dummy" names, mixed up with those of real clans, I strictly confine myself to names borne in historical times by actual clans or groups of clans, adding references to Wüstenfeld's tables, or to original authorities where that seems necessary, Wüstenfeld's tables of the Maaddite tribes are numbered by the letters A, B, C, etc., and the tables of the Yemenite tribes 1, 2, 3, etc,; so that the reader can see at a glance, from the form of the reference, to which of the great divisions of the Arabs each tribe was reckoned by the genealogists. The order of the list is that of the Arabic alphabet, except that I have grouped together various Arabic names for the same animal. To certain names I have added notes illustrating the tribal worship or the evidences of superstitions of a totem type connected with the animal. The contractions B. for Banū, "sons of," and b. for *ibn,* "son," will not cause any difficulty to the reader.

Asad, lion. Of the various tribes of this name the greatest is the Maaddite tribe Asad b. Khozaima (M. 8). Ibn Habīb, p. 30, specifies also Asad b. Mosliya (8 17), B. Asad b. 'Abdmanāt (7 15), and Asad b. Morr (8 17), all in Madhhij, Asad b. 'Abd al-'Ozzā (T. 19) in Coraish, and B. Asad b. al-Hārith (11 22) in the Azd. The name of the Azd or Asd themselves belongs, according to Ibn Doraid, p. 258, to the same root; it has always the article and means apparently "leonine." The Azd b. al-Ghauth (10 10) are one of the greatest Yemenite tribes, with many subdivisions. There are other lion-tribes than these, *e.g.* the B. Asad among the 'Anz, Hamdānī, 118 23; and besides the Asad clans we find among the Azd the B. Forhūd (10 25) or Farāhīd (Ibn Dor. 294 *sq.*), which in the dialect of the Azd Shanūa — to which the clan belongs — means "lion's whelps" (Ibn Khall, no. 219). Yet another lion-stock is Labwān, a *batn* of the Ma'āfir (*Lobb al-Lobāb*). Another is the Lab' (A. 10), a great tribe of 'Abd al-Cais (part of Asad), and finally we have two tribes named Laith, or lion (N. 11; 1 15). On gods in lionform see *RS* 444, and add Photius, p. 1063, ed. Hoeschel. For lions dedicated to Ζεύς Ὄρειος [4] of Sidon (as the result of a command received in a dream, and as an act of piety), see the inscription given by Renan, *Mission de Phénicie,* 397. A connection between the god and a lion is certainly implied. According to Marinus, *Vita Procli,* ch. xix. (ed. Didot, p. 161), Ἀσκληπιὸς Λεοντοῦχος appears at Ascalon, and from the content seems to be the chief god worshipped there. For 'Anath and the lion [see Vogüé, *Mél. d'Arch. orient.* 47, and cp. Ed. Meyer in Roscher's *Lex. s.vv.* "Astarte," "Dolichenus."]

According to Zamakhsharī on Sur. 71 23, the Arabs worshipped their god Yaghūth under the form of a lion; and the existence of a lion-god is independently proved by the name 'Abd al-Asad (R. 21) among the Coraish. That the Coraish worshipped Yaghūth we know from the names 'Abd Yaghūth and 'Obaid Yaghūth (S. 20). But the Meccan religion was syncretistic, the cults of all the tribes that frequented the great fair being represented at the sanctuary; the local and tribal seat of the worship of Yaghūth lay elsewhere. According to Ibn Hishām, p. 52, compared with Yācūt, 4 1022 *sq.*, he was worshipped by the Madhhij and their allies at Jorash, a town in northern Yemen, at the head of the Wādī Bīsha (Hamd. p. I 18), which at the time of Mohammed was inhabited by various Yemenite tribes (Ibn Hishām, p. 954). A few years before the date to which Ibn Hishām refers, there was a great struggle between a number of Yemenite tribes for the possession of this famous idol, which was decided at the battle of Razm, fought on the same day as Badr, the Bal-Hārith and Hamdān being on one side, along with the A'la and A'nom, the hereditary keepers of the idol, who had carried it to these greater tribes for protection, and the Morad being on the other (Yācūt, *ut supra,* and vol. 2 776). The widespread worship of the lion-god in Nejrān and all northern Yemen which this account implies, seems to entitle us to connect with his religion not only the Asad clans in Madhhij but the name of the Asd or Azd. For the main branch of these, the Azd Shanūa, occupied the mountains of northern Yemen not far from Jorash, and in Hamdānī's time the district of Jorash was partly occupied by Azditcs. Further, Azd is represented as son of Ghauth, or rather Ghauth is a tribal name sometimes taken as including the Azd, sometimes as forming a division of them (*Tāj, s.v.*). Ghauth, "protection," and Yaghūth, "protector," cannot be separated; the Ghauth would be grammatically those who stand under the protection of Yaghūth. The name of Ghauth occurs twice in the genealogy of the mythical founder of Jorash (Yāc. 2 61). It appears therefore in every way that the lion-god and the lion-clans are closely connected.

Badan, ibex, is a *batn* of the Kalb (2 30); also a small clan of Bakr-Wail (B. 13), comp. Ibn Doraid, p. 205. Another ibex-clan is Wa'lān among the Morād (*Lobb al-Lob.*). A stock named Wa'la, she-ibex, is mentioned by Ibn Doraid, 211 4; Yāc. 1 235. There were sacred wild goats on the island which Alexander called Icarus, off the mouth of the Euphrates, connected with a shrine of "Artemis," *i.e.* the Arab unmarried goddess (Arrian, 7 20, comp. Strabo, xv. 3 2).

Bakr, a young he-camel. That the camel was a sacred animal in certain worships there are many proofs, [5] but there seems to be nothing to connect it specially with Bakr as a tribal name. The tribe of Bakr-Wāil had for its god 'Aud, of whose character we know nothing. Bakr and Taghlib together worshipped also a god Awal (Lane, *s.v.*) or Owāl (Yācūt, 1 395). Wāil and Awāl seem to be connected. The former is derived by Ibn Doraid, p. 79, from *wa'ala,* "he took refuge," and the latter would then be a variation of *Wi'āl,* "asylum," primarily not the god but a sanctuary. The name Banū Maw'ala, "sons of asylum" (Ibn Dor. 160), lends some plausibility to this view, and the god-name Fols has a similar meaning."

Bohtha, wild-cow, or bovine antelope, a *batn* of Cais 'Ailān (G. 11); comp. *Lobb al-Lobāb,* p. 47, *Ham.* p. 280. Bohtha is also a *batn* of Dobai'a (A. 10). The calves of the bovine antelope are Farācid, the name of a family in Cūfa, whose eponym Farcad (G. 19) is said to be so called as a nickname. Among the Himyarites the antelope is connected with the worship of 'Athtar (Mordtmann and Müller, *Sab. Denkm.* p. 66), and on a Phoenician gem in Mr, Chester's collection it is figured along with the star and dove, symbols of Ashtoreth. Ibn Al-Mojāwir (Sprenger, *Post-Routen,* p. 151) speaks of a S. Arab tribe called B. Hārith or 'Acārib, among whom if a dead gazelle was found it was solemnly buried, and the whole tribe mourned for it seven days. Whether the sacred animal is only the gazelle (as at the Ka'ba), or also the bovine antelope, it is not easy to say. [7] But the bovine antelope supplies stock-names in other forms. Lay b. Adbat (L. 16) is the same with the Taimite Lo'ayy (J. 12), for it was Adbat who delivered the Taim from their Yemenite captivity (see *Additional Note* A, p. 286), and this therefore must be the name of a clan. The Hebrew Leah and Levi have the same root. [8] The sacred stags that accompany the sacred wild -goats in Arrian, 7 20, are probably large antelopes of some kind. Ibn Doraid, p. 187, makes B. Bohtha mean "sons of fornication." This is certainly not primitive, but is easily explained if the great antelope was sacred to the goddess of unmarried love, at whose shrine women, whom the Arabs constantly compare to antelopes, prostituted themselves. The gazelle supplies a name to a clan of the Azd, the Zabyān (10 12).

Tha'lab, Tha'laba, Tho'al, fox, supply many stock-names. Among them are the three clans of Tha'laba (7 17 18 19), called collectively the "Foxes" (*tha'ālib*) of Tayyi (Ibn Dor. 228 9), a Tha'lab among the Kalb (2 17), Tho'āl again among the Tayyi (6 14), and many others.

Thaur, steer, is son of Kalb (2 18), or rather the great nation of Kalb is divided into Kalb and Thaur (Ibn Dor. 314 14). Ibn Khallikān, no. 265, enumerates three other Thaur clans. The calf, 'Ijl, also supplies a clan-name in Bakr-Wāil (B. 16). The wife of this 'Ijl is Kalba, so that here also there is a fusion of a dog and an ox tribe. The steer and cow, as sacred animals or divine symbols of the northern Semites, are familiar to us from the Hebrew golden calves. Agatharchides relates that the Troglodytes on the shores of the Red Sea opposite Arabia gave the name of parent to no human being, but only to the oxen and sheep that supplied their nourishment. [9]

Jahsh, young ass, "a *batn* of the Arabs" (*Lobb al-Lobāb*).

Jarād, locusts, "a *batn* of Tamīm" (*ibid.*). Another locust name is Jondob or Jondab (L. 12), a *batn* of the 'Anbar (Ibn Dor. 129 *sq.*). The Jondob are also a branch of the metronymic B. Jadīla (7 15, Ibn Dor. 228 5). Locusts were not eaten by all the Arabs (see above, p. y6, note); in Islam they are lawful, but the copious discussions of the point by the traditionalists, which are collected by Damīrī, 1 214 *sq.*, show that in the prophet's time there was a doubt as to their lawfulness. The Athenian grasshopper will occur to every reader.

Ja'da, sheep (D. 17), a *batn* of the Ka'b b. Rabī'a. The word is said to be Yemenite (Ibn Dor. 182). [10]

Jo'al, scarabaeus (1 21). Jonda' (N. 11) is also some kind of beetle (Ibn Dor. 105 20). So also we have among the Māzin a clan called *Horcūs* (L. 13), a kind of tick (Ibn Dor. 125).

Hida', kite (7 15), a *batn* of Morad. *Lobb al-Lobāb*, p. 77, has *Hada'* which is the same.

Hamāma, dove. The B. Hamāma are a *batn* of the Azd (L. *Lobāb*). Among the northern Semites the dove is sacred to Ashtoreth and has all the marks of a totem, for the Syrians would not eat it. The testimonies to this effect are collected by Bochart, and show that the bird was not merely a symbol but received divine honour. In Arabia we find a dove-idol in the Ka'ba (Ibn Hish. p. 821), and sacred doves round it. [11] But it is very doubtful if these do not belong to the borrowed features of Meccan worship, and this seems to be confirmed by our finding only one trace of a dove-clan, and it only in an isolated source. In most parts of Arabia doves could not live. In historical times 'Ikrima, hen-pigeon, was a common man's name at Mecca.

Hanash, serpent. The B. Hanash are a *batn* of the Aus (Ibn Dor. p. 260). Another serpent-stock is the *B. A'fā*, Hamdānī, 91 16. We have also the Arācim, or Spotted Snakes, a group of clans in Taghlib. This name is used by Hārith, *Moall.* 1. 16, and is not a mere epithet, for it forms a gentile adjective Arcamī. We find also two clans of Jofī called al-Arcamān in the dual (7 14); and the B. Hayya, another serpent-stock, were sovereigns of the Tayyi in the beginnings of Islam (*Agh.* xvii. 50 7). There is no doubt as to the supernatural character ascribed to serpents by the Arabs, which has been discussed at length by Nöldeke (*Zeitschr. Völker-Psych.* 1 412 *sqq.*). [12] Damīrī, 1 254, tells us that Mohammed changed the name of a man

121

called Hobāb (snake) because it was "the name of a devil," that is of course of a god.

Doïl, a burrowing quadruped akin to the weasel, gives its name to a large branch of the Kinanite Bakr (N. 11).

Dobb, bear, was one of the so-called *Asboʻ* or "wild-beast" clans of Kalb (2 17), and also a clan of Bakr-Wail (B. 20). [13] Dobb as a woman's name among the Hodhail (M. 11, 12) is hardly historical, but seems to point to a bear-clan with female eponym. The bear is still found among the mountains of Hodhail.

Dhiʼb, wolf, is a clan of the Azd (11 16). Among the "wild-beast" clans of Kalb we have both Sirhān, wolf, and Sīd, which means "wolf," but in the Hodhail dialect "lion." There is another clan of B. Sīd in Dabba (J. 12; Ibn Dor. 117 13), and here the son of the eponym is Dhoaib, "little wolf." There are legends of wolves speaking (Damīrī, 1 407), but they are of Moslem origin. [14]

Dabba, lizard (*lacerta caudiverbera*), is the eponym of a widespread tribe (J, 8) reckoned to the alliance of the Ribāb, and so made sons of Odd (see *Additional Note*, A). The plural form *Dibāb* (E. 17) is also a widespread tribe with three branches, Dabb "male lizard," I.lisl, the young lizard of the same species, and Modibb, which is properly "the place of lizards." The diminutive Dobaib is a clan-name among the Jodhām (5 30). That this lizard was a sacred animal there are many proofs. Its flesh supplied the Arabs with medicines and antidotes to poisons, its bones and skin had magical virtues (Cazwīnī, 1 438). Such virtues are generally ascribed by rude nations to animals that are not habitually eaten, and though the Bedouins generally are described as lizard-eaters (*Fihrist*, 58 14), [15] the prophet would not eat the *dabb* himself, and said it was not eaten in the land of his people (Bokh. 6 190). A tradition in Damīrī, 2 88, makes Mohammed allege as the reason for not eating it that a clan of the Israelites had been transformed into reptiles, and he fancied the lizard was sprung from them. "This was before it was known that metamorphosed human beings leave no issue." The idea that lizards are really a clan of men and so must not be eaten has a marked air of totemism. [16]

Dobayʻa, little hyaena, is the name of various tribes (A. 5; C. 15). The hyaena in Islam is not reckoned as one of the carnivorous animals which may not be eaten, and its flesh continued to be sold in the booths between Safā and Marwa (Damīrī, 2 90). The Bedouins still eat it, but, so far as I have been able to learn, rather as medicine than as food. In the Sinai peninsula, according to a MS. note of the late Prof. Palmer, all but one paw is forbidden food. The prophet would not eat the hyaena himself, apparently because, like the hare, it was thought to menstruate, *i.e.* had an affinity with man (Dam. ii. 90 28, compared with i. 24 28). About this affinity to man, or rather to certain men, there are other stories: "the Arabs say there are certain men called hyrenic, and if a thousand men were shut up together With one such, and a hyaena came, it would go straight to him and to no one else" (Damīrī, 2 89 sq.). [17]

ʻAdal, field-mouse (N. 11), a branch of Khozaima.

ʻAnz, she-goat. The tribe of ʻAnz (C. 12) are said by Bakrī, 54 12, to be so named because their ancestor's head was sharp like that of a goat. That totem tribes claim a physical likeness to their totem is usual. The Anz are reckoned to Wail, but as Hamdānī found them in Jorash, they are perhaps not different from the

122

'Ans (7 12), who are closely akin to the group of tribes that worshipped there. As Asd is blunted to Azd before a medial, so 'Anz would be sharpened to 'Ans after the sharp liquid. The great tribe of 'Anaza (A. 6) seems also to be a goat-tribe and to be properly 'Anza, as Ibn Habīb, p. 22 writes the name. That their own traditions make them so appears from Mr. Doughty's travels [*Ar. Des.* 155, cp. *ZDMG* 49 (1895) 501]. Their God was So'air, which I cannot but suspect to be a corruption of Sho'air = שׂעיר the hirsute goat-god. But a passage of Yācūt, ii. 94 11, which would seem at first sight to support this by making goats the victims at the shrine, is corrupt, and as corrected by Fleischer proves nothing.

Ghorāb, raven, a *batn* of Fazāra (*Lobb al-L.*); see also Ibn Dor. p. 297. Ghorāb was one of the names of heathenism which Mohammed made its bearer change (Dam. 1 254). His reason can hardly have been that the raven is a bird of ill-omen, for that is a reason which would have operated equally in the time of heathenism to prevent a man from taking such a name. In fact, two ravens are still a lucky sight in Arabia though one is unlucky. [18] The fact that the raven gives an omen points to its once having had a sacred character among the Semites as it had in Greece in connection with Apollo and Aesculapius. In the Harranian mysteries, dogs, ravens, & ants are called "our brothers" (Al-Nadīm in Chwolsohn, 2 46). [19]

Fahd, lynx, one of the Kalb wild-beast clans (2 17).

Cird, monkey (M. 11), is a branch of the Hodhail, the same as 'Amr b. Mo'āwiya. The original name, of which 'Amr is only a fragment, was no doubt 'Āmr Cird, "worshipper of the monkey," an animal which is still found in the Hodhail district, comp. *ZDMG* 34 374.

Confodh, hedgehog. The B. Confodh are a branch of Solaim (G. 15). Another hedgehog name is Darim (K. 14), one of the greatest branches of Tamīm.

Cahd is a kind of Hijāz sheep, Ibn Dor. 124 6, and the plural Cihād or B. Cahd are a *batn* of the B. Ka'b.

Kalb, dog, with its plurals Kilāb and Aklob and its diminutive Kolaib, are all tribal names. The two Kalbs in Tamīm (K. 17 and L. i 5) are probably of kin with the great tribe of Kalb b. Wabara, Tamīm's ancient allies; but there are dog-clans in many other parts of Arabia, and the Calibbites in the Old Testament are also an ancient dog-tribe. There is a prophecy of the prophet in which he speaks of the baying of the dogs of Hauab [20] at one of his wives, said to have been fulfilled on 'Āisha's march to Basra, before the battle of the Camel. Now Hauab is a water, but is also the mythical daughter of Kalb b. Wabara and mother of Tamīm. A verse in Bakrī, p. 300, speaks of the hand-clappers of Hauab. Does all this point to some religious feast of the dog-kin at this spot? A deity associated with dogs is found at Ilarran (*ZDMG* 29 110), where, as we have seen, the dog is the "brother of man." [21]

Na'āma, ostrich. The B. Na'āma are the B. 'Āmr b. Asad (M. 9), and here again the original name was presumably "worshippers of the ostrich." A demon in the form of a black ostrich (*zalīm aswad*) figures in Maidānī, 1 181 (Fr, *Ar. Pr.* 1 364), and demons are old gods.

Namir, panther, with its diminutive Nomair and the plural Anmār, are all tribal names of wide distribution. A god of the Harranians, Bar Nemrē, son of Panthers, is mentioned by Jacob of Sarug (*ZDMG, ut sup.*), and it may be conjectured that the nickname Abū 'Āmr applied to the panther (Damīrī, 3 398), like the nickname

Omm 'Āmir given to the hyaena, has reference to the worship of these creatures as parents of the stock that did them service.

Wabr, hyrax Syriacus. The B. Wabr b. Al-Adbat (E. 18) are a clan of Kilāb (Ibn Dor. p. 180, Yācūt, 2 43). A superstition that the *Wabr* is the brother of man will be mentioned below (p. 238).

Hawzan is said to be a bird of some kind (Ibn Dor. 177 5). The plural Hawāzin is the name of a great tribe answering to the modern 'Otaiba (F.G. 10).

Yarbū', jerboa, gives its name to a great branch of Tamīm (K. 13) and to a number of other clans. [22]

It is evident from this list that Arabic tribal names are largely drawn from animals, but the full force of the facts can only be seen by taking a view of the proportion which these animal tribes bear to the whole mass of names in any part of the genealogy. To do this one must first strike out names which are really blanks, because no gentile adjective is formed from them, and names like 'Āmr, Taim, Aus, which mean that the clan worships a certain god, whose name has been suppressed by Moslem orthodoxy. Of the names which then remain a very great proportion are derived either from known gods or from animals, and of those which do not fall under one or other of these categories few indeed are personal names in historical times. It will not then be questioned that, so far as the number of tribal names taken from animals goes, the Arabic phenomena agree with the totem theory as fully as can be expected, if we consider that our earliest historical knowledge dates from a time when the whole social order of old Arabia had been utterly dislocated by the great migrations of the Yemenite tribes and other political causes, when the old religion was in rapid decay, and when also, as our previous argument has shown, a new family system had begun to overgrow and transfigure the old structure of society.

To Students of primitive society in general, who have learned what animal stock -names habitually mean, the mass of such names in Arabia must be highly significant; when very primitive races call themselves dogs, panthers, snakes, sheep, lions cubs, or sons of the lion, the jerboa or the lizard, the burden of proof really lies on those who maintain that such designations do not mean what they mean in other parts of the world. That the names are mere accidents or mere metaphors is an assumption which can seem plausible only to those who do not know savage ways of thought.

The second point in the proof that these are really totem names is that the tribesmen believed themselves to be of the blood of the animal whose name they bore and acknowledged physical kinship with it. [23] That they meant less than this when they called themselves sons of the fox, the wolf, the hyaena, seems probable to us only because we have reached a stage of culture in which the difference between man and beast is fully recognised. But the Arabs had not reached that stage; for they call certain men hyaenic and believe that there is an irresistible affinity between them and the hyaena; they readily accept stories of the transformation of human stocks into animals;

[24] and they do not know, indeed the prophet himself does not know at first, that "transformed men leave no offspring." It is plain that this last discovery must have been directed to a practical purpose, and the way in which it comes in, in Damīrī's discussion of the lawfulness of eating lizards, at once suggests that certain animals were not eaten because they were thought to be men in another guise. The proof that it is so lies in the legends still told by the Bedouins; the panther, as the Sinai Arabs told Palmer, whose notes I have by me, was at first a man; afterwards he washed in milk and became a panther and an enemy of mankind. [25] The *wabr* or *hyrax Syriacus* in like manner is not eaten by these Bedouins because he is the brother of man, and "he who eats him will never see his father or mother again." Quite similar is the dislike expressed by the prophet in the *hadīth* to eating the hare and the hyaena because they menstruate — this is a sign that they have a common nature with man. But now we know that the Arabs practised cannibalism at a comparatively recent date (*Additional Note* C), and the prejudices against eating certain animals — prejudices amounting to absolute disgust and based on the theory that these animals are men in disguise — cannot all have sprung up after cannibalism ceased; they must, therefore, in the first instance have been prejudices confined to certain stocks which objected to eat animals of one blood with themselves. And so, too, when we find a whole clan mourning over a dead gazelle, we can hardly but conclude that when this habit was first formed they thought that they were of the gazelle -stock. Thus we have much reason to suppose that when men first called themselves panthers or sons of a panther, lions' cubs or sons of a lion (for the Farahid are of the Banū Azd), foxes or sons of a fox, they really meant what they said. And the argument is greatly strengthened when we observe that, side by side with tribes that call themselves sons of animals, there are numerous cases of tribes that call themselves sons of a god, [26] In some cases where the god-name and the tribename are identical in our lists this is due to a change in the interests of monotheism. Thus among the Dausites who worshipped Dhu '1-Shara we have a clan of his "servants" or "worshippers," 'Abd Dhu 'l-Sharā (10 30), while Ibn Doraid 295 4 has Dhu 'l-Shara simply (supposed to be the name of a personal ancestor). So the names Hārith and 'Abd al-Hārith, 'Auf and 'Abd 'Auf, Cais and 'Abd al-Cais may in many cases be mere variants of one another, and when they are used as personal names the longer form is in all probability original. The Arabs had quite a list of terms which, prefixed to the name of a deity, were used to describe a man or clan as his "increase," his "gift," his "worshippers," his "clients." Thus Ibn Doraid, p. 310, gives as names formed with that of the deity Al-Lāt, Zaid Al-Lāt, Taim Al-Lāt, Wahb Al-Lāt, Sad Al-Lāt, Sakan Al-Lāt, Shukm Al-Lāt, to which others might be added. This implies considerable variety of conception as to the relation between the worshippers and the god, as indeed could not but be the case when many of the gods had ceased to be tribal. But most old tribal names are too well fixed to be explained as abbreviations, and there is abundance of independent evi-

dence that not only the Arabs but all the Semites often spoke and thought of themselves as children of their gods. In Numb. 21 29 the Moabites are called the sons and daughters of Chemosh, and even Malachi calls a heathen woman the daughter of a strange god. The Phoenician cosmogony is throughout based on the idea that gods are the progenitors of men. The same conception appears in Gen. 6 1 *sqq.*, and among the Aramaeans it long survived in such personal names as Benhadad, Barlāhā (son of the god), Barba'shmin (son of the Lord of heaven), Barate, Βαρσέμιος, and the like. [27] To the same class belongs Ναοληλος, that is, as I explain it, "progeny (Arab, *nasl*) of El." There is in Arabia at least one case of an historical clan that had a legend of their descent from a supernatural being. The 'Āmr ibn Yarbu' are called also Banū 'l-Si'lāt, "sons of the she-demon," who according to legend became wife of their father, but disappeared suddenly on seeing a flash of lightning (Ibn Dor. p. 139). We must therefore hold that it was because Arabic tribes claimed to be the children of their tribal god that they took his name. And when we find among such tribes cases like the Banū Hilal, "sons of the crescent moon," or Banū Badr, "sons of the full moon," [28] where the divine being is at the same time one of those heavenly beings which primitive peoples everywhere have looked upon as animals, the interval between divine tribal names and animal tribal names is very nearly bridged over, and one is compelled to ask whether both are not reducible to one ultimate principle such as the totem theory supplies.

To complete the proof of the totem origin of Arabic animal tribes in a quite satisfactory way we ought to have evidence of the veneration of sacred animals by tribes of the same name. But much direct evidence to this effect we cannot expect to find — not because the Arabs had not animal gods, for we know they had, but because our Mohammedan sources draw a veil, as far as they can, over all details of the old heathenism. Before the time of the prophet the greater gods had to a large extent become anthropomorphic, or, if they were not worshipped by images of human form, they were represented at their sanctuaries by a simple pillar or altar of stone, sometimes by a sacred tree. How the god that inhabited the stone or tree was conceived, we generally cannot tell. In some cases in the story of the prophet the genius loci appears as a man or woman protesting against the destruction of its sanctuary (*Moh.* in Med. p. 351, Al-'Ozzā) or trying to slay Mohammed (*ib.* p. 356, Dhāt Anwāt). But the details that would give us insight into the true characters of tribal worship are almost always wanting; indeed we hear very little except about those greater shrines whose worship, all over Arabia, had been very much assimilated to a single type, and that naturally the most advanced. Totemism pure and simple we could not expect to find at such sanctuaries: the most we can look for are traces of idols of animal form, or sacred animals associated with the worship, or simulation of animals on the part of the worshipper and the like. And of things of this kind even the very scanty details handed down to us supply some evidence. Thus the lion-god Yaghūth was indeed no longer a mere tribal god in the time of Mohammed, but there are several lion-clans in the circle of his worshippers.

Two other idols mentioned with Yaghūth in the Coran are said to have had an animal form, *viz.* Ya'ūc, which the commentators make a horse, and Nasr, which is said to have had the figure of a vulture (*nasr*). Ya'uc is said to have been god of the Hamdān or of the Morad or of both tribes; *i.e.* the name is referred to the same circle of tribes which we find engaged in war for the possession of Yaghūth, and so is perhaps only another appellation for the same god (*averruncus*), for Ibn al-Kalbl found no traces of it in poetry and proper names either in Hamdān or among other tribes (Yāc. 4 1022). Horses were worshipped by the Asbadhlyun in Bahrain (Belādhorī, p. 78), but the name is said to be of Persian origin (from *asp*, "horse," Yācūt, 1 237), and if this is correct the cultus also may be Persian. There seems to be no real horse-tribe among the Arabs, which is indeed what we should expect on the totem theory, since the horse is a comparatively modern introduction into the country — much later than the formation of totem tribes can possibly be thought to be. For horse -worship among the Tayyi in the time of Mohammed Osiander cites the words of the prophet to Zaid al-Khail, "I will protect you from the wrath of Al-'Ozzā and of the black horses you serve," Rasmussen, *Addit.* p. 23. The reading, however, is uncertain; *Agh.* xvi. 48, 30 has a black camel instead of the black horses, [29] and Sprenger, 3 387, seems to have read the black mountain, *i.e.* Aja', the sacred mountain and asylum of the tribe. The name of Zaid al-Khail [30] seems indeed to favour the idea of horse-worship, but any two of the three readings could easily arise from the third.

Nasr, the vulture god was an idol of the Himyarites. [31] But of it also Ibn al-Kalbī could find no trace in verses and proper names, so that he supposes its worship to have disappeared with their fall. Yācūt, 4 781, quotes a line in which Nasr is associated with Al-'Ozzā by the Christian poet Al-Akhtal, but that of course is a mere piece of antiquarianism. [32] I find no trace of this worship in the tribal lists, except the name Nasr once in a Yemenite genealogy (9 18), but the vulture -worship of the Arabs is attested by the Syriac *Doctrine of Addai* (ed. Phillips), p. 24.

Of sacred animals at sanctuaries the doves at Mecca is the best-known case. [33] These, according to all analogy, must belong to the Arab counterpart of Ashtoreth, The doves and fishes of Ashtoreth, associated as they are with legends of transformed human beings and prohibitions of their use in food, present all the marks of a totem origin, but it is very doubtful whether at Mecca the doves are not an importation from Syria. The men transformed into fishes by the polyandrous goddess of the island of Nosala, in Arrian, *Hist. Ind.* 31, also belong to Ashtoreth worship and may betray Babylonian influence. Indirectly of course every relic of totemism in the Semitic field makes it also more probable for Arabia, but we cannot build directly on evidence like this. Of simulation of animals in religious rites there seems to be a trace in the practices condemned in ch. 34 of the Christian Laws of the Himyarites, where we read of shameless men who put on masks of animals' skins (δερμάτινα πρόσωπα) and played the devil in the market places and saluted the shame of Satan. [34]

But at the time when our evidence begins, the greater worships of Arabia had passed through so many changes, and the great gods and goddesses had become everywhere so much alike, that the chief signs of early totemism must be looked for rather in the lower superstitions of the people and in the private deities of small groups, just as, among the Hebrews, Ezekiel 8 10, 11 gives us a glimpse of the private worship of unclean beasts and creeping things by the heads of Judean houses at a time when the public religion had long acknowledged no god but Jehovah, At the time of Mohammed, even, the private religion of the Arabs made large use of idols. At Mecca there were idols in every house, and a lively trade in gods was done with the Bedouins (*Moh. in Med.* p. 350). But a whole class of such gods as directly arise from totemism survived Islam by being simply transmuted into *jinn* (genii). We have express testimony in Sūr. 6 100 that the *jinn* were made partners with God, and they are generally conceived as appearing in animal or monstrous hairy form. And these genii have a tribal connection, for we read in Rasmussen, *Adittamenta,* 71 is that the ankle-bone of a hare keeps off the *jinn* of the *hayy* and the household cobolds and the *jinn* of the *'oshra* tree, etc. [35] To the Moslem the old gods are only beings to be feared, but when a hare's foot or a fox's or she-cat's tooth or the inspissated juice of the once sacred *samora* tree (*ibid. et seq.*) are used as charms against demons, [36] the old tree and animal gods are really set to fight with one another. And therefore it is important to note how many such charms are taken from animals that give names to stocks. [37]

It is probable that fuller evidence may still be collected directly connecting superstitions relating to special animals with stocks of the same name. But even in the absence of such evidence the fact that so many of the animals that give names to stocks can be shown to have had a sacred character among the Semites, taken in connection with the independent evidence that the tribesmen really thought themselves to be of the blood of their eponym animal, and meant what they said when they called themselves its sons, makes it really impossible to separate the Semitic facts from the phenomena of totemism found in other parts of the world. And if it be taken with this that we can trace back the social system and rule of kinship in Arabia to the stage which in other parts of the world is habitually associated with totemism the force of the argument from analogy seems overpowering, and it becomes more than a bare hypothesis that the old Arab groups of female kinship were originally totem tribes.

In concluding this chapter I wish to direct attention to a line of inquiry which in all probability might be made to yield good results, if travellers in Arabia would make the necessary observations. It has already been mentioned that totem tribesmen in savage countries often affect a resemblance to their sacred animal, even at the cost of slight mutilations and other self-inflicted deformities. In other cases stocks are distinguished by the patterns of their tattooing, which there is reason to believe were in many cases originally meant as rude pictorial representations of the totem. Now every Arab tribe has its tribal mark (*wasm*), which is branded upon its cattle. No good collection of such marks has yet been published, but there is reason to believe that some of them at least are pictorial in their origin. The scrawlings on rocks which are found all over the peninsula, and which travellers searching for inscriptions are apt to turn from with disappointment, are often old *wasm,* and if collected in sufficient number, with careful notes of the places they come from, might, when compared with the modern camel-brands, have a tale to tell. [38]

I venture to conjecture that in old times the *wasm* was not placed on camels alone but was tattooed on the persons of tribesmen. [39] For the word *wasm* and its synonym *sima* can hardly be separated etymologically from *ism* or *sim,* Heb. šēm (שֵׁם), "a name," and there are sufficient traces in Hebrew usage that שׁם is primarily a stock -name rather than that of an individual. [40] A man's "name" endures as long as he has posterity (Isa. 14 22; Job 18 17, etc.), while conversely "children of no name" (בְּנֵי בְלִי שֵׁם, Job 30 8) are persons without ancestry. A man's name therefore seems originally to be simply his stock-mark. And again, *wasm* must be connected more remotely with *washm,* "tattooing," though on philological grounds one is led to think that the differentiation of the original word into these two forms, with their respective meanings, must be older than the formation of the separate dialects of Semitic speech. The *washm,* as described in the old poets and in the *hadīth* (Bokhārī, 7 58 *sqq.*), [41] is a sort of tattooing of the hands, arms, and gums, imprinted by women on others of their own sex by way of adornment, and it was forbidden by Mohammed along with the wearing of false hair and other attempts to disguise nature. But that tattooing was originally adopted merely for ornament is highly improbable, and among the northern Semites it was certainly practised in connection with religion. The classical passage in proof of this is Lucian, *De Dea Syr.* 59, according to which all the Syrians bore *stigmata* of religious significance on the wrist or neck. [42] To the custom of imprinting marks on the person in sign of consecration to a deity there appears to be an allusion in Isa. 44 5, and another perhaps in Gal. 6 17; the commentaries on these texts and the learned discussion of Spencer (*Leg. Rit. Hebr.* 2 14) may be consulted for further evidence on the subject. Tattooing is condemned as a heathenish practice in Lev. 19 28, but there and in Lev. 21 5 it appears in connection with incisions (*séret, sáréteth*) in the flesh, made in mourning or in honour of the dead. The relation of this last practice to religious tattooing has always been felt to be puzzling; but the difficulty is considerably lessened if the gods to whom worshippers dedicated themselves by stigmatisation were originally totem gods and were afterwards conceived as the fathers of the tribe that worshipped them. The word *séret* reappears in Arabic in the forms *sharat* and *shart*. The latter word means "covenant," but the former is a "token" appointed between men, or "a mark by which men can be distinguished from others" (see, besides the lexx., Ibn Doraid, 295 1). The connection between "covenant" and "token" is plain from such passages as Gen. 9 13, 31 48; but it seems quite certain that the kind of mark originally meant by shart, as well as by the Hebrew word which answers to it, is a mark cut or tattooed on the person. For the root implies this; *sharatāt* has the sense of tattooed marks (Ibn Batūta, 2 192), and *tashrīt* is the term still applied to the gashes over the cheek-bone which are the distinguishing sign of a native of Mecca. [43] All these ramifications of meaning point to the conclusion that *shart* was in old times a tattooed mark by which men who had mutual obligations, *i.e.* men of the same stock, recognised one another; and this, taken with the independent testimony to the religious significance of tattooing among the Semites, goes far to justify the hypothesis that at an early date the tribal mark was a totem mark. In the patriarchal story of Cain, which embodies the old Hebrew conception of the lawless nomad life, where only the blood -feud prevents the wanderer in the desert from falling a victim to the first man who meets him [44] the institution of blood-revenge is connected with a "mark" which Jehovah appoints to Cain. Can this be anything else than the *shart* or tribal mark which every man bore on his person, and without which the ancient form of blood-feud, as the affair of a whole stock, however scattered, and not of near relatives alone, could hardly have been worked?

In later times the Arabs could usually tell to what tribe a man belonged by observing his personal appearance, dress, and habits. This is still the case among the Bedouins, the way in which the hair is worn being one of the chief marks of distinction. In the fratricidal war between Bakr and Taghlib, the Bakrītes, before the battle of Cidda, shaved their locks, that the women who followed them into the field might be able to distinguish friend from foe among the wounded (C. de Perceval, 2 281).

[1] McLennan's paper on "The Worship of Plants and Animals," appeared in the *Fortnightly Review*, Oct., Nov., 1869, Feb. 1870. [Reprinted in *Studies in Ancient History*, 2nd ser., appendix, pp. 491-569.] On the connection between totemism and mythology in general the reader may also compare Mr. Lang's article "Mythology" in the *Encyclopedia Britannica*, 9th ed., vol. 17. [See also Preface, above.]
[2] Animal names are sometimes to be explained as designed to keep off the evil eye. When a certain Arab was born they said to his father, *naffir 'anhu* ("give him a nick-name"). So he called him *confodh*, "hedgehog," and gave him the Kunya, *Abu'l Addā*, "father of the quick-runner" (see Lane, 2824, last col.; *Lisān al 'Arab*, end of art. *nafara*), cp. Doughty, *Ar. Des.* 1 329.
[3] For a list of proper names (some tribal) from trees see Ibn Doraid, p. 328 *sq.* Ibn Cotaiba, *Adab al-Kātib* (ed. Cairo), 27, ed. Grünert, p. 29; [cp. Landberg, Études sur les dialectes de *l'Arabie méridionale* (Leyden, 1901): Hadramoūt, 1 350].

For bird names see Ibn Cotaiba, 27 *sqq.*, and compare, perhaps, *Hodhail* — there seems to be a myth of its death in Damīrī, *s.v.* (see Guidi, *Ka'b ibn Zoheir Banāt Su'ād*, p. 75) — *ya'kūb*, partridge (Lagarde, *Uebersicht*, p. 107 *sq.*, identical with עֲקֹב-?), *cawācil*, B. Hish. 288 (the same as *cawācila*, Wüst. 18 24), perhaps "partridges," though other explanations are given. *'Ocab*, the "eagle"-standard of Morra (Nābigha, 21 7, ed. Derenbourg), may also be cited [RS 226]. [For a tribal name derived from a fish Robertson Smith adds *'Anbar*, a fabulous sea-monster, probably a reference to the spermaceti whale. It is less likely that the name means "perfume" (ambergris) here. (Private communication from Nöldeke.).]

[4] The "mountain Zeus" can hardly be any other god than the Eshmun whose mountain sanctuary Eshmunazar built, and Zeus is necessarily the supreme god. [From a MS. note.]

[5] [*RS.*, reff. *s.v.* 'camel.'] The camel in Arabia observes the laws of blood and refuses "*inire matrem*" (*Mir. Ausc.* no. 2).

[6] Prof. W. Wright suggests to me that Wail may be really identical with יוֹאֵל. For this name, which is Phoenician as well as Hebrew (*CIS* 1, no. 132; cp οὐάελος, Wadd. 2496), can hardly be connected with Jehovah-worship, and from the compound form יאפעל, on an inscription in the Louvre, seems to be the name of a god, perhaps the Iolaos of Polybius [7 9]. Compare further the Arabian king Ya'lu or Ya'ilu, on an inscription of Esarhaddon, which Schrader, *KAT*, 2nd ed., p. 24, and Fried. Delitzsch, *Wo lag das Paradies?*, p. 1 63, unnecessarily connect with the Hebrew יְהֹוָה. For the identification of Wail and Joel see Nestle, *Israel. Eigennamen* (1876), p. 86 [Nö. *ZDMG* 42 (1888) 471, *Oxf. Heb. Lex.* 222].

[7] [Cp. RS 466, Wellhausen, *Heid.* (1) 102, (2) 106.]

[8] The Hebrew word Leah is the diminutive (cp. Heb. *sĕ'er*) with a feminine ending (לֵאָה = לְאָוָה), and this is confirmed by the *nisba*, לִי. [From a MS. note.]

[9] On Bacchus Zagreus as a bull, and on the probable derivation of his worship from Crete, see Lenormant in *Gaz. Arch.* 1879, p. 18 *sqq.*

The Τύχη βουπρόσωπος of Lydus, *Mens.* 4 33 is doubtless the Τύχη-Ashtoreth of Greek Asiatic cities.

[10] The worship of a ram by a Berber tribe of Mt. Atlas (*Bakrī*, ed. Slane, 161 14) is doubted by Goldziher, *ZDMG* 41 39.

[11] [The protecting of doves is a pre-Islamic custom at Mecca, Nābigha 5 38, cp. "a town in which the dove is safe," a paraphrase for Mecca, Cais b. Rocayyāt, ed. Rhodokanakis, p. 296. — I. G.]

[12] For a totem-serpent in Mesopotamia see *RS* 445. According to *Agh.* iii, 4 7, the Adwān were "the serpent of the earth," which is explained in Lane (1986 *c*, from TA) as a tribe, strong, malignant, and cunning, not neglecting to take blood-revenge.

[13] [Cp. the name Abū Dobb, Azracī, ed. Wüstenfeld, 481 2. — I. G.] Parallel to the *Asbo'* are the *Ahjār*, clans of the B. Nahshal named from stones, cp. Doughty, *Ar. Des.* 1 17. With the *sim'*, the fabulous wild-beast, we may perhaps compare the Sab. tribe-name סמעי or סמע and a divine patron (שׂיע) of the same name (D. H. Miiller, Sitzb. Berl. Akad. 1886, 2 842 *sqq.*, Halevy, nos. 628, 630), but Miiller prefers to read Sama' from the form of geographical names in Hamdānī.

[14] For stories of were-wolves cp. Macrīzī, *de Valle Hadhramaut* (ed. P. B. Noskowÿj, Bonn, 1866), 19 *sq.* [and *RS* 129, n. 2]. It is only figurative when the B. Ka'b b. Malik b. Hanzala are called wolves of *ghada* (Camus, *s.v. ghada*). The wolf of *ghada, i.e.* one frequenting the trees of that name is regarded as especially dangerous and as the tribe lived in *Ghadā* the figure is obvious (see Lane, *s.v.*).

[15] Cp. Yācūt, iii. 473 13 with the explanation on the page following. It would seem that lizards and the *hisl,* or young of the lizard or the hyrax, were used as food in time of famine.

[16] Cp. Doughty, *Ar. Des.* 1 326 [*RS* 88].

[17] The hyena's skin is mentioned by Lydus (*De Mensibus,* 3 52, p. 50, 1. 1) as a charm against lightning. [See *RS* 129, 133.]

[18] Good as well as bad omens are drawn from ravens. Lane, 563, first col. [cp. Wellh. *Heid.* (1) 149, (2) 203].

[19] Chwolsohn, in his notes on this passage of the Fihirst, has omitted to cite Porphyry, *de Abstin.* 4 16, where it is related that in the mysteries of Mithras the fellowship of man with animals is indicated by calling the *mystae* lions, the women lionesses, and the ministrants ravens. The two sets of mysteries which present this common feature in all probability are not merely similar but historically connected.

[20] According to Goldziher the evil omen at Hauab probably preceded the prophecy. He cites Ya'cūbi, 2 215, Yac. 2 353 for the development of the story (*Lit. blatt* p. 27 *).

[21] See further RS (1) 29 *sq.* The trait in Bacchic orgies described by Theodoret, H.E. 5 20 (Migne, 3 1241), where the orgiasts wear the aegis and run about rending (διασπῶντες) dogs, is probably eastern; it is not the Greek rite. It should be the divine animal that is torn. According to Phylarchus, frag. 34 (Müller, *Fr. Hist.* Gr. 1 343), women, dogs, and flies were not admitted to the temple of Kronos.

[22] What is to be said as to the religious connections of the jerboa bears only indirectly on Arabia. In Arabic the male jerboa is called 'akbar, the Hebrew עְכבָּר . 'Akbar or 'Akbor is a man's name among the Edomites (Gen. 36 38), the Judaeans (2 Kings 22 12) and the Phoenicians [*CIS,* 1, nos. 178, 239, 247, 344, 510, etc.]. And this name seems to have a religious connection, for in Isa. 66 17 to eat the mouse (*'akbar*) and the swine is taken as a clear sign of apostasy from Jehovah. We shall see in *Additional Note* F, that this passage refers to a mystic rite implying the worship of a mouse-god. Such a deity exists in the Sminthian Apollo, who was not originally conceived as the destroyer of mice, since there were sacred mice in his temple (Aelian, 12 5), and the mouse is his usual symbol. Now Apollo as a mouse-god is in the Iliad a sender of pestilence, a combination which cannot be explained on Hellenic ground, but becomes clear from i Sam. 64, where golden mice are offered by the Philistines as a propitiation when they are visited by the plague. Hitzig, to whom this explanation is due (*Urgeschichte der Philistäer,* p. 201 *sq.*) confirms it by reference to Herod. 2 141, where we find that the retreat of Sennacherib, which we know from the Bible to have been caused by a plague, was commemorated in Egypt by a statue holding a mouse, and that the legend said that mice destroyed the arms of the Assyrians. The worship of Apollo as Smintheus is probably therefore Semitic; it belongs to regions where Semitic religious influences were very strong, *e.g.* Crete and Rhodes. Apart from this combination, however, there is general evidence that the heathenish Hebrews worshipped a variety of unclean creatures (שֶׁקֶץ, "vermin"), to which the mouse belonged (see Additional Note F). The town of 'Ukbarā on the Dojail may be taken as probably indicating that mouse-worship was known also among the Aramaeans. Among the Arabian Bedouins in later times the jerboa was ordinarily eaten; indeed the Arabs, in the hunger of the desert, will eat almost anything, and we cannot expect to find any law of forbidden food extending beyond a narrow circle. But the 'Āmr b. Yarbū' were probably in the first instance 'Āmr Yarbū' "jerboa worshippers." And it is at least a curious coincidence that their mother is a lightning-goddess and so akin to the divine archer Cozali, who in so many ways answers to Apollo.

In Cyprus the mouse eats iron, which illustrates Herod. 2 141 (Arist. *Mir. Ausc.* 24 *sq.*).

[23] [See *RS* chap. 3, *passim.*]

[24] Cp. Ibn Mojāwir in Sprenger, *Post-Routen,* 142.

[25] Kremer, *Stud, zur vergl. Culturgesch.,* i. p. 4, thinks that washing in milk is here a sin against food (as when the prophet forbids a louse to be killed with a date stone, Damīrī, *s.v.* قَمْل 2 309 *infra*). This may be so, unless it was originally panther's milk.

[26] [Cp. RS 42 *sqq.*]

[27] The same conception perhaps underlies Phoenician names like אחתמלכת, "sister of the queen," *i.e.* of Ashtoreth, as compared with מתמלכת, "handmaid of the queen" ([cp further *RS* p. 45 n. 2 and see] Stade, *ZATW* 6 330 *sq.*, Kuenen, *Gesammelte Abhandlungen,* 206).

[28] Cp. the Banū 'l-Shahr al-Harām (*Agh.* viii. 82 10, cited by Wellh. Held. (1) 5 [not in the second edition]), who, like Νουμήνιος, will have been born at that time, but this does not seem to explain a tribal name.

[29] So, as Goldziher (in a private communication) cites, Sohaili on Ibn Hishām, p. 947 (ii. 212 11).

[30] His real name was Zaid Manāt (Wellh. Heid. (1) 4, (2) 7).

[31] Cp. Muller, *ZDMG* 29 600, Meyer, *ib.* 31 741, and Nöldeke. *ib.* 40 186 [and see *RS* 226, n. 3].

[32] A better reading in Lisān, 13 6 ascribes it to Ibn 'Abd al-Jinn (so Tab. 1 791), and at 7 60 to 'Abd al-Hacc.

[33] [See RS 219, 294.]

[34] See further *RS* 4.35 *sqq.*, and cp. 293, 467, 474 *sqq.*

[35] So Imraulcais, 3 2. Sihāh (*s.v. rasa'a*) says the jinn ride on foxes, gazelles and porcupines, but avoid the hare because it menstruates [cp. RS 129, n. 2]. They ride on others doubtless as 'Anāth rides on a lion, De Vogüé, *Mel. d Arch.* p. 46 *sq.*

[36] [Cp. on this Goldziher, *Abhandl. s. Arab Philologie,* 1 208.]

[37] [On the analysis of the nature of the jinn and its bearing upon Semitic totemism see *RS* 119-139. Cp. also Westermarck's criticisms, *Journ. Anthrop. Inst.* 29 252-269 (1899).]

[38] The *wasm* of the B. Minkar had the form of a mihjan and was called *shi'b;* see Lisān, 1 484 foot, 485, where other matter bearing on this topic will be found. On the wasm, also called *nār,* cp. Rasmussen, *Additamenta,* p. 76, 1. 11 of

Ar. text [and *RS* 480. For specimens of *wusūm,* see Burckhardt, *Bedouins and Wahabys,* p. 113 (1830); Wetzstein, *Globus,* xxxii. (1877), p. 255 *sq.*; Burton, *Land of Midian,* p. 321, with plate (London, 1879); Sachau, *Reise in Syrien u. Mesopotamien,* pp. 119, 134, 136 (Leipzig, 1883); Conder, *Palestine Exploration Fund Quarterly Statements,* 1883, pp. 178-180: Ewing, *ib.* 1895, p. 163; Schumacher, *Across the Jordan,* 67 *sq.,* 90, ZDPV 1902, p. 116; Doughty, *Arabia Deserta,* 1 125 *sq.*; Bent, *Southern Arabia,* p. 369. For analogies outside the Semitic field cp. A. L. J. Michelsen, *Die Hausmarke* (Jena., 1853); R. Andree, *Ethnographische Parallelen* (*neue folge,* Leipsic, 1889), pp. 74 *sqq.*

[39] *Agh.* vii. 110 26. A captive engages to find ransom or return to his captor with all his people. Finding no ransom, he brings his family who become *holafā* of his patron and are tattooed with his camel-mark [cp. also *RS* 148, n. 2].

[40] That ٱسم is derived from سمة was the opinion of the school of Cūfa. This view is rejected on very narrow grammatical grounds; see Ibn Ya'īsh, *Sharh al-Mofassal,* 1 26 *sq.* Prof. Wright, who has long taught the derivation of *ism* from *sima,* confirms it by observing that the verbal form سمّ side by side with Syriac ܫܡ is plainly secondary. [Cp. W. Wright, *Book of Jonah,* p. 43.]

[41] [Cp. Labid, *Mo'all.* v. 9, Tarafa, *Mo'all.* v. 1. — I. G.]

[42] [See *RS* 334, n. I, and *Ency. Bib..,* art. "Cuttings of the Flesh."]

[43] It may be noted that Al-Asma'ī, cited by Jauharī, derives the name of the *shorat,* or military police attached to the court of the Caliphs, from "the token that they appointed for themselves to be recognised by it." See, however, Fraenkel, *Aram. Fremdw.* 239 [and on *sharata* in general, Wellh. Heid. (2) 125].

[44] Compare Wellhausen in *Comp. Hex.* (3) 8 *sq.* [and, on the mark of Cain, Stade, *ZATW* 14 250 *sqq., Akad. Reden u. Abhandl.* 229 *sqq.*

Chapter Eight - Conclusion

The Arabs retained a tribal constitution longer than the other Semitic races, and we know much more about their tribal system than we do even about that of the Hebrews, whose primitive organisation was profoundly modified, at an early date, by the conquest of Canaan, the transition from pastoral to agricultural life, and the absorption of a considerable part of the aboriginal population. The argument for the prevalence of totemism among the early Semites must, therefore, always start from Arabia; but no one who has given attention to the subject will be prepared to believe that the development of Arabian totemism can be subsequent in date to the Semitic dispersion. If the argument in Chapter Seven is good for anything all the Semites must have passed through the totem stage, and traces of this are to be looked for among the northern as well as the southern Semites. But Syria and the region of the Two Rivers advanced in social and political life so much more rapidly than Arabia that in these districts we cannot look for more than very fragmentary relics of the primitive system. Such relics appear to be present in sufficient number, and some of them have already been incidentally mentioned in illustration of parallel Arabian facts. But it may be useful to recapitulate here in more orderly form a few of the chief heads of evidence, without going into more detail than is necessary to show that the north Semitic data are quite consistent with the theory that the Arabs passed through the totem stage and that totemism began before they were separated from their northern kinsfolk.

We have first to note the existence among the northern Semites of tribes with animal names. On this topic I may refer in general to my article in the *Journal of Philology*, 9 75 *sqq.* (1879), though I should not now venture to insist upon all the points of evidence there put forward in a tentative way.' The strongest and best case perhaps is that of the ancient inhabitants of Mount Seir, whose clans or cantons, enumerated in Gen. 3G, contain a startling proportion of animal names with or without the addition of an adjective termination. The animal names, such as Young Lion, Hyaena, Wild Ass, Antelope, Ibex, Kite, occur side by side with god-names, just as in the Arabian lists. For יעוש (E.V. Jeush) in verse 14 is the exact phonetic equivalent of the lion-god Yaghūth, and עקן (Akan) or יעקן (ver. 27, i Chron. 1 42) is probably connected with Ya'uc. The genealogy presents the same kind of confusions as characterise the Arab lists; thus the Wild-Ass clan (ענה) is variously represented as the daughter, the brother and the son of the Hyaena clan (צבעון). These confusions show that the original principle on which the social organisation was based had already become unintelligible when the so-called "genealogy" was written down.

That the division of Israel into twelve tribes did not assume its present shape till after the conquest of Canaan is recognised by most recent inquirers, and the names of the tribes, which in part still await explanation, are not reducible to a single principle, nor indeed are they all of equal antiquity. But the most ancient division of the Israelites is between Rachel and Leah, both of which are animal names, "ewe" and "bovine antelope." The nomadic populations of southern Palestine, which ultimately became incorporated with Judah, also present animal names, of which the most important is that of the Calibbites (Caleb) or dog-tribe.

In the paper already referred to I have argued that many place-names formed from the names of animals are also to be regarded as having been originally taken from the totem-clans that inhabited them. This argument might easily be developed and strengthened, but it is not necessary to do so here. I may observe, in passing from the Hebrews, that there are more animal names in the old genealogical lists than have usually been recognised. The explanation of Leah as an antelope-name, which is now generally accepted, is only a few years old.

Of the ancient tribal divisions of the Canaanites, Phoenicians and Aramaeans, who adopted a settled life and formed more advanced political institutions at an early date, we know very little, but the Hamorites or sons of the he-ass at Shechem are noteworthy. There is also a class of Aramaic personal names like Bar Kalbā, "son of the dog" (*Addai,* 17 11), Bar Daisān, or in Greek Bardesanes, "son of an ibex," [2] which can hardly be separated from the names like Benhadad, Barba'shmin, in which a man is called son of a god. Those, therefore, point either directly to the worship of animal gods regarded as the fathers of their devotees, or else to animal tribes, originally of totem character, from which patronymics were formed. [3] Ultimately the patronymic might come to be treated as an ordinary personal name, just as a modern Jew may be called Levi without regard to his descent.

Of the worship of animal gods by the northern Semites, and of the sanctity attaching to living animals, examples have been noted in chapter vii. The sacred doves and fish of Ashtoreth present every mark of a totem origin, especially the very characteristic one that the worshippers of the goddess would not eat of them (Xen. *Anab.* i. 4 9; Diod. 2 4; Lucian, *Dea Syr.* 14; Philo ed. Man. 2 646; Athenaeus, 8 37; Neanthes Cyz. a*p.* Porph. de *Abst.* 4 15). The later Ashtoreth worship was a fusion of several older cults, and had spread over all Syria, but the form to which the sacred fish belong is that Derceto or Atargatis who was worshipped under the form of a fish with a human countenance in her temple at Ascalon, and of whom the legend ran that she was a woman transformed into a fish (Diod. *l.c.*), while her son, according to Xanthus the Lydian (*ap.* Athen. *l.c.*), was named Ichthys or "Fish" (Dagon).

Observing further the distinct statement of Diodorus that the sacred fishes were actually worshipped as gods, and remembering that the region to which this religion belongs is one in which the oldest deities were certainly tribal and the worshippers habitually called themselves children of their gods, we have in this instance every possible mark of a primitive totemism, and may be dispensed, for our present purpose, from examining in detail the other evidence as to sacred animals and animal gods among the northern Semites. [4] But the subject is large and important enough for a separate investigation, and the range of facts on which investigation might be brought to bear is wider than may appear at first sight. Animal deities often lurk in unexpected places, as one may see from Lagarde's very ingenious identification of Eshmūn-Iolaos as a quail-god (*Gr. Ueb. der Prov.* p. 81). [5]

For the present, however, it is sufficient to observe that northern Semitic facts throw no obstacle in the way of the hypothesis that the Arabs passed through the totem stage, and that they entered it before they were differentiated from their brethren who in historical times lived outside the peninsula. This view is opposed to current prejudice, for totemism is commonly looked at only in its bearings on the history of religion, and in this aspect has to contend with a very current opinion that the astral character, so deeply impressed on Semitic religion wherever Babylonian influence reached, is of primeval antiquity. But I would ask the supporters of this opinion whether the identification of deities with heavenly bodies is not habitually found where tribal religion has given way to national religion of a syncretistic type.

The astral deities belong to wide circles of clans, but their local worships retain features of totem not of astral type, which bear evidence to an earlier prevalence of much more primitive superstitions. The oldest unambiguous sign of belief in gods that dwell in the sky is perhaps the use of burnt-offerings, whose fragrant smoke rises towards the seat of the divine power. [6] But this is not the earliest type of Semitic sacrifice; it is preceded by the form, which to the last remained common in Arabia, in which the gift of the worshipper or the blood of the sacrifice is simply poured out at a sacred place or smeared on a sacred stone. [7] The late prevalence of this ritual is not favourable to the idea that astral worship was the oldest form of Semitic religion. But it is still more important to observe that the later astral worships afford no clue to the most significant features of Semitic faiths, their tribal character and their association with the belief that the tribesmen are the children of their god — a very different idea from the more advanced belief that men generally are children of one great Father, or creatures of a celestial power. The advantage of J. F. McLennan's totem hypothesis over all previous theories of primitive heathenism is that it does justice to the intimate relation between religion and the fundamental structure of society which is so characteristic of the ancient world, and that the truth of the hypothesis can be tested by observation of the social organisation as well as the religious beliefs and practices of early races. It is the social side of totemism with which we are concerned in the present investigation, and to this aspect of the matter we must now return; that is, we are to look on the totem-stock as the ancient Arabian kindred group, before the development of the modern family, at a time when kinship was not counted by degrees but all were kin who bore a common totem stock-name and (probably) impressed on their bodies a distinctive totem-mark.

Among primitive peoples totemism is found in association sometimes with male and sometimes with female kinship, but McLennan's researches led him to conclude that in all cases totemism with male kinship has been derived from a preceding totemism with kinship through the mother only. So far as the Arabs are concerned there can be no question that, in pursuing the hypothesis that they passed through a totem stage, totemism combined with polyandry and female kinship is what we have to consider; for not among the Arabs alone, but among all the Semites, relics of the last-named institutions survived to a late date. Evidence of this in the case of the northern brethren of the Arabs has been incidentally brought forward at various points of the present volume; the survival of polyandrous practices at religious feasts is particularly noticeable in the present connection, and with this may be taken Nöldeke's important observation that, in religious acts, the Mandaeans, who retain so many relics of old Semitic heathenism, employ the style "*M*, son of *N*," naming the mother and not the father of the person designated. [8]

Now we have seen at the close of chapter vi. that where totemism is associated with female kinship, and wives are obtained by capture or purchase from alien stocks, we must expect to find in each local horde members of as many totem-stocks as have contributed child-bearing women to the horde. The heterogeneity thus introduced into every horde of a race divided into totem-stocks will be most marked where the hordes are exogamous; for in that case no man can possibly have a son of his own stock.

Exogamy is so constantly found in all parts of the world in connection with totemism and female kinship that, if the Arabs had the last two institutions, it is against all analogy to think that they could escape having the first. The origin of exogamy is not yet explained, though there is reason to hope for important contributions towards its explanation from the posthumous papers of J. F. McLennan: [9] but there can be little question that it is due to general causes which come into play at a certain stage in all early societies. And in point of fact, at the stage of development which we are now considering, bars to marriage, if they existed at all, could hardly take any other form, kinship not being reckoned by degrees but simply by participation in a common totem-stock. It is probable therefore that, for a time at least, the ancestors of the Arabs must have been exposed to the full force of the causes that tend to diffuse all the stocks existing in a district through each of the local hordes. [10] Let us consider what the effects of this would be and compare them with what we know of the distribution throughout the peninsula of tribes or clans bearing the same totem names.

The state of things which, upon the hypothesis now before us, must have existed among the remote ancestors of the Arabs may be realised by looking at what is actually observed among the aborigines of Australia, where under a system of female kinship and exogamy — i.e. prohibition of marriage between people of the same stock or totem — we find precisely the same stock-names diffused through every local tribe over a great portion of the continent. The members of each stock, "though scattered over the country, are yet to some intents as much united as if they formed separate and independent tribes; in particular the members of each family (totem-stock) are bound to unite for the purpose of defence and vengeance, the consequence being that every quarrel which arises between the tribes is a signal for so many young men to leave the tribes in which they were born, and occupy new hunting-grounds, or ally themselves with tribes in which the families of their mothers happen to be strong, or which contain their own or their mother's nearest relatives. This *secession,* if we may so call it, is not always possible, but it is of frequent occurrence notwithstanding; where it is impossible, the presence of so many *of the enemy* within the camp affords ready means of satisfying the call for vengeance; it being immaterial, according to the native code, by whose blood the blood-feud is satisfied provided it be the blood of the offender's kindred" (J. F. McLennan, *Studies in Ancient History,* p. 90 *sq.*) [11]

The Australians, whose social system is characterised in this extract, are exogamous and continue to practise marriage by capture. The consequence of this is that the interfusion of totems is carried as far as possible, a single family containing numbers of two or more stocks. It is plain, however, that a family so constituted, or even a horde made up of such families, is an extremely unstable body. Common blood, as indicated by the common totem, is the only permanent bond of union, and manifests itself as such whenever a blood-feud arises. The consequence of this is that members of the same stock must habitually gravitate towards one another and tend to form small fellowships, which would accompany one another in hunting or in forays for the capture of women and other purposes, and would ultimately come to hold certain property in common apart from the rest of the horde. Such groups might form the starting-point for a possible advance in the social system, and that in more than one direction. If the local hordes long continued to be in relations of constant and permanent hostility to one another, the practice of marriage by capture would probably go on until the idea was firmly established that woman was little better than a chattel. Thus marriage by capture would by and by come to be supplemented by marriage by contract, and it would be a question turning merely on the scarcity of women whether the woman who was sold as a wife became the property of a single husband or of several kinsmen. In the latter case, a custom of *ba'al* polyandry with female kinship would be established, which in turn would give rise to a recognition of paternity and pave the way for the transition to male kinship. When that stage was reached the children born in a group of men of any stock would be of the blood of their fathers, and the natural tendency of men of the same stock to gravitate together no longer having to contend with the disruptive action of the old rule of kinship, totem tribes would be formed exactly corresponding to the Arabian *hayy*. And just as is the case in Arabia, totem tribes of the same name would be found in various parts of the country, wherever representatives of the old stocks had been carried in the times when they existed only in interfusion with one another.

Further, as the theory supposes that the totem tribes were formed within a circle originally composed of friendly members of various stocks, we should expect to find in the various parts of the country confederations of several tribes more or less permanent in character. Many of these confederations might be very loose indeed, because the blood-feud was still wholly a thing between stock and stock. And the formation of the stocks into tribes able to stand by themselves would in one way tend to make the relation between men of different bloods still looser than it had been in the days of interfusion. But, on the other hand, there might be many circumstances that would lead several totem tribes to knit themselves into a closer unity, *e.g.* for purposes of defence, and such a course would be facilitated, after male kinship was established, by the fact that men could not suddenly become forgetful of the old bonds of mother-blood. Within a circle composed of stocks that had habitually intermarried for some generations, the various tribes, though now of distinct blood on the father's side, would be linked together by many bonds of female kinship, and in all probability children would begin to worship their mother's as well as their father's god. If now in such a circle one totem-stock, let us say the Dogs, had a great numerical preponderance, women of the Dog-tribe would be found as wives in all the other tribes in greater proportion than women of any other stock, and by and by the god of the Dogs might come to be a kind of common god of the whole confederation, without displacing the minor gods of each stock. Combine this with the principle that worshippers are children of their god (which is only a modern way of expressing the old principle that they are of common blood with their totem), and you have at once sufficient basis for the rise of a belief that in some sense all members of the confederation are Dogs and that the Dog is the great ancestor of the minor totem gods. Thus we can understand the formation of a great nation like the Kalb with minor totem clans under it. In other cases, where the various totem tribes that formed a confederation were nearly balanced, a confederate religion might be formed by the adoption of a new god, belonging to a higher development of religious ideas, and then we should have such a great tribe as the Cais, with a name not totem in form but having totem names in its subdivisions. On the other hand a group of tribes that did not succeed in forming a common religion and deriving all its branches from a supposed divine ancestor would be so unstable that it might be broken up at any moment and that its very existence and name might soon be forgotten.

The steps in religious progress which correspond to such a social development are that the totem first becomes an animal-god, and then comes to be thought of as a divine ancestor more or less completely anthropomorphic. If the last stage was reached before the introduction of kinship through males, the divine head of the stock would necessarily be feminine, and this conception might readily acquire sufficient fixity to survive the introduction of male kinship. But in that case the descent from the eponyma would come to be traced through a son, and this would naturally give rise to the mother and son worship of which examples have already come before us.

This summary sketch of a possible line of progress which would account for many of the phenomena of Arabian society rests throughout on the classical discussion in the eighth chapter of J. F. McLennan's *Primitive Marriage,* and ought to be compared with his fuller statements and arguments, in which many difficulties which may suggest themselves to the reader have been satisfactorily disposed of. The general soundness of his construction (based on an induction of facts of which very few were derived from the Semitic field) derives striking confirmation from its applicability to the very part of the world which was least in his eye when he essayed the task of tracing the general lines of human progress in respect of marriage and kinship; but it is plain that no general theory can embrace all the details of every individual case, and the case of Arabia presents certain phenomena which it may be well to look at separately.

We have found evidence in certain parts of the peninsula, and still more among the northern Semites, of an early prevalence of *beena* marriage. We have also found indications that women did not always and in every part of the Semitic world occupy the low position which would be determined by the prevalence from time immemorial of marriage by capture or purchase; on the contrary, there are traces of an unambiguous kind pointing to a high position of woman, and even to female sovereignty, down to a comparatively recent date. These phenomena call for some farther remark, especially as *Primitive Marriage* deals very briefly with monandry accompanied by female kinship, reasons being assigned for holding that it is a comparatively rare and exceptional custom. Let us go back to the stage of savage society in which the habitual practice of marriage by capture, followed by the rise of a law of exogamy, had produced the state of things in which the same totem-stocks are found in every part of a wide district, diffused through a number of thoroughly heterogeneous hordes. We have seen that in such a case the men of the same stock in any one horde would tend to gather together in rudimentary families, but with this important difference from later families that, if a wife from abroad was brought into the family, her children would be of different blood from the men under whose charge they grew up. And we have hitherto supposed that women would be habitually introduced in this way, first by capture and then by purchase. But this supposition is not inevitable. The custom of capture might come to an end without a system of purchase taking its place. A family of brothers might prefer to keep their sisters with them. The latter would then receive visits from friendly members of other stocks and bear children who would grow up under the protection of their maternal uncles. Or, if the women of such a rudimentary family sometimes left their home to accompany men of other stocks, they would not necessarily be permanently lost to their kinsfolk. For, if we may judge from what took place in Arabia, unions between the sexes would often be of a very temporary kind, and mothers with their young children would constantly be drifting back to their own people. Thus if a group of neighbours of different stocks lived for some generations in undisturbed friendly relations, the fragments of stock-groups which it contained would tend to consolidate into as many families or small clans as there were stocks. And, as the blood-bond was stronger than the bond of neighbourhood, the horde or circle of friendly families would very much present the aspect of a miniature confederation of discrete clans of female descent.

The difference between such a circle of friendly neighbours and the loose confederations of several kinship-tribes that we meet with in Arabia in the later ages of heathenism is that the Arabian *hayy* with male kinship was a perfectly stable unity, and could go on multiplying from generation to generation without loss of homogeneity and local continuity, so long as it had room to expand; whereas the groups of mother-kin which we have been looking at would be essentially unstable, unless they were kept within very moderate size. For the theory of such a group is that brothers and sisters live together, and that the children borne in the group are their uncles' heirs, the men of the group being content to have no wives at home, but merely to visit, in a more or less temporary way, women of other stocks in their neighbourhood. This plan obviously could not succeed unless groups of different stocks were always within easy reach of one another; and if the whole circle of friendly people became large and spread over a considerable range of country, each stock would necessarily be divided into a number of small groups, instead of holding together and occupying broad pastures to the exclusion of neighbours, as the later tribes of male descent did. This, however, is on the assumption that exogamy continued to be the rule; if exogamy disappeared before a movement towards male kinship began, a large tribe of female descent might readily be formed. For the occurrence of a blood-feud of some duration might force the various fractions of the same stock to come together for mutual defence; and if the feud developed into a protracted war, they might never separate again, but remain together in the seats that they had occupied. In truth, one can see that an event of this kind might naturally bring about the disappearance of exogamy. For while the common totem-stock was distributed over the country in a number of small divisions, enough of family feeling, as distinct from stock feeling, would have sprung up to lay the foundation of the recognition of degrees of kinship, and this, taken along with the fact that the state of war had put an end to the old facilities for forming relations with women of other stocks, might operate to bring about the substitution of a law of forbidden degrees, such as prevailed among the Arabs before Mohammed, for the old absolute prohibition of marriage within the same stock.

The conditions for a development of this sort are, it would appear, three in number. (1) A distribution of totem -stocks with female kinship through a number of hordes, in the way exemplified in the case of the Australians and other rude peoples. The examples show that this is possible, and J. F. McLennan, in his *Primitive Marriage,* has gone far to show that such a distribution would necessarily arise, through the inevitable practice of marriage by capture in every primitive race during its early struggles for existence. Following on this we must have (2) a period of more peaceful character, in which marriage by capture went out of use and Nair polyandry (or perhaps *beena* marriage) took place regularly between interfused and friendly stocks; and then (3) a period of war, which not only broke the friendly relations between different stocks, but forced men and women of the same stock to come together in large groups for mutual defence. The last two conditions appear to be satisfied by what we know of the history of southern Arabia.

For many centuries Yemen was enriched by the incense trade, and by its position as the emporium of eastern commerce; the tanks of Ma'rib spread fertility around them, and the peninsula was intersected by busy caravan routes. In this period the name of Arab was associated to western writers with ideas of effeminate indolence and peaceful opulence. But social institutions had not kept pace with this prosperity, for towards the close of the golden age of Yemen Strabo describes a marriage-custom which corresponds closely with Tibetan polyandry. Even this stage, we must think, had been reached only by advanced communities, or perhaps only by the upper classes, to which Strabo directly refers; [12] Nair polyandry must once have been universal and can hardly have died out, for it is in this region that we meet with the Queen of Sheba, and at a later date with a law of succession to the throne by sisters' children, and it is in Yemen that the most persistent traces of polyandry of the Nair type are found down to quite modern times. But now it is well known that the decay of commerce, the dilapidation of the tanks and the closing of the trade routes were associated with a violent disruption of the old order and a great movement of the tribes accompanied by long and bitter wars. This period of universal disorder is represented in Arabian legend as a vast migration of Yemenite tribes, following directly upon the *sail al-'Arim* or bursting of the tanks. It affected a large part of the peninsula, and as the only permanent bond of society was still the bond of blood, it must have tended to bring together considerable hosts of people, mainly of the same stock, in the very way which has been hypothetically sketched above. That in the migrations the principle on which men held together was in great measure that of female kinship was not wholly unknown to later tradition (Bakrī, p. 18). A kinship-tribe formed in this way, and having given up its strict exogamy, which, if it had lasted so late, could at least hardly survive through such a period, would be a great totem tribe of female descent, and might naturally come to regard itself, as several great Arab tribes actually did, as being sprung from a female eponym. But unless it then went on to observe a rule of strict endogamy, the heterogeneity so inseparable from female kinship would soon reappear, especially as a protracted period of warfare and constant migration would almost inevitably lead to the revival of marriage by capture. If this new process of disintegration from within again went on for generations, the female tribe of descent would once more become a thoroughly heterogeneous tribe with many interfused stocks; but the period of the Yemenite migrations lies within a very few generations of the ultimate victory of male kinship. That victory probably came fast, for, as we see from Strabo, the beginnings of the new system had already been made in certain circles by the aid of Tibetan polyandry, and the long struggle for existence in harder circumstances, leading to a revival of female infanticide and capture of women, would tend to make this kind of marriage common. But some time was needed to complete the change, and in the interval marriages with aliens would introduce into a community of female kinship a certain number of minor groups of other stocks. And therefore, when the change came, the community might indeed still be mainly of one old stock and refer itself as a whole to one great mother, but it would contain certain clans or sub-groups with other stock-names. It is easy to see that these, as well as any allies that had come into the community in other ways, would be regarded as junior branches of a greater whole, and ultimately, when male kinship was fully established, would be affiliated to the main stock in the way already indicated at p. 265 *sq.*

The Arabian peninsula is large enough to make it probable that in different parts of it the order of social progress varied very considerably; and in the nature of things the sparse and warlike nomadic populations of the upland deserts must have had a very different history from the peaceful tribes of the more fertile Yemen. We are not, therefore, at all bound to suppose that all parts of Arabia reached male kinship at the same date or by the same path.

What is certain is that all the tribes arrived at the same goal, and that the tribal system had become practically uniform at the time of the prophet. With this it agrees that either of the two courses which have been hypothetically sketched in the preceding pages leads to essentially the same ultimate result, though some of the phenomena may fit one form of the hypothesis better than the other.

The soundness of the general principles which underlie both forms of the hypothesis seems to receive a remarkable confirmation in a fact which has always puzzled historians, namely that so many of the names of Arabian "nations" which were known to Ptolemy and other western writers, before the trade routes to Yemen were closed, had entirely disappeared before the time of the prophet, and that new tribes before unheard of had sprung into prominence in their place. If in the time of Ptolemy the more important nations had already been constituted on the later tribal principle, it is difficult to believe that so many of them could have entirely disappeared, and still more difficult to believe that in the comparatively brief interval an entirely new set of tribes could not only have sprung into existence but could have come to regard themselves as founded on an ancient blood-bond so strong as the blood-bond was in Arabia. The difficulty however disappears if we consider that the later *hayy* inherited the traditions of the old diffused totem -stock. The Dogs, the Lizards, the Panthers, had always been present in Arabia and had always been united by bonds of blood. But so long as they were diffused in small groups or Nair families over every pasture-ground, living side by side with families of other stocks, they escaped the notice of foreign inquirers. The names that Ptolemy would hear would necessarily be the names of the political combinations of men of many stocks that occupied a particular district. He could not know or care to know that beneath these shifting and unstable combinations there was another and stronger principle, which at any moment might be brought into action and shatter his so-called nations into fragments by uniting the men of the same stock against their nearest neighbours. When the great period of war and migration began, all bonds except the bond of blood would snap like tow, the old "nations" would in many cases disappear, and in every case the stocks would emerge into new political importance, which was soon rendered permanent by the complete victory of that law of male kinship which secured the homogeneity of the kinship-tribes from generation to generation.

It still remains to say something, at least by way of conjecture, as to the history of the most northern branches of the Arab race and of the northern Semites in general, which ran a very different course from the southern tribes.

The Semites are one of the great migratory and conquering races of antiquity, and the beginnings of their migrations must date from a very remote period. We cannot suppose that the movements which spread the race over all the lands between the Tigris and the Mediterranean were effected by small bands, for all our evidence goes to show that the process was not one of gradual occupation of unsettled territory, but that wherever they came they had to do battle with earlier occupants. The invading hordes therefore must from the first have been aggregates of several stocks held together by their common enterprise and common dangers. A nation which is in the position of an invading army needs more organisation than a band of hunters in a common hunting-field, and this need would be naturally met by people of the same stock going together. Throughout the ages of war and migration all things would conspire to facilitate the formation of *dārs* of kinsmen, women either remaining with their brethren, but receiving the visits of men from an allied *dār*, or returning to their kinsmen, and bringing their children with them, if for a time they had betaken themselves to a group of another stock in a different part of the host. Something of this sort appears to have prevailed at a much later date, but under similar conditions, among the warlike Saracens of the Roman frontier. At the same time no doubt the advance of the conquerors would be marked by many captures of women. But conquest on a great scale could hardly fail to introduce slavery, and the children of slave-women of altogether foreign type and strange language would probably even at this early time be regarded as slaves. Or if they were in certain cases taken into tribal fellowship with their conquerors they would be so only by an act of adoption and would therefore be cut off from their mothers' stock. Thus among the hordes that overspread the northern Semitic lands it was possible even with female kinship to make great progress towards the principle that the stock-group is also a body which not only rallies together for special purposes like the blood-feud but habitually moves and acts together. And it is also reasonable to think that, this custom having acquired a certain fixity, the conquered lands would be occupied according to the distribution of stocks, and that property in land or watering-places, as well as in herds and cattle, would be stock property, or that, when individual property came to be recognised, a man's heirs would be those of his own stock — in the first line his sisters' children.

The victorious progress of the Semites, if we may judge from what happened in historical times in the same lands, was accompanied partly by the extermination of the older inhabitants, partly by their subjugation to a kind of serfdom, and partly by their gradual retreat to parts of the country still unsubdued. Accordingly for long generations the invaders were always face

145

to face with the enemy and had the strongest motive for restraining mutual feuds. Thus there would be every facility for a system of friendly marriages. And at first these would be more naturally of the *sadīca* than of the *ba'al* type, because members of the conquering race would not readily allow their daughters to pass into a position closely analogous to that occupied by captives of a race to which they already felt themselves superior. Marriage by purchase, therefore, might not become common, or at least would be considered less honourable, till the period of conquest was past; and thus it is very intelligible that we find *beena* marriage so prominent in the ancient Hebrew traditions, that it appears to be regarded as the oldest type of marriage, and that the woman's tent, appropriate to this type of union or to Nair polyandry, appears to have been long retained as a necessary part of the apparatus of the marriage ceremony. If, however, marriages by purchase came in, or if wars began again between the neighbouring Semitic stocks, while female kinship was still the rule, the stocks would again tend to acquire a marked degree of heterogeneity, which might be modified by shifting of the population, those of the same stock always tending to cohere, but could not be wholly overcome till the rise of male kinship, the advent of which would probably be accelerated by the causes already spoken of at p. 209. A people which had in its midst many concubines taken from a subject race would soon form a preference for marriages which made the husband his wife's lord and made the children also belong to him, and contracts to this effect would be devised accordingly. If this practice got a firm footing before *beena* marriages became uncommon, or if exogamy had by this time gone out, the original totem-stock in any settlement of the conquerors would still constitute the mass of the population, and the minor stocks, now consolidated into stable clans, would ultimately come to be regarded as subdivisions of it. If on the other hand the establishment of male kinship was long deferred the local settlement would cease to be mainly of one blood. The neighbours of different stocks would, however, be likely to connect themselves by religious ties through the worship of a local deity (borrowed perhaps from the old inhabitants), and ultimately on the establishment of male kinship this god would become the eponym and father of a group of clans, each of which would still retain, in addition, its old stock-deity. Thus we should expect to find in such a conquering nation a descending scale of tribes and clans, with many of the old totem names retained in the lower divisions and some perhaps in the higher also, while in other cases animal names of totem origin would survive only in the names of places which in historical times were peopled by a mixture of several stocks.

Some such hypothesis as this seems to be sufficient to account for the traces of primeval totemism that are found north of the Arabian desert. But it must of course be remembered that the period of migration from Arabia to Syria and the neighbouring lands was a very long one, and that the conquest of the fertile lands from the desert was only effected by the advance of wave upon wave of emigrants, probably during centuries. Throughout this period there must have been a continual ebb and flow through all the northern parts of Arabia, the nomads now pressing forward beyond their barren limits and anon being thrust back into the wilderness. Any social changes that went on in the conquered lands might therefore readily react on all the northern Arabs, from Jebel Shammar to the Belcā and the Euphrates, who from time immemorial have constantly moved northwards in great confederate hordes to seek summer pasture and plunder in watered regions even when they had no hope of making permanent conquests. It has already been noted that the word *ba'l* is a loan word in Arabic, and this perhaps indicates that some tribes of the Arabs learned the practice of *ba'al* marriage from their cousins in Syria. The Hebrews, who were not the first Semitic conquerors of Canaan, and had gone through many vicissitudes in various lands, were perhaps already constituted in tribes of male descent before they fell upon the Amorites; the metronymic tribes of Leah and Rachel belong to a remoter period, and the traditions of *beena* marriage are also referred to a time long before the conquest of Canaan. [13]

[1] [On the article in question, and the theory in general, see J. Jacobs, *Studies in Biblical Archeology* (London, 1894), pp. 64 *sqq.*; G. B. Gray, *Studies in Hebrew Proper Names* (London, 1896), pp. 86 *sqq.*; cp. also Zapletal, *Der Totemismus* (Freiburg, i. S., 1901), pp. 29 *sqq.*; S. A. Cook, *Jewish Quarterly Review*, 1902, p. 416 *sq.*; *Lévy, Rev. Ét. Juives*, 1902, pp. 13-26.]

[2] [But see Nöldeke, *ZDMG* 40 185.]

[3] Hoffman, *Syr. Acten Pers. Märt.* p. 137, corrects the name of the father of Bardesanes in Barhebraeus, *Chron. Eccl.* 1 47, from ܐܚܐ ܢܘܢܐ to ܢܘܢܐܡ ܐܚܐ, "my fish is [his] mother," observing that *nūnā* is here feminine because the fish is the goddess Atargatis. This correction, if accepted, clinches the connection between names like Bar Kalbā on the one hand and Bar Ba'shmīn on the other. The name of Bar Daisān is said by Barhebraeus to be taken from the river Daisān, because he was born on its bank.

[4] See *Additional Note* F.

[5] For Ešmun-Iolaos and the quail, see Gruppe, *Culte u. Mythen*, I. p. 380 *sq.* [and *RS* 469].

[6] [See *RS* 236, 379 *sqq.*]

[7] Sacrifices and offerings of this type are not confined to Arabia (for which cp. Sprenger, *Leb. Moh.* 3 457 *sq.*, Wellh. Heid. (1) 115, (2) 118, and Ch. 2, above), but are attested also among the northern Semites. See, for the Phoenicians, Philo Byb. *ap. Eus. Praep. Ev.* i. 10 8 (*Fr. Hist. Gr.* 3 566); and for the Hebrews, i Sam. 14 34 *sq.* compared with 2 Sam. 23 16 *sq.* The oil poured by Jacob on the stone at Bethel is an offering of the same class; comp. Judges 9 9.

[8] So later in Arabic magical formulas: Nöldeke, "Das arab, Märchen vom Doctor und Garkoch" in the *Abhandl. d, Königl. Akad. d. Wissensch.* (Berlin, 1891), p. 33 [and Goldziher, *ZDMG* 48 360]; and in Syriac, Cambridge Univ. Library, Add. 1167, ܘܩܠܒܐ ܚܙ ܦܟܕܡܐ (Wright, *Syriac Catalogue*, p. 6). [Also in later Jewish

magic (L. Blau, *Altjüd. Zauberwesen,* 85); and in Latin and Greek curse-tablets *Rhein. Mus. f. Phil.,* 1900, p. 263 *sq.* - I. G.]

[9] [See the *English Hist. Review,* Jan. 1899, pp. 94-104, reprinted in *Studies in Ancient History, second* series, ch. vi.]

[10] It is important to observe that Ibn Al-Mojāwir relates of the B. Hārith, the tribe which buried a dead gazelle with the same formalities and lamentations as if it had been a kinsman [*RS* 444], that they refused to eat or drink at the hand of a woman, and would rather have died of hunger and thirst than break this rule. For such a custom seems to point to a time when the men and women were not allowed to eat the same food, and in totemism with exogamy a man and his wife must always have different laws of forbidden food.

[11] [Sir George Grey, *Journals of Two Expeditions of Discovery in NorthWest and Western Australia,* vol. ii. chap. xi. p. 225 *sqq.*]

[12] That different classes of society should have different marriage laws is easily understood, and as the condition for the rise of male kinship, whether through Tibetan polyandry or otherwise, is a system of marriage in which the wife is under dominion, it is easy to understand that in an advanced society like that of Yemen, where there were well-marked social grades, the upper classes who could afford to buy women, or the military classes who had opportunities of capture, might be the first to develop Tibetan polyandry. In Africa we find cases in which a man has one "Bossum" wife whose children are his, but may have other wives whose children belong to their mothers' people. So in the case recorded by Strabo, the family of chiefs who had one "Bossum" wife between them to keep up their stock in the male line may very probably have had Nair connections with other women. In Rowlandson's translation of the *Tohfat al-Mojāhidīn,* p. 63, we read: "With regard to the marriage of the Brahmins, when there are several brothers in one family, the eldest of them alone enters into the conjugal state, the remainder refraining from marriage, in order that heirs may not multiply to the confusion of inheritance. The younger brothers, however, intermarry with women of the Nair caste without entering into any compact with them, thus following the custom of the Nairs, who have themselves no conjugal compact." That is, the younger brothers join a polyandrous society in which female kinship is the rule, and "in the event of any children being born from these connections, they are excluded from the inheritance." In a somewhat ruder state of society all the brothers would share the one wife, but at the same time might practise Nair polyandry.

[13] See *Additional Note* G.

Additional Notes

Additional Note A - The Affinities of the Codā'a

As the question of the affinities of the Codā'a has an important bearing on the most interesting period of Arab history, I propose in this note to enter into some further details, and in doing so to clear up an obscure passage in Tebrīzī's commentary on the *Hāmasa,* which will then help us to understand the relations between Kalb and Tamīm on which Jarīr and Al-Farazdac lay so much weight.

The proof passages for reckoning Codā'a as Ma'addite may easily be multiplied; see, for example, Ibn Khallikān, no. 595, and Ibn Hishām, p. 7, who makes Codā'a the eldest son of Ma' add, from whom he has his *konya* of Abū Codā'a. Bakrī, in the dissertation on the migrations of the Arab tribes which stands at the head of his geographical dictionary, goes at great length into the movements of the Codā'a, throughout assuming that they are Ma'addite, and quotes verses which show that the various tribes of Codā'a called themselves so (from Mofadd, 32 8; see Goldziher, *Muh. Stud.* 1 91). Thus Balī and Bahrā are of Ma' add (Bakri, p. 19 *sq.*; the same verses are in Yācūt, 4387, which I mention in order to point out that in Yācūt's remark on them, ibid, line 8,

ـﺴﻌﺪ must be corrected into ﻗﻌﺪ; for ﻗﻌﺪ see 'Āmr, *Mo'all.* 40). Again, Bahrā and Kalb are called Ma'addite in verses quoted by Bakrī, p. 56, and Yācūt, 4 129. When, however, one finds that Ghassān is also reckoned to Ma'add in Yācūt's form of these verses, and that Bakrī, pp. 13, 37, records that Sakūn and Sakāsik, and indeed the Kinda generally, were sometimes called sons of Ma'add, one begins to ask whether Ma'add had any definite meaning, or whether he was not, as he is sometimes called, "the father of the Arabs" generally; just as the prophet uses "sons of Ishmael" in so wide a sense that some thought it necessary to hold that all Cahtān was Ishmaelite (*Kāmil,* p. 264). This, however, is not so; in the time of Justinian, Maaddeni and Homeritae were distinct, and the latter gave sovereigns to the former (Procop, ed. Dind. 1 100, 106), so that Arab tradition is right in speaking of the old enmity, and of the wars in which Ma'add strove to throw off the Himyarite yoke. In like manner we learn from Nonnosus that at this time Ma'add and Kinda were distinct, and there seems no reason to doubt that at least the princely houses of Ghassān and Kinda were of Yemenite origin. But in the time of Justinian these distinctions were rather national and geographical than genealogical. One can gather from Nonnosus, comparing him with Procopius, and with the Arabic accounts which make the region of Batn Marr near Mecca the original centre of the Ma'addite Arabs, that Ma'add must have been practically the group of tribes which already had a religious (and trading) centre at Mecca, and whose mutual feuds were at least softened by the institution of the

149

months when war was forbidden. Now the Sakun and Sakasik are connected by Bakrī with the seats of the Kindites in this district at Ghamr dhū Kinda, and so their local connections were all with Ma'add. Indeed, the Kindite princes who ruled in Ma'add seem at length to have reckoned themselves to that nation and not to the Yemenites, as in a verse of Imrau 'l-Cais (Ahlwardt, no. 44, 1. 3), where indeed, as in other cases where Ma'add is mentioned in old poetry. there is a variant avoiding the word. Ghassān was dependent on Rome up to the time of Islam, and probably could not have been called Maaddite by any one till Islam, but it had close associations with Codā'a, and at the battle of Marj Rahit (a.h. 64) Ghassān Sakūn and Sakāsik all fought alongside of Kalb against Cais.

From all this it seems pretty plain that in old times Ma'add was not a genealogical term at all; it became so because tribes organised on the principle of blood-feud seek to establish real or fictitious bonds of blood to cement every political alliance, and thus all traditions of political alliance were ultimately translated into the language of kinship. But that Codā'a belonged to the Ma'addite alliance — primarily an alliance against Himyar — in very ancient times, can be still shown from the series of poems referring to the battle of Al-Baida preserved in the Hamāsa, pp. 162 sqq., and illustrated by a tradition, referred to Abū Riyāsh, which Freytag has totally misunderstood, but which can still be made intelligible and yields very interesting results. To make it intelligible we must read ‏سعد‎ for ‏سعد‎ (as in the passage of Yācūt already amended) in three places, p. 164, I. 25 (to agree with 165, 1. 2), ibid. 1. 26 ('Abd Manāt is a tribe of Kalb, and this, says our author, is not inconsistent with the fact that it is Ma'addite, for Codā'a was then referred to Ma' add and only became Yemenite later) and ibid. I. 28 (where we must also omit ‏وهم‎, repeated from the preceding word, and put ‏معانة‎ for ‏معاوية‎ after 'Tabarī, i. 1111 2, "The Sa'd Hodhaim are a tribe of the sons of Ma'add and Mo'āna, their father being Sohār or Sa'd Hodhaim of the race of Codā'a [Tab. ut sup. 1. 4] and their mother 'Ātika bint Morr b. Odd "). [1] But again, in 11. 25, 26 the explanation that the 'Abd Manāt are the Ribāb or allied tribes of Taim 'Adi and 'Okl is a gloss, representing a later state of things than that contemplated in the verses, for in them Taim is still only the ally of Kalb or 'Abd Manāt and not completely fused with them. The gloss would give us two Taims, one an ally of 'Abd Manāt and one a part of that tribe, which is wrong. Really the old allies did not become one tribe till later. Further, in p. 165, 1. 6 the distinction between Kalb and 'Abd Manāt seems to be a gloss; the 'Abd Manāt were Kalb by Abū Riyāsh's own account, and it is not clear that any other Kalb were engaged. These confusions have reacted on the opinions of the commentator on the authorship of the verses; the first of the four poems, as Rückert saw, is by a man of Kalb, not by a Himyarite (though of course Kalb is Himyarite according to the later view); so also is the third, while the second and fourth are spoken by the Taim.

I now proceed to the story as it comes out with these corrections. The allied Maʻaddite tribes of Taim b. Morr, ʻAbd Manāt (a branch of Kalb) and Sohār leave their seats under pressure of famine and go foraging into Yemen. The Sohar have a brush with the Himyarite natives, and knowing that the blood they have shed will call for vengeance, retreat into Maʻaddite country. The ʻAbd Manāt, who being Kalbites are of Codāʻa and near of kin to the Sohar, are now left to bear the brunt of the bloodfeud with Himyar, but they are gallantly helped by their allies the Taim and gain a great victory at Al-Baidā. But (p. 168) the Himyarites again assemble and utterly defeat the Taim, slaying and taking captives, who languish in Saba' till, in answer to their appeal, the Tamīm send an army to their deliverance under the chieftains Al-Namir and Al-Adbat. From the verses quoted to illustrate this last part of the story it appears that the appeal and deliverance of the captive Taimites was part of the traditions of Tamīm (Jarīr, Al-Farazdac) and the Ribāb (Dhu 'l-Romma), and that the chieftains who led Tamīm to Yemen were looked on as their earliest national heroes. Hut why are the Tamīm the natural helpers of the Taim? The reason is that the Taim are simply a fraction of the Tamīm who have attached themselves by alliance to the Kalb. For, in the first place, they are Taim b. Morr and Tamīm is Tamīm b. Morr. Again Jarīr makes the Ribāb, *i.e.* the confederation of which, in later times at least, Taim was the leading member, one of the four great houses of Tamīm (the Ribāb, Saʻd, ʻAmr, Hanzala, *Agh.* 16 117; see also *Kāmil,* 248 7). Further, Ibn Habīb says (*Agh.* 18 163) that all the Tamīm were called ʻAbd Taim and that Taim was their idol. This of course is a confusion; Taim is not a god-name, but means "worshipper of" a god. Moslem scrupulosity drops the god-name and thus at length Taim comes to be misunderstood. What does appear is that Tamīm were also called Taim-.i", worshippers of a god whose name we no longer know. Such names, formed from the tribal religion, were naturally used to distinguish members of confederations; the Taim and the ʻAbd Manāt among the Ribāb are distinguished by their worship like the Taim Al-Lāt and Aus Manāt at Medina. Thus the allies who fought at Al-Baidā under the name of the Ribāb were a section of the Kalb and a section of the Tamīm. Their alliance proved permanent, and the two groups were gradually so far merged together that finally all the Ribab, whether Kalbite or Tamīmite, were cither reckoned to Tamīm (Jarīr), or at least esteemed near kinsmen of Tamīm and so separated from Kalb. This alliance of Kalb and Tamīm on the very threshold of the history of the Northern Arabs enables us to understand the weight which the poets of Tamīm, Jarīr and Al-Farazdac, attach to the ancient friendship of these two tribes (*Agh.* 19 25, 44 *sq.*). "Tamīm to Kalb and Kalb to them are truer and closer than Sadā (Madhhij) to Ilimyar"; "No two *hayys* were united by stronger bonds than Tamīm and Kalb, and no Codaite had aught to fear among us, though the cauldrons of war were boiling over." Plainly this account of the battle of Al-Baidā and its consequences rests on old tribal tradition; and it is also confirmed by the name of the "castle of Al-Adbat" and the traditions connected with it (Yāc. 1 311).

But now to our surprise we find that over against the tradition of Abū Riyāsh in Al-Basra there stands a totally different account of the battle of Al-Baida preserved in the 'led, 3 93, and by Nowairī, on the authority of the great genealogist of Kufa, Hishām b. Mohammed Al-Kalbī, in which the leader of the Ma'addites against Himyar is a hero of Cais-'Ailan, — that mythical or semi-mythical 'Āmir b. al-Zarib who is hardly different from the "Amalekite" 'Āmr b. al-Zarib, the fabled father of Zebbā or Zenobia (Tab. 1 756). This version stands quite alone, and has no verses or collateral tradition to support it. But Al-Kalbī naturally followed the later genealogy of his own tribe, and could not make their history begin with a war against their new allies and supposed brethren of Himyar. He therefore puts their enemies of Cais in their place.

There are still one or two points about the relations of the Codā'a which are worth looking at as illustrations of the way in which the genealogists manipulate facts. In Abū Riyāsh's tradition the allied tribes of Ma'add are Tamīm, Kalb, and Sohār or Sa'd Hodhaim. Kalb and Sohār are brothers (both being of Codā'a), Tamīm and Kalb are allies (Ribāb). The later genealogists were not ignorant of this close connection, but when they separated Kalb from Ma'add they could express it only as a relationship through women. So 'Ātika mother of Sohār becomes the sister of Tamīm. Conversely Hauab daughter of Kalb b. Wabara is mother of Tamīm and all his brethren (Yācūt, 2 352) whom she bears to Morr b. Odd, and in *Agh.* 8 179 the 'Āmila, a branch of 'Abd Manāt, are said to be so called from their mother, a woman of Codā'a.

But the close connection of the Kalb with the Tamīm and their brethren comes out in yet another way. The Sfrandfather of Tamīm and 'Abd Manāt is Odd. Now the Arabs themselves knew that Odd or Idd is only a phonetic variant of Wodd or Wadd, the god of the Kalb (Yācūt, 4 912 *sq.*; Ibn Doraid in *Tāj,* 2 292; Krehl, p. 62). The worship of Wodd among the Kalb was official, for the custody of the god belonged to the princely house (Bakrī, p. 34). When Tamīm and 'Abd Manāt are made sons ot Odd they too are made sharers in this tribal religion. The 'Anbar, a branch of Tamīm, are also said by some genealogists to be really of Bahrā and so Codaites, *Kāmil,* p. 264 *sq.*

[1] [But see Nöldeke, *ZDMG* 40 186.]

Additional Note B - The Marriage of Khadija

In the text I have tried to give such an account of Khadīja's marriage and property as is consistent with the traditions accepted by the leading authorities. But it is only necessary to read the mass of contradictory traditions brought together by Sprenger, *Leb. Moh.* 1 194 *sqq.* (with which may now be compared Tabarī, 1 1127 *sqq.* to see that very little was known about Khadīja, and that what was known was in part deliberately falsified. Thus as regards her marriage, Wācidī, cited by Tabarī, 1 1129, prefers the tradition that Khadīja's hand was given away by her father in his cups; but another tradition from Ibn 'Abbas through 'Ikrima says that her father was dead and that she was given away by her uncle. Have we any right to build on either tradition? Khadīja had been twice married before, and this fact, if we may accept the statement in the last sentence quoted from Tabarī in Ch. 3 of the present work, would have made it possible for her to acquire the right of disposing of her own hand. But the discrepancies in the tradition seem to show that there was something about Mohammed's marriage that it was thought decorous to conceal; perhaps too there was something not very creditable about the way in which she had acquired her property, which is also left obscure. The emphasis laid on her nobility of birth, which, combined with her great wealth, made her hand to be sought by all men, is suspicious; if she was so desirable a match, it seems strange that one of her former husbands, Zorāra the Tamīmite, by whom she had a son, was alive as late as the battle of Badr. An Arab is slow to divorce a rich and noble woman by whom he has a son. And indeed Mohammed's marriage with the woman he served does not look like a *ba'al* marriage at all; it can hardly have been of his free will that a man of such strong passions had no other wife as long as "the old woman" lived. Khadīja's mother Fatima was of the Banū 'Āmir b. Loayy, and these seem to be the same Banū 'Āmir whose women still contracted mot' a marriages at Mecca in the first years of Islam (Wilken, *Matriarchaat,* p. 10; at p. 16 Wilken suggests that the 'Āmir b. Sa'sa'a are meant, but that is less likely, as the latter were not a Meccan clan). If *mot'a* marriage was common among the Banū 'Āmir, it is possible that Khadija was herself the offspring of such a marriage, and had been brought up with her mother's people to follow their customs. This would account for her independence and property, but would indicate that her social position was low. (It may perhaps be noticed that in B. Hish. p. 100, a woman offers a hundred camels for marriage (?) with Abdallah b. Abd-al-Mottalib (Tab. i. 1078 8). But the story has circumstances which make it worthless as evidence.)

Additional Note C - Female Infanticide

The practice of infanticide is spoken of and condemned by the prophet in several places (Sūr. 6 141, 152, 17 33, 81 8). The motive which he assigns is poverty: the parents were afraid that they could not find food for all their offspring. Other authorities say that the motive was pride, the parents being afraid that their daughters might be taken captive and so bring disgrace on their kin. These two motives would hardly come into operation together, and the details of the evidence appear to show that they belong to distinct varieties of the practice. According to *Agh.* 12 150, the murder of female children for fear of disgrace began with a chieftain of Tamīm, *viz.* Cais b. 'Āsim the Sa'dite, a contemporary of the prophet. Moshamraj the Yashkorite had made a foray on the Sa'd and carried off, among other women, the daughter of a sister of Cais, who was assigned to the son of her captor and, when Cais appeared to ransom her, declined to leave her husband. Cais was so indignant that he killed all his girls by burying them alive and never again allowed a daughter to live. One daughter born in his absence was sent by the mother to her own kin, and on Cais's return he was told by his wife that she had been delivered of a dead child. Years passed on till the girl grew up, and came one day to visit her mother. "I came in," so Cais himself told Mohammed, "and saw the girl; her mother had plaited her hair, and put rings in the side-locks, and strung them with sea-shells and put on her a chain of cowries, and given her a necklace of dried dates. I said, 'Who is this pretty girl?' and her mother wept and said, 'She is your daughter,' and told me how she had saved her alive; so I waited till the mother ceased to be anxious about her; then I led her out one day and dug a grave and laid her in it, she crying, 'Father, what are you doing with me?' Then I covered her up with the earth, and she still cried, 'Father, are you going to bury me? are you going to leave me alone and go away?' but I went on filling in the earth till I could hear her cries no longer; and that is the only time that I felt pity when I buried a daughter." Cais's example, says our author, found imitators, till every chief destroyed his daughters for fear they might cause him shame.

It is plain that the murder of a daughter under the circumstances described in this horrible story is altogether different from the ordinary type of infanticide in savage nations, which is practised on new-born infants. The Arabic accounts, therefore, are correct in representing Cais as an innovator, but not in making him the inventor of child-murder. Maidanī (Fr. *Ar. Pr.* 2 16) cites authority to show that the practice had once been general, but before the time of the prophet had nearly gone out, except among the Tamīm. But among them it was not confined to great chiefs like Cais; Al Farazdac's grandfather Sa'sa'a, a contemporary of Cais, was honourably distinguished for his efforts to put down the practice (Nowairī in Rasmussen, p. 66 *sq. Kāmil,* pp. 276 *sqq. Agh.* 19 2 *sq.*) [1] by buying from the fathers the life of their children. This points to penury as the real cause of the custom, as the Coran says; and as regards most cases, the *Kāmil* is probably right in saying that pride and the fear of disgrace were mere pretexts. The prevalence of infanticide at the prophet's time among the Tamīm and their neighbours, or, according to other authorities, among the Tamīm, Cais, Asad, Hodhail, and Bakr-Wāil, is connected by the *Kāmil* with a terrible seven years' drought, and such an occurrence might well give new life to an ancient usage which was already beginning to offend the more advanced minds. But infanticide was not a new thing, nor was it limited to one group of tribes; the mother of 'Āmr b. Kolthūm, daughter of Mohalhil the Taghlibite, was sentenced by her father to be destroyed but saved by her mother (*Agh.* 9 182). This must have been about A.D. 500, or earlier; and more than a century later, Mohammed, when he took Mecca and received the homage of the women in the most advanced centre of Arabian civilisation, still deemed it necessary formally to demand from them a promise not to commit child-murder (Ibn al-Athīr, Būl. ed., 2 105). In Arabia, as among other barbarous peoples, child-murder was carried out in such a way that no blood was shed: the infant was buried alive, and often, if we may believe Zamakhsharī on Sūr. 81 8, the grave was ready by the side of the bed on which the daughter was born. The same authority says that girls were sometimes spared till the age of six, and then adorned and led forth by their father and cast into a pit in the wilderness. This, however, seems to be rather a kind of human sacrifice, such as we know the Arabs to have practised, for the father said to the mother, "Dress her up that I may bring her to her mothers" (so Pococke, *Spec.,* ed. White, p. 324; the Calcutta ed. has

احمائها for اماتیها, which must be wrong), *i.e.* to the goddesses or *Banāt allāh.* [See further, *RS* p. 370, n. 3.]

According to the proverb (Fr. Ar. Pr. 1 229), to bury a daughter was regarded not only as a virtuous but as a generous deed, which is intelligible if the reason was that there would be fewer mouths to fill in the tribe. And so in *Hamāsa,* p. 4, we find that 'Osaim the Fazarite did not dare to save alive his daughter Lacīta, without concealing her from his people, although she was his only child. This implies that the custom, was very deeply rooted indeed.

As to the extent to which child-murder was practised as late as the time of the prophet, we have some evidence in the fact that Sa'sa'a claimed to have saved a hundred and eighty daughters (*Kāmil,* p. 679). A detail in this story shows a curious connection between child-murder and the law of inheritance: a father says, "if it is a colt we will make it partner in our wealth, but if it is a filly we will bury it." The same connection occurs in a tradition of Ibn 'Abbās (*Kāmil,* 678 15), who, in explaining what the Coran says about child-murder, adds that no inheritance or share was given except to warriors. It is not easy to see the connection unless we can suppose that at one time among the Arabs, as in some African tribes, the sons were of the father's kin and the daughters of the mother's. Then it would be at once intelligible why they have no share in the inheritance, and why the tribesmen have no objection to their death, but rather desire it. The father, however, seems usually not to have killed the daughter himself, but to have bidden the mother do so. This appears in the story of 'Āmr's mother, in Zamakhsharī's account, and in the prophet's charge to the women of Mecca, and is perhaps an indication that the custom took shape before the rise of paternity.

Indeed, that the pressure of famine had far more to do with the origin of infanticide than family pride had, can be doubtful to no one who realises the fact— vividly brought out in Mr. Doughty's travels — that the nomads of Arabia suffer constantly from hunger during a great part of the year. [2] The only persons who have enough to eat are great men, and these it was who, following Cais's precedent, gave pride as the reason for killing their daughters. To the poorer sort a daughter was a burden, and infanticide was as natural to them as to other savage peoples in the hard struggle for life. The Arabs, like most savages, seem to have been driven to practise other checks to the growth of population. It appears from the traditions that the عزل was not confined to the case of captive women (*Sharh al-mowatta'*, 3 77 *sq.*) The objection of the Arabs to the غيلة (intercourse with a nursing mother, *Kāmil*, p. 79), which was supposed to hurt the suckling, may have similar connections, and would at any rate afford an additional motive for infanticide.

A word may be said in conclusion as to Wilken's conjecture that the wars of the Arabs would tend to an excess of females over males. It is so in modern Arabic warfare, in which women are treated as sacred. But this is not old law, for it was Mohammed who forbade the killing of women and children. The wars of the old Arabs were of two kinds, plundering excursions and wars of revenge. In a plundering excursion, of old as in the present day, not much blood was shed, the object being rather to take prisoners. Of course women were captured oftener than men, but we see from the Hodhalite poems that these captives were often simply taken to the slave-market of some such trading-place as Mecca and sold out of the country. According to Wellh. *Moh. in Med.* p. 221, there were centres of the export slave-trade at Medina, Taimā, and Khaibar, and the operation of this trade must have been to increase the scarcity of women, especially in the weaker tribes. Sometimes all the women of a settlement were surprised in their men's absence, and many stories show that a chief point of strategy was to save the women and children.

In a war of revenge every male was slain who could be reached, but here again the custom of selling the women into foreign slavery would prevent any great inequality of the sexes from arising. In the older wars women went into battle with the warriors of the tribe, an antique custom which was revived by the Meccans at Ohod, and in the heat of the fray no distinction of sex would be observed. We must think of the earliest Arabs as pure savages; the women followed the warriors, despatching and mutilating the fallen, and Hind at the battle of Ohod made herself a necklace and anklets of the noses and ears of Moslems and even gnawed the liver of her arch-enemy Hamza. When this was so women certainly would not be spared in hot blood, and even captives must at one time have often been slain. In truth the early Arabs were not only savages but cannibals. In later poetry the expression of a desire to drink an enemy's blood is a figure of speech, but Ammianus, 31 16, relates an actual case. Procopius, *Bell. Pers.* 1 19, speaks only of anthropophagous Saracens in remote parts, as indeed the Arabs of the Hijāz still accuse distant tribes of drinking their enemies' blood. But such accusations are rather reminiscences of obsolete practices than pure inventions; [3] in *Agh.* xvi. 50 14 Yazīd the Blood-drinker (*shārib al-dimā*) appears as a chief of the Tayyi. Another reminiscence of cannibal times is the vow of a mother to drink wine from the skull of the slayer of her son (Ibn Hishām, 567 14 = *Agh.* iv. 41 22).

Actual cannibalism under pressure of hunger appears in *Diw. Hodh.* no. clxi. *sqq.* In the state of society to which these indications point, female captives would hardly have been spared at all unless women were usually scarce.

[1] In *Agh.* xix. 3 i it appears that this had never been done before. The father's motive is expressly said to be poverty.
[2] [*Travels in Arabia Deserta* (Cambridge, 1888); see Index, *s.v.* "Hunger."] On the foods used in famine, including dried blood, *'ilhiz,* see Yāc. 3 474.
[3] [Khālid b. Ja'far licked the brains that clung to the sword with which he had cleft the head of Zohair b. Jadhīma (*Agh.* x. 17 5). According to Ibn Batūta, 1 285, at Medina they licked the blood of the man who had been killed in blood-revenge (*la'acū damahu*). For other examples see Jacob, *Altarab. Beduinenleben* (1895), 90, n. 2, and Goldziher, "Ueber Kannibalismus aus orientalischen Quellen," *Globus,* 70, no. 15 (1896). On the practice of cannibalism for superstitious and medical reasons see Ousāma ed. Derenbourg, 24 19, Ta'rīkh al-Sūdān, ed. Houdas, 48, 'Alī Mobārak, *Khitat,* vi. p. 2. — I. G.]

Additional Note D - Notes on Polyandry

Eusebius mentions γαμεταί and θυγατέρες without distinguishing the cases. His allusion to the connection with Astarte worship is not so precise as to justify me in saying that the licence was only at the temple. It seems to be real polandry as in the Syro-Roman law-book. According to Socrates (*HE* 1 18) wives were common (polandry), and also τας παρθένους τοῖς παριοῦσι ξένοις παρεῖχον πορνεύεσθαι. The prostitution of maidens to *strangers only* was also the rite at Byblus (Lucian, *Dea Syr,* 6), Babylon (Herod. 1 199), and apparently also Cyprus (Justin, 18 5). Barhebraeus repeats only the first half of Socrates' statement.

Sozomen (v. 10 7, p. 194) remarks that the cruelty practised under Julian on the holy virgins of Heliopolis probably took place because it had been forbidden καθὸ πάτριον αὐτοῖς πρότερον, ἐκπορνεύεσθαι παρὰ τοῦ προστυχόντος τὰς ἐνθάδε παρθένους, πρὶν τοῖς μνηστῆρσι συνελθεῖν εἰς γάμον, and connects this prohibition by Constantine with the destruction of the temple of Aphrodite. Elsewhere (i. 8 6, p. 18) he says that Constantine forbade the Phoenicians of the Lebanon and Heliopolis to practise prostitution of maidens πρὶν τοῖς ἀνδράσι συνελθεῖν, οἷς νομίμῳ γάμῳ συνοικεῖν εἰώθεσαν, μετὰ τὴν πρώτην πεῖραν τῆς ἀθεμίτου μίξεως. The statement of Ploss (*Das Weib,* 2nd ed. 1 302) concerning the Phoenician custom on the authority of Athanasius seems to rest upon a misunderstanding of the passage in *Contra Gentes,* 20, which gives only the usual Christian statements.

[With the קְדֵשׁוֹת may be connected *CIS* 1, nos. 253, 256, where the temple-slaves have the name of their mother but not that of the father, עבדשת is a man in no. 279, but certainly feminine in no. 385 (עב]לשת) if correctly restored, and there is some doubt, therefore, whether the parent in no. 256 is a man or a woman. In no. 378 the daughter is styled the "handmaid of the gods" (אמתאלהׄ); [1] her name is אבבעל ("father [is] Baal"), and that of her mother is גדנעמׄ[ת]. In all these instances the worship is that of תנת who is rendered Artemis in no. 116 (עבדתדת = Ἀρτεμίδωρος = *virgo celestis,* but nevertheless is called "mother" (אם) in Nos. 195, 380 (*Rel. Sem.* p. 56 n. 2).] [2]

[1] Cp. the name Amat-Šamaš, who is designated the servant of Šamaš, in an old Babylonian contract of the time of Samsu-satana (*Keilschrift. Bibliothek,* 4 43, no. 2; cp. also Meissner, Beitr. z. altbab. Frivatreckt, no. 16).
[2] In *CIS* no. 251 *sq.* the parentage is uncertain, but in nos. 247-250, 254, the father's name is given.

Additional Note E - Mother and Son as Associated Deities

Among the Nabataeans Al-Lāt is "the mother of the gods "; to them therefore, as to the Arabs of Herodotus, to the people of Tāif in the time of the prophet, to the Taim Al-Lāt in Medina and other tribes in various parts of Arabia, she was the great goddess, the Rabba, as she was called at Tāif. When therefore Epiphanius describes the annual feast at the old Nabataean capital of Petra, the virgin or unmarried mother of the great Nabataian male god Dusares or Dhu 'l-Sharā can be no other than a form of Al-Lāt. [1] The name Χααβοῦ, which Epiphanius gives to her, has been discussed by Mordtmann and Rösch (*ZDMG* 29 99 *sqq.,* 38 643 *sq.*), and the latter has seen that the word must be identical with *ka'b, ka'ba,* "a die or cube," such a form as the Ka'ba or "four-square house" at Mecca. [2] Now Suidas tells us that at Petra Dusares was worshiped in the shape of a four-square stele, and hence Rosch thinks that Epiphanius gives the name of the image of the god to his mother. This, however, is not so. Al-Lāt's image at Tāif was a four-square white rock, still pointed out in Mohammedan times under the mosque (Yācūt, 4 337; Cazwlni, 2 65), presumably that mass of white granite, now shattered with gunpowder and shapeless, which lies beyond the walls, below the great mosque to the S.W. My guide called this stone Al-'Ozzā, and gave the name of Al-Lāt to a rounded mass, rising from the summit of the more southerly of the two eminences within the town, and now partly buried in rubbish; but the stone outside the town was shown as Al-Lāt to Hamilton and Doughty. In like manner De Vogüé found at Salkhat a square stele dedicated to Al-Lāt, just as a similar stele with an inscription published by him was dedicated to Dusares. We conclude then that there were two such stones, half idol, half altar, at Petra. Indeed a stone (*nosb, massēba*) in which the god or goddess was supposed to live — so it is put in the accounts of Al-Lāt at Tāif [3] — was the usual idol of an Arab sanctuary, beside which the sacrificial blood was poured out, or under which, at Dumat al-Jandal, a boy was yearly buried (Porph. *de Abst.* 2 56).

The Nabataean worship at Petra is therefore the worship of an unmarried goddess and her son, each being represented under the form of a block of stone squared. The same worship of two deities is attested elsewhere in the Nabatajan region. In Numb. 33 13 Alush is rendered by Al-Wathanain, "the two idols," in the Arabic version published by Lagarde, the translator probably thinking of the shrine at Elusa, of which we shall have more to say presently (*ZDMG* 25 566); and Mordtmann has recently shown from inscriptions that Al-Sanamain in the Haurān bears its name of "the two images" from the worship of Fortune (τύχη) and Zeus (*ibid.* 39 44; cp. Wadd. 2413 *f-k*). [4] So too in Herodotus 3 8 the worship of Al-Lāt (Alilat) is associated with that of a male deity Orotal whom the historian identifies with Dionysus. [5]

Further insight into the nature of the worship of the Nabatcean supreme goddess is obtained from what Jerome, in the life of S. Hilarion, c. 25, tells of the festival of Venus at Elusa in the wilderness of Kadesh. According to Epiphanius this feast was held on the same night as that at Petra, and his words imply that here also the worship was that of a mother and child. Jerome too says that Venus was worshipped at Elusa "*ob Luciferum cuius cultui Saracenorum natio dedita est.*" The expression "*ob Luciferum*" is strange, but certainly implies a connection between the Venus of Elusa and the Lucifer whom he again names as a god of the Saracens in his commentary on Amos 5. Let us consider who Venus and Lucifer are. The Arabic goddess usually identified with Venus is Al-'Ozzā. [6] Thus Procopius tells us that Al-Mondhir sacrificed a captive to Aphrodite, while a Syrian historian tells us of his human sacrifices to Al-'Ozzā (Nöldeke, *Gesch. d. Perser u. Araber,* p. 171; comp. Isaac of Antioch, 1 210, 220). The Westerns also persistently believed that the worship at Mecca was Aphrodite-worship. The ground for this seems to have been twofold; on the one hand the great Arabian goddess was identified with the planet Venus (Ephr. Syr. *Opp. Syr.* 2 457; Is. Ant. 1 246), and on the other hand her rites resembled the obscene worship of the Oriental Aphrodite (Ashtorcth). She was, according to Ephraim, represented as forming polyandroiis relations (*ut sup.* p. 458; compare for the conception of the planet Venus as an unmarried goddess her name ﮐﻮﮐﺐ = Κόρη, Hoffm. *Pers. Märt.* p. 129), and therefore at her festivals women were allowed to prostitute themselves (p. 459). [7] The astral element in these practices may be, as Ephraim supposes, Chaldean, and the practices themselves were common enough at Syrian shrines, *e.g.* at Baalbek; but it is clear that the Arabian ritual was similar, indeed Barhebra.nis on Ps. 12 9 speaks of the obscene feasts of the Edomites (Nabataeans?) where the women made a sevenfold circuit, as at Arabian shrines, round an image of Beltis or Aphrodite on the top of a Palestinian mountain and then practised promiscuous uncleanness. According to Tuch the Venus of Elusa was the goddess Al-Khalasa or Al-Kholosa (*ZDMG* 3 193 *sq.*), [8] whose worship reappears at Tabāla in Yemen. And here also there was, according to a tradition of the prophet in Yācūt, ii. 462 24, a feast thronged by the women of the Daus. The difference of name between the goddesses at different seats of Venus-worship is of no importance; Al-Lāt and Al-'Ozzā are merely titles, and Al-'Ozzā, "the mighty goddess," must be the highest title of a female deity and not different from the mother of the gods. We see from Ephraim's explanation of her character that a single male god associated with her could only be her son. She had no husband, and therefore, as Epiphanius represents her, was an unmarried though not a chaste deity. But what now is the relation of Jerome's Lucifer to Epiphanius's Dusares? They ought to be the same, for to Epiphanius the worship of Χααβοῦ and Dusares at Petra is identical with that of Venus-Khalasa and Lucifer at Elusa. And so the Dausites, who according to Yācūt worshipped Khalasa at Tabāla, were also, according to Ibn Hishām, p. 253, worshippers of Dhu 'l-Sharā or Dusares. [9] And this is confirmed by various arguments. Mordtmann (*ZDMG* 32 565), following Lagarde, *Ges. Abh.* p. 16, has shown that Lucifer is a title of the god Azizus, *i.e.* 'Aziz, the masculine counterpart of 'Ozzā, who was worshipped at Edessa in the time of Julian, but was, as his name shows, an Arabian divinity, many Arabs having already settled in that region. In various Dacian inscriptions 'Azīz appears with the titles *bonus puer posphorus* (sic) *Apollo Pythius*. [10] As Phosphorus he is Jerome's Lucifer, as *puer* he is Epiphanius's divine child Dusares, and finally as Apollo Pythius he is an archer-god. The Arabian archer-god, whose bolts are lightnings and his bow the rainbow, is Cozah (Tuch, *ut supr.* p. 200), who was the god of the Idumaeans (Jos. *Arch.* xv. 7 9) and has been plausibly identified with the Idumaean Apollo (Jos. c. *Ap.* 2 10). But Dhu 'l-Sharā is most easily taken as meaning the lightning-god, and thus seems to be only an epithet of the widespread Cozah. In the case of 'Aziz, Dhu 'l-Sharā, Cozah, all genuinely Arabic, it is pretty clear that the conception of the lightning -god is older than his association with the star Phosphorus. His mother also, very probably, was not originally planetary; and certainly the cultus and attributes are much more easily derived from a general prevalence of ancient polyandry than from a planetary myth. Yet there is so inveterate a prejudice that the idea of a goddess mother is simply borrowed by the Arabs from the Syrians, and that the Arabic male god in any pair was originally the husband of the corresponding goddess, that it is worthwhile to follow up the traces of such pairs at points remote from the Syrian frontier.

The temple at Tabāla is sometimes called the Yemenite Ka'ba, sometimes Dhu 'l-Khalasa. The image here, like that of Al-Lāt at Tāif, was, according to Yācūt, a white flint-stone with a sort of crown sculptured on it; and this stone no doubt, and not the temple, was what originally bore the name of Ka'ba. The term Dhu 'l-Khalasa is sometimes taken to mean the temple, but old accounts, especially the life of Imrau 'l-Cais in the *Aghānī,* make Dhu 'l-Khalasa the name of a god worshipped there, who administered an oracle by arrows, like Hobal at Mecca. I see no reason to doubt that this is correct; the oracle by arrows is appropriate to the archer-god Dusares, who was worshipped by the Dausites, the frequenters of the shrine of Tabāla, and Dhu 'l-Khalasa can be best taken, after the phrase ذو بطنها "son of her womb," and such Yemenite tribe -names as Dhū Hosain, to mean son of Al-Khalasa. Imrau 'l-Cais was angry with the deity, who forbade him to avenge his father, and dashed the arrows in his face, foully abusing the god's *mother.*

Let us pass now to Mecca. Here also the Ka'ba, as De Vogüe conjectures, was presumably not at first a house, but the four-square sacred stone. There were and still are two sacred stones at the Ka'ba, the black and the white, both built into the wall and touched by worshippers in the Tawuf And the Coraish had two great deities, AI-'Ozzu and Hobal, whose names, in this order, the goddess coming first, were their rallying cry at Ohod Hobal, in Mohammed's time, had an anthropomorphic statue, which represented him with arrows in his hand — *i.e.* as an archer. This of course is a much later thing than the sacred stones, but it seems to show that he was conceived as a god of the same type with Dusares or Cozah; Cozah was also worshipped at Mozdalifa, in the Meccan feast. As the goddess at Tāif and Tabāla was worshipped as a white stone, we may suppose that the white or southern stone was the original Meccan goddess, the black stone her son; and these will be the originals of Al-'Ozzā and Hobal. The white stone is now much less important than the black, but had it not once been very important it would hardly have been spared at all when the heathen symbols, except it and the black stone, were destroyed. That Al-'Ozzā was conceived as a mother with two daughters appears in a verse ascribed to Zaid b. 'Āmr (*ZDMG* 7 490) [11] and that her worship had a leading place at the Ka'ba appears from the sacred doves still protected at Mecca, from the figure of a dove in the Ka'ba in heathen times, and from the golden gazelles of the Zemzem well. On Phoenician gems the gazelle is a symbol of Ashtoreth, like the dove, and in S. Arabia the antelope is sacred to her male counterpart 'Athtar (Mordtmann and Müller, *Sab. Denkm.* p. 66). On the whole, therefore, the Byzantine writers are hardly drawing altogether on their imagination when they regard Venusworship as the chief thing at Mecca. There, as at Petra and Tabāla, the very name Ka'ba seems to point to a supreme female deity.

Inquiries in this region are complicated by the fact that the sex of the Arabian deities is not seldom uncertain. In Yācūt's account of Tāif we see an effort to change even Al-Lāt into a male figure. In the same way Sowā', the great deity of the Hodhail, is often spoken of as a god, but seems to have been really worshipped in female form (Krehl, p. 67). Now Sowā' is associated with a male god Wadd, who was represented at Dumat alJandal as an archer (*ibid.* p. 65), so that here again we seem to have the same pair. It would appear from Porphyry that the great deity of Dumat al-Jandal, worshipped in the form of a block of stone, was originally a goddess; for the sacrifice of a virgin is the same which was made by Al-Mondhir and other Arabs to Al-'Ozzā, and which was so common at the shrines of goddesses in Syria (comp.

ZDMG 39 45). That maidens were sacrificed to "their mothers," *i.e.* the goddesses, by being thrown into a pit and buried, we have learned to know as an Arab custom. So again in the Himyarite inscriptions the sun is a goddess, and the fact that even in Hebrew Shemesh is often feminine makes it probable that this is the original type of sun-worship, and that the North Semitic male sungod is later. In Arabia itself Dusares, and Cozah at Mozdalifa, seem to have ultimately been viewed as sungods, but this is secondary and connected with the modern view which made the male deities greater than the goddesses. In general it is very difificult to fix the precise attributes of Arabian deities after they began to be compared with those of other nations. Dusares, for example, is to Hesychius a Dionysus, as the god associated with Al-Lāt was to Herodotus. In both cases the point of contact is presumably the orgiastic character of the worship; but this in itself goes far to prove that the Orotal or Dionysus of Herodotus was worshipped, not as the husband of a chaste goddess, but as the son of a goddess who was already the patron of polyandry or promiscuity.

In Arrian's *Indica,* 37, we find yet another Greek rendering of the male partner of Aphrodite or Al-'Ozzā; the Island of Cataca (Kish) was sacred to Hermes and Aphrodite. Ikit as Pliny calls the island Aphrodisias the female deity is here also the greater of the two. So too the island of the Sun (*ibid.* 31) had formerly belonged to a Nereid, *i.e.* a goddess, who practised polyandry with all who visited it and then changed them into fishes. One might give other evidence, but enough has been said to show that in old Arabian religion gods and goddesses often occurred in pairs, the goddess being the greater, so that the god cannot be her Baal, that the goddess is often a mother without being a wife and the god her son, and that the progress of things was towards changing goddesses into gods or lowering them beneath the male deity. An early trace of the transformation of the supreme goddess into a supreme god is found by comparing Herodotus's Urania or heaven-goddess with the Uranus who takes her place in Arrian 7 20 as the only Arab deity except Dionysus. But it is probable that this transformation is due to the Greek narrator, and that "the visible heaven that embraces all the stars and the sun himself" was still, as the description suggests, the great mother of all. Certainly all Semitic analogy leads us to think that the heaven that contains sun and stars would be viewed as their mother, just as in Isa. 14 12 the day-star (Jerome's Lucifer) is son of the twilight sky in whose lap he floats. *Samā,* heaven as opposed to earth, is often, if not usually, a feminine noun, and the Himyarite god Dhū Samāwī (*Sab. Denkm.* p. 10 *sq.*) is probably the son of heaven rather than its lord. It is well worth inquiry whether in North Semitic religion also the goddess mother is not older than the goddess wife, and whether this does not explain certain features of Greek religion which have Eastern connections and yet are quite distinct from Baal and Ashtoreth worship. But this is not the place for pursuing such questions. [12]

[1] Dhu 'l-Shară = Abraham, "husband of Sara" (Lagarde, *Mittheil.* 2 185), but on the analogy of ذُوْ الْحَمَلاتِ it would be rather "son of Sarah," cp. Lag. *Uebers.* 92 *sq.*
[2] See Lydus, *De Mensibus*, iii. § 34, wlio derives κυβέλη ἀπό τοῦ κυβικοῦ σχήματος.
[3] [Doughty, *Ar. Des.* 2 516 describes it as "an unshapely crap; in length nearly as the 'Uzza, but less in height, and of the same grey granite."]
[4] Cp. also the two *ghari* at Hira and Faid (Wellh. *Heid.* (1) 39 *sqq.*, 2nd ed. 43 *sqq.*, 244 [see *RS* 210 n. 2]).
[5] Orotal-Dionysus would be Dusares [*RS.* 193]. Of various conjectures about him note also O. Blau's in *ZDMG* 18 620.

[6] قُرْعَ ضَوز Yācūt, 1 837 — Porta Veneris, explained by زَهْرَة, a city and temple of the Sabians in Harran.
[7] Hence Ashtoreth is the same as Artemis (Hoffmann, *Opusc. Nest.* 95 15 *sqq.* Ashtoreth is called Αφροδιτη, Beltí, Αρτεμις the goddess [الدبلا]. She is Baal's wife and a morning star at the beginning of winter). Similarly Tanith-Artemis of the Carthaginians is a virgin-mother [*RS* 56 and n. 2], ami at Carthage she appears to he identical with Dido [*RS* 374, n. 1, cp. Barton, *Hebraica*, 4 50 *sq.* (1893)].
[8] [This is doubtful, though the identilicalion of Elusa with the mod. Khalasa still holds good; *RS* 57 n., *Heid.* (2) 48, 244.] Αλασαθος (Wadd. 2042, 2047) is not to be connected with Khalasa (baethgen, *Beit.* 103), but is certainly עלושה; see Nöldeke, *ZDMG* 42 474 *sq.*
[9] Dusares, the god of Bostra, is called in Damascius ap. Photius (ed. Hoeschel, p. 1062) Θεανδρίτης, the Θυανδρίτης of Marini Proclus, xix. (ed. Didot); cp. inscr. 4609 (Pape, *Gr. Eigennam.* ed. 3).
[10] But 'Azīz is rather a title than a name, cp. Ibn Hish. 131 1 الوادى عزيز هذا.
[11] Ibn Hish. 145 8. Is it possible that the two daughters are Lāt and Manāt who in the Coran are, along with Al-'Ozzā, the three daughters of Allāh?
[12] The Phoenician Herakles seems to appear as son of Astarle (Asteria); so Gruppe, 1 360 *sq.* The same autiior finds the pair ApolloLeto without Artemis in one form of the Greek legend (p. 524 *sq.*).

Additional Note F - Sacred Animals

Of sacred animals in the later heathenism of Syria we find a somewhat extensive list in Lucian, *De Dea Syria*. In the enclosure of the temple at Ilierapolis there were sacred bulls, horses, eagles, bears, and lions; in the lake there were sacred fish; the dove was so holy that whoever touched one was unclean for a day; swine were neither sacrificed nor eaten, but it was a question whether this was because they were unclean or because they were sacrosanct. The sanctity of so many different kinds of animals at one shrine is a mark of the syncretistic character of the worship. Such syncretism was universal in Syria under the Roman Empire, as the symbols on coins and gems

163

show, and indeed the forces that produced it had been at work since the period of Assyrian conquest, as wc learn from 2 Kings 17 24 *sq.* At the beginning of the Chaldean period it was only small peoples in obscure corners, like Moab, that were still "settled on their lees" and retainetl the flavour of antiquity (Jer. 48 11). Accordingly, the fact that sacred animals are interpreted in later times as mere symbols of divine attributes proves nothing for the original character of the religions to which they belong. When every great cult was based on a combination of older worships, the introduction of priestly allegory was inevitable. If half a dozen local or tribal deities with animal attributes were fused into one, the animal in each case was of necessity interpreted as a mere symbol. In many cases it is still possible to show that in older times every sacred animal had a distinct local connection; the horned Ashtaroth of Bashan (Ashteroth Carnaim, Gen. 14 5) is a distinct local type from the fish-shaped Derceto of Ascalon; and the horses of the sun (2 Kings 23 11) have quite another source from the boar, also identified with the scorching summer sun, which slew Adonis and gave its name to the Syrian June (*Khazīrān*). The symbolical explanation no longer appears so plausible when we go back from the later syncretism to such local animal forms as the Fly-god (Baal-zebub) of Ekron, the Fish-god (Dagon) with his fish-shaped mother (Derceto) at Ascalon, and the cow-headed Astoreth of Sidon, whose lover is Zeus Asterios, the white bull-god of Gortyna (a deity who has nothing to do with the stars, but is simply עשתר, a form already known from the 'Ashtar-Kamosh of the Moabite stone, and corresponding to the Himyaritic 'Athtar, the male counterpart of 'Ashtoreth; comp. the Hebrew הצבא עשתרות). [1] For the purely allegorical interpretation of animal myths is open to the gravest objections, as has been well shown by Mr. Lang, and in the local cults the animals associated with the gods are themselves objects of divine reverence, which extends not to particular sacred animals alone, but to all doves or all fishes. That gods were first anthropomorphic, and then were figured with animal characters, is a most perverse assumption; the second commandment and the scene in Ezekiel 8 10 show that among the Hebrews the opposite is true. In Ezekiel the animal-gods are worshipped by the heads of Judaean clans through pourtrayed images, and so it is in Deut. 4 16 *sq.*; but in Exod. 20 4 the true translation is "thou shalt not make a graven image, nor shalt thou worship any visible form that is in the sky or on the earth or in the waters," *i.e.* any star, bird, beast, or fish.

But perhaps the most important evidence is that derived from forbidden foods. A prohibition to eat the flesh of an animal of a certain species, that has its ground not in natural loathing but in religious horror and reverence, implies that something divine is ascribed to every animal of the species. And what seems to us to be natural loathing often turns out, in the case of primitive peoples, to be based on a religious taboo, and to have its origin not in feelings of contemptuous disgust but of reverential dread. Thus, for example, the disappearance of cannibalism is due to reverence, not to disgust, and in the first instance men only refused to cat their kindred. It is noteworthy that we constantly find a parallel drawn between cannibalism and the eating of the flesh of certain animals; the Egyptians and Phoenicians, says Porphyry, would rather have eaten human flesh than that of the cow (*De abst.* 2 11). In totem religions such expressions are not mere rhetoric, but precisely describe the feeling that a man's totem-animal is of one race with himself.

We have all formed our first ideas about forbidden meats from the Levitical prohibitions of the Pentateuch, and in doing so have been accustomed to understand the term "unclean" as conveying an idea of physical foulness. But the Hebrew word אמט, *tāmē,* is not the ordinary word for things physically foul; it is a ritual term, and corresponds exactly to the idea of *taboo,* which is found among all early peoples. [2] The ideas "unclean" and "holy" seem to us to stand in polar opposition to one another, but it was not so with the Semites. Among the later Jews the Holy Books "defiled the hands" of the reader, as contact with an impure thing did; among Lucian's Syrians the dove was so holy that he who touched it was unclean for a day; and the *taboo* attaching to the swine was explained by some, and beyond question correctly explained, in the same way. Among the heathen Semites, therefore, unclean animals, which it was pollution to eat, were simply holy animals. And this is confirmed by the laws of the Harranians, though they, like the Hebrews, had reached a general classification of animals whose flesh was forbidden, viz. quadrupeds with incisors in both jaws, and birds of prey, as well as the camel and the dove. This classification includes the dog and the raven, which in the mysteries are called brothers of the inystce: the swine and the ass are also expressly mentioned, the former of which we have seen to be sacred, while the latter must have been adored in some Syrian circles, otherwise the fable that the Jews worshipped the ass, and the Gnostic association of the swine and the ass with their Sabaoth, are unintelligible.

With all this it agrees that such unclean, *i.e.* sacred, animals were indeed sometimes sacrificed and eaten, but only in mystic rites (ἔν τισι τελεστικαῖς θυσίαις, Julian, *Orat.* 5 176, cited by Chwolsohn, 2 83; see also Movers, Phoenizier, 1 219 *sq.,* 404 *sq.*) [3] It is such mysteries that are referred to in Isa. 65 4 *sq.,* 66 3, 17, as Spencer long ago saw, observing that by partaking of this magic food the worshippers "tanquam sacramento et ritu magico se Daemoni consecrasse et δαιμονολήπτους evasisse." If the old Cambridge theologian had been trying to describe the sacramental mysteries of totem-religion he could hardly have expressed himself more accurately. The only difference is that in these Asiatic mysteries the persons who consecrate themselves by assimilating the very substance of the divine animal are no longer a totem-kin but a selected group of *mystae.*

But again, these mysteries first come under our notice at the very time when, as we know from the prophets, the old heathenism of Western Asia had been driven to despair by the progress of Assyria; when no man felt secure in the worship of his father's gods, and when new rites of more powerful piacular efficacy were eagerly sought from all quarters. This was just the time when such mysteries would become most popular and when the Hebrews most needed to be guarded against them. And it is at this time, first in Deuteronomy and then in Leviticus, that we find a list of forbidden foods laid down in writing and enjoined on all Jehovahworshippers. The most notable feature in the Levitical prohibitions is that they correspond so closely with those of the heathen Semites and yet are expressly set forth as belonging to Israel's peculiar consecration to Jehovah. And only second in importance to this is the fact that the terms שֶׁקֶץ and שִׁקּוּץ are indifferently applied to unclean beasts and to the gods of the heathen, but to nothing else. The unclean creatures, therefore, are the divine animals of the heathen, such animals as the latter did not ordinarily eat or sacrifice, but did eat in those mysteries, of higher potency, which now, in the breaking up of the old society, were losing their tribal character and offered their temptations to *mystae* of any race. That these abhorred rites were of totem character, that they proceeded on the doctrine that the worshippers and the sacrosanct sacrifice were, or became, of one nature, is shown (1) by the fact that the brotherhood of man with the sacred animals was expressly taught in the Harranian and Mithraitic mysteries; (2) by the fact that in Isa. 66 3 the sacrifice of a sow [4] or dog is put on one line with those piacular human sacrifices which also become so common in the seventh century B.C.; and perhaps also (3) by the ritual: for the dog's neck in Isa. 66 3 is broken, *i.e.* the creature is slain without shedding blood. This feature is not accidental, for, as Movers points out, it recurs in Greek mysteries of a similar kind; its meaning must be that the blood of the victim is not shed, and that therefore the life which lies in the blood is not lost, but is shared among the participants (Deut. 12 23). With this it agrees that these sacrifices are boiled and yield a magical hell-broth (Isa 65 4), and that in Zech. 9 7 the shiccūsīm or sacrifices of sacred animals are called "bloody morsels": comp. the N.T. πνικτά, and Spencer's dissertation on Acts 15 20 (iii. 1 4). Only thus can we understand the stress laid by Ezek. 33 25 on the guilt of eating "with the blood," the association of the same offence in Lev. 19 26 with heathenish auguries and superstitions, and the penalty of excommunication attached to the eating of blood in Lev. 7 27. That many of the heathen ate blood, but only in religious ceremonies, as an act of communion with their gods, is attested by Maimonides, and his accounts, however uncritical, are not wholly imaginary. In old Israel, eating with the blood meant eating what had not been sacrificed to Jehovah by pouring out the blood to him (1 Sam. 14 33 *sq.*). This meaning disappeared with the Deuteronomic legislation, and a new meaning is required to explain the importance attached to blood-eating, not as a mere neglect of Jehovah, but as a manifest sign of idolatry. In Ezek. 18 6, 11, 15, 22 9 we must probably read הַדָּם for הֶהָרִים, as in 33 25; the corruption is the same which underlies the Septuagint text of Lev. 19 26.

That the Hebrew list of forbidden toods is largely made up of the names of creatures that there could be no temptation to eat under ordinary circumstances is naturally explained by the theory just put forward; it will be noted also how many Arab tribes have their names from obscure "creeping things." In some cases a real or supposed resemblance to man probably guided the choice of an animal god; the jerboa is very like a manikin, with his erect bearing and hand-like forepaws. In Lev. 11 27 all animals that have digits are pronounced unclean.

[1] [See *RS* 310.]
[2] [See further *RS*, especially 152 *sqq.*, 446 *sqq.*]
[3] [See RS 290 *sqq.*, 357 *sqq.*, etc.]
[4] For the pig in Greek expiations see J. de Witte, *Gazette Archeol.* 1879, pp. 129 sqq. *Ann. De l' Inst. Arch.* (1847) 19 426 *sqq.* Zeus purifies Ixion by applying pig's blood to his hands (Eustathius on Iliad, T. p. 1183).

Additional Note G - Evidence From Nabatean and South Arabian Inscriptions

Prof. J. Euting's *Nabatäische Inschriften aus Arabian*, [1] Berlin 1885, which reached mc too late to be used for the text of my argument, supplies some important evidence bearing on the family and social system among the Nabatseans, the great trading people of northern Arabia. Prof. Nöldeke, in a note on p. 79 of Euting's work, directs attention to the independent position of women indicated by the inscriptions. Women construct expensive family graves, which they dispose of apart from their husbands, and we even find a provision that daughters' children shall be interred in their grandmother's sepulchre. All this, Nöldeke adds, is in harmony with the great place occupied by women on Nabataean coins. In looking at these facts more closely we have first of all to note that these Nabatseans had male kinship, a man's *konya* being regularly taken from his father. We should therefore expect that the family grave as among the Hebrews, at Palmyra, and among the later Arabs, would descend in the male line, so that, though daughters might be buried in it, a daughter's sons would be buried in their father's sepulchre. Many of the inscriptions present nothing inconsistent with such a supposition, and in *CIS* 2 209 it appears by express statement that the sepulchre was to descend in the male line. On the other hand when a man makes a tomb for himself, it is sometimes expressly provided that his daughters and their children shall have a perpetual right of burial in it (nos. 119, 212, 215). This shows that heritable property could be transmitted through women, and so agrees with the evidence of other inscriptions that married women could hold property apart from their husbands (see especially no. 213). That is so under Mohammedan law also, and thus far there is nothing to decide whether the independent position of women had survived from a time when all kinship and inheritance was through women, or whether the Nabataeans had once had laws as unfavourable to women as those of Medina, but had abolished these as civilisation advanced.

But now let us observe that a sepulchre had a sacred character, so that it could not be alienated, like ordinary property, by the heir into whose hands it fell. It was, so to speak, entailed, and the entail was under religious sanction (nos. 199, 200, etc.). These provisions may in part be regarded as precautions against the violation of the tomb if it fell into the hands of strangers, who might cast out the bodies of the old occupants; but this is not in itself sufficient to explain provisions like those of no. 198, in which it is forbidden not only to alienate the grave but to allow any stranger to be buried in it. It can hardly be doubted that the family sepulchre is connected with the family religion. No one can be buried in it who does not belong to a certain social and religious community based on kinship. And from this point of view the transmission of a right of burial through women becomes very significant, resembling the Mandaean use of the *konya* taken from the mother in religious ceremonies. The tomb is one of the *sacra* of the family in an exclusive sense, and therefore the entails show that such *sacra* could be transmitted in the female line. They were also transmitted in the male line in the times of which we have record; but such a twofold line of transmission is necessarily a modern thing, and implies that the old stock-system had been broken down by the introduction of a new kind of kinship. From this point of view we are led to regard the transmission of sacred family rights from mother to child as a relic of an old law of female kinship. It is in matters connected with religion that old rules continue to hold after they have become obsolete in other quarters.

This being granted we can see also in these inscriptions relics of a custom of *beena* marriage. In no. 209 we have a list of persons other than the sons and daughters of the founder and the posterity of his sons who may be specially granted a place in the grave by the heir of entail for the time being. They are his wife, his wife's daughters, a "kinsman" (*nasīb*), or a son-in-law. The word *nasīb* is obscure, but cannot mean as it would in later Arabic a kinsman in the male line; [2] for these had a right to burial without special permission. I presume that it must mean a descendant in the female line, *e.g.* a daughter's child, for, on the analogy of other inscriptions, these could hardly be excluded. In that case the order of the permissions is at once clear. A man may wish to share his tomb, in the first place, with his own wife; then her daughters by a former marriage, who presumably followed her to his house and were brought up "in his bosom" (*Sūr.* 4 27), may be allowed to lie with their mother (compare the cases in nos. 198, 205, where a woman makes a tomb for herself and her daughters); in the third place a man's daughters' children may be brought into the grave, and this being so it is reasonable that their father should rest with them and with their mother, who (as one of the posterity) appears to have the right of burial without express permission. The son-in-law is taken into the family of the dead, just as in *beena* marriage he would be taken into the family of the living.

There are several inscriptions in which a woman erects a sepulchre for herself and her children, without mentioning their father. In nos, 198, 205, the tomb passes from mother to daughters, and sons are not mentioned, whether because there were no sons or because they would share their wives' tombs does not appear. But in nos. 216, 223-225, the grave is designed for all the posterity of the foundress, who thus appears as the true head of the family of the dead to the exclusion of her husband. Again we see that the old family system, obsolete in political life, prevails in the grave.

These results are in full agreement with what we have learned in *Additional Note* E, as to the mother and son worship of the Nabataeans.

[Evidence for the existence of polyandry among the ancient Arabians has been found by Glaser (*Münch. Allgem. Zeit.; Beilage,* 1897, Dec. 6, p. 7), and Winckler (*Zeit. f. Ethnol.* 1898, Jan., p. 29 *sq.*; *Altorient Forsch.* 2 81-83 [1898]). It rests upon the fact that in certain inscriptions a man is described as the son of two or three fathers. Thus a king Nash-ī-karib is son of two kings, brothers, but it still remains uncertain whether the two brothers have only one wife or several in common. In another case a man appears as the son of a man and his father.] [3]

[1] [Since re-edited in the *CIS, pars secunda,* 1. i. fasc, 2, to which reference is made throughout in this note.]

[2] [So *CIS,* following Euling, "socer."]

[3] Winckler compares the names Ahab and Ahat-abi-ša a daughter of Sargon (cp. also *Beitr. z. Assyr.* 4 47 72). On the looseness of marriage-relations in modern Yemen, see Landberg, *Arabica,* 4 26 35 5 168.

www.ingramcontent.com/pod-product-compliance
Lightning Source LLC
LaVergne TN
LVHW091258080426
835510LV00007B/305